ON PLATO'S *STATESMAN*

Cornelius Castoriadis

Assistance for the translation was provided by the French
Ministry of Culture.

On Plato's "Statesman" was originally published in French in
1999 under the title *Sur "Le Politique" de Platon.* © Editions du
Seuil, September 1999.

Stanford University Press
Stanford, California

Printed in the United States of America
on acid-free, archival-quality paper

Library of Congress Cataloging-in-Publication Data

Castoriadis, Cornelius.
   [Sur Le politique de Platon. English]
   On Plato's Statesman / by Cornelius Castoriadis ; edited and
   translated by David Ames Curtis.
      p.   cm
   Includes bibliographical references and index.
   ISBN 0-8047-4144-1 (alk. paper)—ISBN 0-8047-4145-x
   (pbk. : alk. paper)
      1. Plato. Statesman I. Curtis, David Ames. II. Title
JC71.P314.C37 2002
320'.01—dc21   2002070647

Original Printing 2002

Last figure below indicates year of this printing:
11   10   09   08   07   06   05   04   03   02

Typeset by Alan Noyes
in 10.9/13 Adobe Garamond and Lithos Display

ON PLATO'S *STATESMAN*

MERIDIAN

Crossing Aesthetics

Werner Hamacher

Editor

Edited and Translated by
David Ames Curtis

Stanford
University
Press

———————

Stanford
California
2002

Contents

Books by Cornelius Castoriadis in English

CL   *Crossroads in the Labyrinth*, trans. Martin H. Ryle and Kate Soper (Cambridge, Mass.: MIT Press; Brighton, UK: Harvester Press, 1984).

CR   *The Castoriadis Reader*, ed. David Ames Curtis (Oxford, UK, and Malden, Mass.: Blackwell, 1997).

IIS   *The Imaginary Institution of Society* (1975), trans. Kathleen Blamey (Cambridge, Mass.: MIT Press and Cambridge, UK: Polity Press, 1987; cor. paperback edition, Cambridge, UK: Polity Press, 1997 and Cambridge, Mass.: MIT Press, 1998).

PPA   *Philosophy, Politics, Autonomy*, ed. David Ames Curtis (New York: Oxford University Press, 1991).

PSW1   *Political and Social Writings*, vol. 1, *1946–1955: From the Critique of Bureaucracy to the Positive Content of Socialism*, trans. and ed. David Ames Curtis (Minneapolis: University of Minnesota Press, 1988).

PSW2   *Political and Social Writings*, vol. 2, *1955–1960: From the Workers' Struggle Against Bureaucracy to Revolution in the Age of Modern Capitalism*, trans. and ed. David Ames Curtis (Minneapolis: University of Minnesota Press, 1988).

PSW3   *Political and Social Writings*, vol. 3, *1961–1979: Recommencing the Revolution: From Socialism to the Autonomous Society*, trans. and ed. David Ames Curtis (Minneapolis: University of Minnesota Press, 1993).

WIF   *World in Fragments: Writings on Politics, Society, Psychoanalysis, and the Imagination,* ed. and trans. David Ames Curtis (Stanford: Stanford University Press, 1997).

N.B.: An extensive bibliography of writings by and about Castoriadis in a dozen languages can be found at the Cornelius Castoriadis/Agora International Website, http://aleph.lib.ohio-state.edu/bcase/castoriadis.

Foreword

Castoriadis and the Statesman

PIERRE VIDAL-NAQUET

This small book has a history that makes a lovely story. It started out as a Castoriadis seminar on one of Plato's most difficult dialogues, the *Statesman*, recorded on audiotape week after week between February 19 and April 30, 1986, before an audience of students from the École des Hautes Études en Sciences Sociales.

A first raw draft of the transcription was made by Pascal Vernay, with the collaboration of three of his friends, in 1992, and submitted to Cornelius, whom we called Corneille. He was at once surprised ("I didn't know that I had written a new book"), delighted, and severe, as he was toward himself. Since that time, the text has been reworked, filled in, and clarified on a few points of detail. Thus was born, while Corneille was still alive, a team whose collaboration continues after his death and that proposes to publish in their entirety, and with the requisite rigor, the seminars led by Cornelius Castoriadis. An encyclopedic task if there ever was one.

Vernay tells us the basics in his Introduction. Of his work, I can say what he could not say: how remarkable it is, and in what way it is so. Plato is an author who condemned writing, a perverse gift of the Egyptian god Thoth, in the *Phaedrus* and also, as a matter of fact, in the *Statesman*. The written law cannot hold its own vis-à-vis science as embodied in the philosopher in power. The poets are to be chased from the city of the *Republic*; and writing is only a *deuteros plous*, a second best, a lesser evil in relation to living speech and memory. Between impossible speech and theoretical writing, Plato chose a sublime compromise: the dialogue. The dialogue is to speech what myth is to truth. The transcription of Castoriadis's seminar we owe to Vernay is the result of a similar compromise; it is certainly closer to the spoken word than the Platonic dialogue is, but it is purposely situated between the oral and the written. There have been, for certain famous seminars, transcribers who, while claiming to be perfectly faithful, have sown confusion and sometimes ended up looking ridiculous. Such is not the case with the seminar on the *Statesman*.

When I presented Cornelius Castoriadis's candidacy at the École des Hautes Études en Sciences Sociales twenty years ago, I recalled a dialogue that had taken place at Ferney apropos of Voltaire. "It's only in Roman law that I find him a bit weak," said a famous professor . . . of Roman law. "And as for me," replied d'Alembert, "that's my opinion, too, concerning mathematics." I was trying to explain to my colleagues that, as a specialist in ancient Greek culture, I did not find Castoriadis at all "a bit weak" in this sector and that, quite the contrary, I had much to learn from him. And I have indeed learned much from him. It happens that it was apropos of Athenian democracy that, during the winter of 1963–64, I had my first dialogue with Castoriadis. Since the time of another winter, that of 1956–57, I had been acquainted with *Socialisme ou Barbarie*, the review he ran with Claude Lefort, and by the end of 1958, I had made a first fleeting contact with the group, but I knew the man only very little and very superficially.

With Lefort and a few others, Corneille participated in a circle of thinkers, with Saint-Just chosen as "patron saint."[1] François Châtelet, Jean-Pierre Vernant, and myself were asked to take up the cause of Greek democracy and present it before this group. In 1962, Vernant had published *Les Origines de la pensée grecque* (*The Origins of Greek Thought*), in which he explained that Greek thought was the daughter of the city and was modeled upon the political sphere [*le politique*].[2] Châtelet had written *La Naissance de l'histoire* (The Birth of History), a book in which he showed that history, too—as a discipline founded by Hecataeus, Herodotus, and Thucydides—was closely connected with the civic structure.[3] For my part, with Pierre Lévêque, I had just finished *Clisthène l'Athénien* (*Cleisthenes the Athenian*), a book on Cleisthenes, the founder—after Solon, but in a more radical way than Solon—of the Athenian democracy.[4]

I was young and, to tell the truth, a bit full of myself, proud beyond reason of my new knowledge. How had democracy been born? At Chios, perhaps—although few still believe that—then at Athens. I saw it as having been instituted around two experiences—tyranny, which was creative

of forms of equality, and colonization, a source of political inventions—
and on a foundation: slavery. I rapidly came to understand that I had before me not some amateurs but real experts, and that Castoriadis, in particular, was intensely familiar with all the major texts, those of the
philosophers, the historians, and the tragedians. As for democracy, far
from being merely "formal" (as imbeciles were saying), it was the very example, at Athens, of the self-institution of society.

I would not necessarily countersign everything Corneille wrote about
ancient Greece. If it were otherwise, what purpose would a dialogue with
someone's oeuvre serve? Nevertheless, we are talking about a great oeuvre
and a robust way of thinking. The reader has in his hands one of the
finest texts this incredibly fertile mind produced. A dialogue of Plato's,
the *Statesman*, a dialogue with Plato, and, as Vernay says, "a tremendous
fragment of philosophical *agora,* in which Plato and Castoriadis confront
each other at their most resourceful, with an issue at stake: democracy."

~

There are many ways of studying Plato. Castoriadis proceeds, according to an image from the *Phaedrus*, like a good butcher: he brings out
what he calls the *Statesman*'s "quirky structure," with its three digressions,
its eight incidental points, and its two definitions, "neither of which is the
good one from Plato's point of view." Here, Castoriadis's work could be
contrasted with that of another exegete who spent a great deal of time on
Plato: Leo Strauss. Like Castoriadis, Strauss followed the text quite
closely—to the point of modeling himself upon it. But the result in
Strauss's case is a constant justification of the most minor details of the argument. Castoriadis, on the contrary, is very particular about differing
with the text, showing that what is, in appearance, secondary is in reality
essential—this is the case, for example, with the myth of the reign of
Cronus—and that the denunciation of the Sophists accommodates itself
quite well to the use of sophistical procedures. He shows perfectly, too,
how, with the "resignation" Ulrich von Wilamowitz-Moellendorff spoke
of, the *Statesman* takes us into the heart of what is the mark par excellence
of the late Plato: blending, acceptance of the mixed, even of the *metaxu*,
of the intermediate; democracy is the worst of the regimes governed by
laws; it is the least bad of anomic regimes.

When I was a student, a book by Karl Popper, *The Open Society and Its
Enemies*, set out to attack the "spell" of Plato head-on.[5] He made of Plato

a "reactionary" thinker who hurled such slogans as "Back to the tribal patriarchy." In that form, the attack completely missed its target. Plato was not reactionary in the sense that, for example, Charles Maurras was;[6] he did not dream of an impossible regression. A study of the *Laws* demonstrates his perfect knowledge of the legal and political mechanisms of fourth-century Athens, and it was to a foreigner from Athens that he entrusted the task of sketching out, on Crete, the very detailed scheme for a new city, "second in unity" in relation to the city of the *Republic*. It remains the case, however, that while Plato knew the world surrounding him and the one that came before him, he hated that world. And his hatred did not apply only to the democracy whose contemporary he was—which when he died in 348 B.C.E. was already confronted with Philip of Macedon—but in the first place to the instituting democracy, that of Pericles, whom he attacked directly or indirectly in the *Gorgias*, caricaturing him under the name of Callicles.

With the sole exception of the *Laws*, there is no dialogue of Plato's that is not clearly situated before the death of Socrates or at the moment of the latter's death, in 399. All Plato's characters are therefore men of the fifth century, even though Plato takes all possible and imaginable liberties with the chronology. The example of the *Menexenus*, that cruel pastiche of Pericles' Funeral Oration in Thucydides—a pastiche put in the mouth of Aspasia, a woman, a courtesan, and, what is more, Pericles' official mistress—shows that Plato knows perfectly well where to strike: not at the "demagogues" of the "decadent" period but at the very heart of the city that claimed to be the educator of Greece.[7]

From its first lines, the *Statesman* tells us that to treat the sophist, the statesman, and the philosopher as if they were "of equal value" is to make an "outrageous remark." It is the royal man, who alone is ultimately worthy of governing the city, that the Stranger from Elea comes to seek at Athens, not the citizen capable—as demonstrated by the myth in the *Protagoras*, which undoubtedly reflects the great Sophist's view that every human being has at his disposal a modicum of political know-how—of expressing an opinion on the great problems with which the city is confronted, if not on technical questions. Perversely, Plato plays upon the ambiguity of *technē*, as if statesmanship [*la politique*] were some kind of technical knowledge. But the whole question is precisely whether the king can rule the city without destroying its foundations.

The "king" in Greece, as Castoriadis rightly remarks, was a marginal figure. At Athens, he was an archon, an annual magistrate, chosen by lot.

His duties were purely religious. His wife, the "queen," wed Dionysus. At Sparta, the two "kings" were an archaeological curiosity. Their duties were basically military. The greatest of the Spartan generals during the Peloponnesian War, Lysander, belonged to a royal line, but he was never "king."

The Athenians can be heard to say without any complex, via a character from Aristophanes' *Wasps* (around 422 B.C.E.), that their power "yields to no kingship" (line 549), and before that, via Pericles and via Cleon, that they exercise something like a "tyranny"[8] over the allied cities—that is to say, that they are to Mytilene and to Samos what Oedipus is in appearance to Thebes—ruler not by right of birth but by the fortune (*tuchē*) of history. As for the real kings, they were located on the outer edges of the Greek world: in Epirus, on Cyprus, and especially in Macedonia.

It remains the case that, beside the King par excellence, who reigned over the Persian empire, the royal personage was an important and even capital figure in fourth-century Greek political thought. Plato was not alone in this. Even though it purports to be the story of the education of the founder of the Achaemenid dynasty, Xenophon's *Cyropaedia*, which is nearly contemporary with Plato's *Republic*, is a treatise on how Greek cities can make good use of the providential man. The same goes for Isocrates' *Evagoras*, a eulogy for a Cypriot king. Plato, Xenophon, and Isocrates herald a time that became one of kings, after Philip and especially Alexander, who corresponds rather well to the *panbasileus* evoked by Aristotle in the third book of his *Politics*; indeed, Aristotle was the educator of Alexander after having been Plato's disciple.

Xenophon, Plato, and Isocrates became the prophets of the Hellenistic world. Needless to say, the city did not disappear. It was still an essential framework for life in the age of the first Roman emperors, but in the Mediterranean world and even in the Greek world, it ceased to be a preponderant factor. The greatest town of the Hellenistic world, Alexandria, which was "near Egypt" and not "in" Egypt, was in fact a *town* more than a city. The Greeks there were citizens, but they had no part in the government of their town. It was in vain that Cleomenes, a revolutionary king exiled from Sparta, attempted at the end of the third century, under Ptolemy IV, to incite them to freedom. Alexandria was not an autonomous decision-making center. It is in this sense that it can be said of Plato, as Castoriadis does, that he played a "considerable role in . . . the destruction of the Greek world." One can go even further than this and state that in the Later Roman Empire, starting with Diocletian, we find philosopher-kings who claimed to govern according to Plato's principles. Diocletian himself tacitly did so in an edict (from 301) that set a maximum price for all merchandise, the preamble of which is nourished by Plato's philosophy.

~

For Castoriadis, philosopher and theoretician of the political sphere, society has to tend toward a mode of explicit self-creation, a self-creation incessantly renewed by what he calls—and this is the title of his most famous book—"the imaginary institution of society." For Plato—creator, after the Milesians and the Eleatics, of philosophy—it is the "royal race" alone that can be defined as "self-directive" (*autepitaktikē* [*Statesman* 260e]). For Castoriadis, the Athenians' immortal contribution to political thought is their integration of historicity. That is how the Corinthians depict them to the Spartans in book I (68–71) of Thucydides;[9] for Plato, the statesman's whole effort is aimed at blocking the historical process.

As for the imaginary, Plato does in fact make abundant use of it—whether it is a matter of a mere image (like the abundant comparisons borrowed from the vocabulary of the various trades), of a paradigm (like that of weaving),[10] or of myths (like the one that plays a central role in the *Statesman*, which Castoriadis competently analyzes). But neither the myth nor the image nor the paradigm gives us access to the "incorporeal realities that are the most beautiful and the greatest." For these "most precious" realities there are, as Plato tells us expressly, no "images created in order to give men a clear intuition of them" (*Statesman* 285e–286a).

It remains the case, however, that Plato plays, with great panache, upon the very thing he denounces! He uses the paradigm of weaving, for example, in order to make of the king a weaver who weds courage and gentleness the way his craftsman model unites the warp and the woof in order to manufacture a fabric. The paradigm of weaving is far from taken at random. Castoriadis sensed this very well, and works written subsequent to his seminar have established this in the greatest detail: weaving furnishes Greek thought, both mythical and political, with one of its most precious tools of analysis.[11]

Cornelius Castoriadis did indeed come to Paris, coming from Athens, as the Stranger came from Elea (Velia), in Magna Graecia, to Athens in order to be there a "teacher of truth," teacher of a truth who wanted not to stifle but to promote freedom.

Introduction

"Living Thought at Work"

PASCAL VERNAY

It was during the winter of 1992 that Cornelius Castoriadis read the present transcription of these seven seminars held at the École des Hautes Études en Sciences Sociales (EHESS) in 1986. His notes, corrections, and additions have, of course, been integrated into the text you are about to read. The judgment he gave was a bit contradictory. Amused, at first: "I didn't know I had written a new book"; then generous: it's "an excellent job"; finally, reserved, because "some of the points aren't ripe enough" to envisage publication. Yet here we have these seminars published, and, what is more, in an unauthorized form. Why, then, have we not respected his wish not to see them in print?

First of all, and this is the most circumstantial reason, because in early 1992 Corneille was busy preparing the fourth and fifth volumes of the *Carrefours du labyrinthe* (Crossroads in the Labyrinth) series and above all preoccupied with putting together [a planned multivolume work to be entitled] *La Création humaine* (Human Creation).[1] Planned, thought out, and elaborated for almost twenty years, "La Création humaine" was to be found—albeit in raw form—in the transcriptions of the more than 200 seminars held at the EHESS since 1980. The rewriting of a history of philosophy commentary—to speak too quickly, and even though this commentary had its place in the overall publication of his great work—did not figure at that time among his priorities: he wished to begin with "heavy" philosophy, ontology, therefore, and to get to Greece and to politics only six or seven volumes later. Alluding to the relative "greenness" of this work on Plato was therefore also Castoriadis's way of telling us: I've got something else to do at the moment.

The second element involved in weighing this matter relates to the high degree of excellence Corneille required of himself and of what he signed. This was not just about elegance, formal perfection—although the pertinence, the virulence, of certain condensed conclusive formulas garner our support as much as the arguments preceding them do; and although, in addition, Castoriadis, who detested approximations and needless repetitions, used footnotes to refer to already solidly established points, whence the extreme density of most of his writings. It was about completion: a text is finished when it can stand on its own, when its theses, arguments, and supports have been sufficiently tested beforehand, polished with criticism in order to resist attacks. From the standpoint of such completion, of this capacity for self-defense, these seven seminars have quite strong backing; it is not a mere textual commentary you are about to read, but rather a tremendous fragment of philosophical *agora*, in which Plato and Castoriadis confront each other at their most resourceful, with an issue at stake: democracy.

Finally, and this is precisely what might have bothered Corneille, there is the insufficiently reworked oral nature of the presentation. Yet this is today what for us makes this long commentary so precious: our rediscovery of that ever so trenchant, convincing, energetic, provocative, droll voice—in a word, a voice that fills us with enthusiasm—which makes up a bit for the pain we feel in having lost him. And it is also, for his usual readers, testimony to a hitherto unknown Castoriadis, who reflects while he is speaking, collects himself, corrects himself, and does not hesitate to harp on what his listeners absolutely have to take in. And then there is the most precious thing of all: getting a feel for his thinking, which, at the end of a seminar, tries to find itself, gropes about a bit confusedly, and then takes on its full breadth, all its rectitude, at the beginning of the next seminar.

This living speech—preserved, rediscovered—has nevertheless been reworked.[2] The recordings of the seminars have, of course, served as the basis. First, the most scrupulous, faithful, and exhaustive transcription possible was made, an unpackaged transcription, it could be said. Then the formal errors or fumbles of all kinds (grammatical, syntactical, etc.) were rectified, the citations corrected, but without harming the way his speech unfolds. After that, in a third stage, attempts were made—as discreetly as possible—to improve the overall readability: turning two sentences into one, or vice versa, transforming some of the excursuses into notes, setting back into their place within the overall commentary some developments that, as Castoriadis himself had pointed out, had been forgotten, and, finally, indicating, surely in a bit too heavy-handed and formal a manner, the articulations of the argument, of the exposition, either because he had neglected to insist upon them or because they had been drowned out, lost in the overall exposition. As for words and phrases in Greek, we have chosen to transliterate according to the system Castoriadis himself used: a Latin character (or two) for a Greek letter, using the usual accents to indicate the length of vowels (thus, *é* {Americanized in this translation to *ē*} for eta, *ô* (Americanized to *ō*} for omega, *e* for epsilon, etc.). Nonetheless, in the case of longer quotations integral to the play of the questions and answers, we give the Greek text—that of Auguste Diès (Paris: Les Belles Lettres, 1960, 1975).

A few rudimentary thematic points, it seems to us, might be useful here in order to place these seven seminars in the context of Castoriadis's sixteen years of teaching at the EHESS. Here is a very rough summary. The years from 1980 to 1986 were basically devoted to Greece, to the creation of philosophy and democracy—with more precise and specific analyses here and there of Anaximander, Heraclitus, the tragedians, Pericles' Funeral Oration, Plato's *Statesman*, and so on. Then, from 1987 until 1992, Castoriadis took up anew the great problems of philosophy, confronting his "parent ideas" [*idées mères*] with the analyses of the "four greats" from the history of philosophy: Plato, Aristotle, Kant, and Hegel. Finally, the years 1993, 1994, and 1995 dealt almost exclusively with the human psyche, starting from, with, and sometimes against Freud.

To situate this commentary on the *Statesman* within his overall labor during the 1985–86 school year, here, finally, is the summary Castoriadis himself wrote for EHESS's annual report, under the title "Institution of Society and Historical Creation: Democracy and Philosophy in Ancient Greece":

> The 1985–86 seminar endeavored to bring out first the differences and oppositions between the Greek political imaginary and the modern political imaginary.[3] As opposed to direct participation in power and self-government in the democratic cities and to the absence there of the State, of "ideology," of an extrasocial basis for the institution, and of constitutional illusions, there are in modern times the imaginary of "representation," the omnipresence and

the all-powerfulness of a bureaucratic State that lies beyond the bounds of the political game, the cloaking of governmental power as such, and "ideology." But on the other hand, as opposed to the limitations placed upon ancient political activity, there is a lifting of the limits of modern political action: extension of formal sovereignty to the whole of the population; universality, by right, of the political community (wherein, it is true, the nation remains a lump undigested by political philosophy); and a challenging, by right, of all institutions. Finally, as opposed to the ancient political ethos of brutal frankness (no justification of slavery existed before Aristotle), there is the instituted duplicity of modern times (which originates in monotheism, on the one hand, and imperial Rome, on the other). In the background, there was, for the Greeks, being as *chaos/kosmos* and the acceptance of mortality; for the Moderns, the subject (God and his successive placeholders, culminating in the substantive individual) and the illusion of immortality.

Plato constitutes the point of passage between these two worlds. His unitary ontology and his identification of being with the good, which are radically foreign to the Greek imaginary, later became central to modern thought and practice. Profoundly hating the democratic universe and its arborescences ("sophistry," rhetoric, political activity, even poetry), he constructs—by strokes of historical falsification, rhetoric, sophistry, theatrical scenes, and demagogy—a false image of it that was later to have weighty historical effects: when referring to Plato, one still talks about "Greek political thought," whereas he is the total negation thereof. He pulled off a great historical operation, transforming the de facto destruction of the democracy into a de jure downfall. Greek political thought is to be sought, rather, in democratic political creation, and that creation ends basically in 404 (or 399). The very difference between Socrates and Plato symbolizes this: Socrates remained in the city, whereas Plato withdrew from it; Socrates was a soldier, gave sons to the city, and served as a magistrate, whereas nothing of the kind is known about Plato.

At the same time, though, Plato created philosophy for a second time. He invented imaginary schemata of great potential; he was the first to articulate and to instrument his schemata in and through a tremendous deployment of ensemblistic-identitary means, the first to aim at and to achieve a system with pretensions to exhaustiveness, but also the first to be able to put his own results back into question. More than just philosophical reasoning, Plato created philosophical Reason—*Logos*—and that is why, even among his adversaries, philosophy remains Platonic.

The *Statesman* was chosen as an object to be worked upon in detail: more than just a difficult transition between the *Republic* and the *Laws*, it is also an extremely rich dialogue in its own right. But it is above all a dialogue whose apparent and real quirks (two definitions, neither of which truly comes off, three major digressions, and eight less long digressions or incidental points) make it, of all Plato's writings—and perhaps even of all philosophical writing—the one in which can best be seen living thought at work.

On the Translation

Once again, the main challenge of the present translation has been to translate Castoriadis while endeavoring to be faithful to his own distinctive translations from ancient Greek.[1] As Castoriadis himself noted in "The Discovery of the Imagination": "The translations of passages . . . are my own. Often they diverge considerably (and sometimes on 'elementary' points of meaning) from existing translations. I have worried little about elegance" (*WIF*, p. 216). In his *Statesman* seminars, Castoriadis makes use of Auguste Diès's standard Guillaume Budé French translation. But he departed therefrom when he felt he himself could better translate Plato's text and elucidate its meaning. Translations of Plato differ rather substantially, if not wildly, within any one modern language, let alone between two or more. There would have been no way of capturing the specificity of the terminology, phrasing, and flavor of Castoriadis's renditions through direct use of existing English translations for the *Statesman*. (The same goes for other Platonic dialogues he quotes and further ancient Greek authors he cites, remarkably well, from memory.) I have therefore again opted to render the distinctiveness of these French translations, whether Diès's, Castoriadis's own, or a combination thereof, directly in English myself. This has often required consultation of the Greek original, Diès's French, and an English translation (Hamilton and Cairns's *Plato: The Collected Dialogues*), and I have incorporated nuances of all three into the final English version given here.

The French original of these seven Castoriadis seminars prepared by Pascal Vernay and reviewed by the speaker himself offers a good running guide to the general locations in the *Statesman* where Castoriadis offers translations of dialogue. Standards for providing citations and references are considerably stricter in the English-speaking world. Included, therefore, are specific additional references in scrolled braces "{}"—also noting "cf." and a reference in such braces for quotations of not fully certain origin or for Castoriadis's more general paraphrases. These added references should aid the reader who wishes to follow the commentary closely; any errors in them are my own.

In a number of instances, Castoriadis quotes or makes passing mention of other authors. In the past, I checked with Castoriadis directly concerning unreferenced quotations. Since I can no longer do this, I have now added some references myself, in consultation with the team of French editors. In some cases, however, this was not possible.[2]

As with his polyglot writings, Castoriadis's spoken seminars span several languages, as if "no one language, or even three or four, could bear the weight of his thought."[3] Interestingly, a significant number of English words steal into Castoriadis's lectures. These include: "second best" to translate *deuteros plous* throughout, "busybody" as the best translation of *polupragmonein* (2/19), and numerous colloquialisms—"Tell that to the marines!" (2/19), "jam session" (3/12), "They will laugh him down" (4/23)—as well as his paraphrase of President Reagan's "political maxim" (4/30).

Also worthy of note are a few neologisms in French, English, or both languages. *Comitant*—Castoriadis's neologism for Aristotle's *sumbebēkos*—has again been translated as "comitant."[4] Note here my own subsequent discovery that "comitant" does indeed—or at least did—exist in English. It thus is not a neologism in our language. The *Oxford English Dictionary* notes that this now "rare" term comes from *comitānt-em*, past participle of *comitāri*, "to accompany"—precisely the sense Castoriadis intended when creating his French neologism! (A search of several French dictionaries turned up no comparable existing, rare, or even obsolete term.) *Interrogativité* appears to be another Castoriadis neologism, this one improvised on the spot. I have created the English "equivalent," placing *interrogativity* in quotation marks at its first appearance. There is a French word *sensorialité*. It is of relatively recent origin—1970, according to the *Grand Larousse de la langue française*, where it is defined as "the set of functions of the sensorial system, that is to say, of the specialized sensorial apparatuses, or organs of the senses, as they are classically distinguished." Lacking an English equivalent, I have used (coined?) *sensorial-*

ity, it being a short stretch from the extant English adjective with Kantian connotations. ("Sensory makeup" might have given too exclusively passive an idea of Castoriadis's conception thereof.) The 1951 coinage of another French word Castoriadis uses—*démiurgie*—is attributed to André Malraux. This neologism comes from the Greek *dēmiurgia*, meaning creative activity, workmanship, handicraft. I have merely rendered the word into "English"—*demiurgia*—thus availing myself of a minor prerogative contained in the creative activity of the translator.

Following standard editorial practice, first names have been supplied for all but the most obvious persons mentioned. Here again, any errors are my own. I have consulted the *Oxford Classical Dictionary* for spellings of classical names and places. "Sophist" appears in uppercase when referring to those specifically understood to fall into that category, but in lowercase when meant (as far as I could tell) more generally.

Nonsexist language is employed throughout: unspecified persons are arbitrarily designated as "she" or "he." This practice, already employed previously, was developed in consultation with Castoriadis.

One nuance of the French text has not been rendered into English. Plato's *Statesman* concerns knowledge, in particular the *epistēmē* of the "statesman." Both *savoir* and *connaissance* may be translated as "knowledge"; but the former has a more formal connotation, while the latter often implies rather a familiarity, as in knowing (*savoir*) that one knows (*connaît*). Short of indicating each specific appearance, it is impossible to reflect this distinction in the translation.

Finally, we come to the title itself of Plato's dialogue. In Greek, it is *Politikos*; in French, *Le Politique*. The English translation, the *Statesman*, is rather unfortunate, Castoriadis himself noted.[5] Had these seminars been delivered by him directly in English, one could imagine him prefacing his remarks with something like the following:

> Now, the English title, the *Statesman*, is particularly intolerable. I've said on many occasions that the Greek term *polis* is not to be translated as *city-state*, for the Greeks didn't have a separate state apparatus. To call the person who was to be occupied with the running of the *polis* a *statesman* is, even in Plato's perverse construction concerning the so-called royal man, totally unacceptable. Yet here we have the term enshrined in tradition as the common translation of Plato's dialogue. We cannot pretend that this reality doesn't exist and so must use this wholly unsuitable term; let us simply keep in mind its inadmissibility each time we employ it.

Likewise, when talking about the art of this "statesman" we refer to his "statesmanship," whereas the Greek original speaks of *politikē*, which in French is *la politique* and in English usually is translated as *politics*.

I would add to this imaginary aside the fact that, as opposed to *la politique* (politics/statesmanship), *le politique* can mean not only the statesman but also "the political" (or "the political sphere"), a relatively recent term derived from Carl Schmitt's *das Politische*, which Castoriadis did not eschew.[6] I have endeavored each time to choose the correct term in English—*statesman* or *the political, politics* or *statesmanship*—according to context. The reader may now judge for herself whether I have successfully sorted out the nuances and ambiguities, or whether alternative readings might be called for.

ON PLATO'S *STATESMAN*

Seminar of February 19, 1986

I was telling you the last time that Plato played quite a considerable role in what can be called the destruction of the Greek world. In the eyes of history, he transformed a de facto destruction into an apparently de jure destruction. That is to say, if the Athenian democracy collapsed in the end, it was ultimately in the order of things—not in the sense in which Herodotus says, "All that is great must become small," and vice versa, but because it was fundamentally rotten, a regime dominated by the ignorant crowd, the impassioned and passionate crowd, and not by the wise man or by wisdom, the just man or justice. Thus, rather than being a historical tragedy, the fall of Athenian democracy becomes a case of immanent philosophical justice.

This he did, in one respect, if I may phrase it thus, "positively": he advanced the idea that there can and should be an *epistēmē* of politics [*la politique*], a sure and certain knowledge enabling one to be guided in the political domain; that, in the end, this *epistēmē* of statesmanship [*la politique*] relies upon a transcendent knowledge; and even that it relies upon transcendence itself. It is in this sense, ultimately, that the regime described in the *Laws* can and should be considered—to speak hastily and facilely—to be much more moderate than that of the *Republic*. Plato, as one says, watered down his wine as he aged. That doesn't happen to everyone, but it happened to him.

Yet, even though it is more moderate, the regime of the *Laws* remains all the same basically a theocratic regime. And it is this regime that, in a sense, opens the way not only to the critique of the democratic regime but also to the quite ambiguous critique of the law as such. I shouldn't say *ambiguous*, moreover, but *very clear*, when this critique is read in the

I

Statesman (294a–c) and when it allows Plato to justify his claims to be going beyond written law in the name of a higher form of knowledge.

And it's indeed Plato who completely overturns the Greek conception of justice as a question that remains constantly open within the city: Who is to give what, and who is to have what? This question constantly poses the problem of distribution among the citizens and at the same time thus opens the way to further questioning [*une interrogation*]. He therefore overturns this definition and makes of justice what could be called and has, moreover, been called in modern times a holist, or holistic, property, a property of the whole. For Plato—this is the conception from the *Republic*, this is the conception from the *Laws*—justice is the fact that the city as a whole is well divided, well articulated, and that, within this whole of the city, each has his place and doesn't try to obtain another one. According to the famous phrase from the *Republic*, justice consists in τά αὐτοῦ πράττειν καὶ μὴ πολυπραγμονεῖν (*Republic* 433a), minding your own business, doing what's yours, what belongs to you, what is your own, what corresponds to your place, without trying to busy yourself with everything, to be a busybody—this English word being, moreover, the best translation of *polupragmonein*.

But at the same time, it's in Plato that for the first time we have an attempt to ground, in right and in reason, a hierarchy within the city. In the Greek city, the existence of freemen and slaves or of the rich and the poor is a fact. With Plato, this supposedly becomes a right—that is, something that rests upon the different natures of the individuals of which the city is composed. To do this, I said, Plato engaged throughout his work in an immense operation that turns anything to good account and that manifests a strange inconsistency, which I have even qualified as perversity—I stand by this word. Plato constantly rebukes the rhetoricians, yet he himself proceeds rhetorically in an immense number of instances. He tries to garner one's conviction, and he succeeds in doing so—the proof? we're still talking about him—by playing upon the plausible, the probable, the likely, by playing even upon the wellsprings of shame, respectability, and modesty. He does so by working on the soul of the listener, and not only on his reason, in order to try to show him that there is good and evil, that a decent man can only be on the side of the good. Those who are evil blush in the dialogues, like Thrasymachus at the end of the first book of the *Republic*: "Thrasymachus agreed to all that . . . but reluctantly and with great difficulty . . . and then I saw something I had never seen before: Thrasymachus blushing" (350d).

It's the same thing as regards the Sophists. Plato rebukes them, but he is himself an incomparable sophist. One cannot count the number of intentional sophisms and paralogisms that are there in the dialogues. The *Republic* itself is one huge articulated sophism, a multi-leveled and multi-staged sophism.

The two preceding considerations show that what Plato says against the demagogues can be turned around against him—except that, in his case, it isn't an everyday, physically present *dēmos* that he's stirring up, that he's churning up, and that he's trying to carry off in a certain direction. It is the *dēmos* of the lettered men and women of history, of the work's readers over the centuries. And for the same reasons, moreover, he, too, is an *eidōlopoios*, a manufacturer of simulacra—what he accuses the Sophists of being—in, for example, everything he recounts about the differing natures of human beings, which goes to justify their division into classes in the *Republic*, or the conscious, impudent lies proffered in the third book of the *Laws* concerning the history of Athens, and so on.

And at the same time, this is someone who, if one goes deeper, is, one could say, lacking in modesty. He has, that is, an immodesty of the mind, the immodesty of an argumentative person. To prove this, I need only cite the accusation lodged in the *Gorgias* {515dff.} against the politicians of Athens and, notably, against Pericles, where it is said that if those people were truly, as reported, so just, so intelligent, they would have raised [*auraient élevé*] their sons in corresponding fashion. And this is said by someone who was himself a pupil [*élève*] of Socrates, the disciples of whom included, on the one hand, Alcibiades and, on the other, a dozen of those who later became the Thirty Tyrants! That's the result of what Socrates taught, according to Plato's logic! And, secondly, this is said by someone who raised no son of his own, neither good nor bad, neither in the direction of justice nor in the direction of injustice. He's got a lot of cheek, as is said in common parlance, or, in a more noble language, the immodesty of someone who is a philosophical arguer.

Comparing Alcibiades and Plato, one could say that in a sense—though, to support the comparison, to push it further, one would have to read the *Symposium* in detail, which we cannot do here—Plato is a sort of inverted Alcibiades. Considerably younger than Alcibiades, undoubtedly thirty years his junior, Plato sublimates this passion for power that Alcibiades couldn't master and that led him to do what he did in the history of Athens; Plato transposes it onto another level, the level of writing, of schooling, of counsel given to the powerful and to tyrants. That is what he did, it seems, in Sicily with Dionysius and then with Dion.

But at the same time, there's a sort of indifference on his part to the city that raised him. Again, this contrasts him with Socrates. For Alcibiades, Athens is purely and simply the instrument of his own might. When the Athenians recalled him from Sicily,[1] he passed over to the side of Sparta and then came back to Athens. Likewise, Plato is completely cold toward Athens; he rebukes it, and not just the democracy. He does retain a kind of racial pride, so to speak, which is to be found again at the end of the *Laws* {969c–d}, when the Lacedaemonian and the Cretan agree among themselves that they could never have succeeded in resolving the problem of the good city without the Athenian who accompanies them during this long philosophical march—a march both literal and figurative. Plato therefore retains this one point of honor; but as for the content and substance of Athens, of the Athenian historical creation, he detests it. In any case, he simply uses his situation as an Athenian citizen to profit from what he has learned, to profit from Socrates, who is a son of the city, to profit from the *paideia* {education} streaming out from Athens, and to profit from his own position. And he uses it finally to found his own school in the gardens of Academus, profiting from the liberalism, from the love of liberty, of the Athenians, who, once again, allowed someone to open a public-education establishment that rebukes their city, instead of putting him to death right away, as the ephors would have done in his beloved Sparta.

To this dimension would have to be added the concern with the aesthetic appearance of one's life, a concern that, unless I am mistaken, appears for the first time in antiquity with Alcibiades, thus dissociated. Plato himself undoubtedly cultivated—and cultivated until the end—the aesthetic appearance of his life and made sure that his followers, his pupils, the entire Academy, constantly contributed to the fabrication of this myth of Plato, which passes by way of many things—including, probably, the fabrication of letters, about which I'll say a word in just a moment.

From all these standpoints, we can reflect upon these two children, these two pupils, who were by far the two most brilliant Socrates had: Alcibiades and Plato. Undoubtedly, too, at this time (at the end of the fifth century and the beginning of the fourth; thus, after the tragic poets and after Thucydides), they were the two most brilliant Athenians in quite different domains—but both of them were already perverse and did not love their *polis*.

Why this influence of Plato's? I shall come back to this question at the end. In this influence must be seen, on the one hand, what is due to Plato himself, which we have already seen: a whole series of operations, the strategy he puts into effect. But there is also what is due to later times. Here, things are relatively simple. I won't talk about Karl Popper, who created a kind of counterprejudice. One cannot call Plato *totalitarian* or make him into the father of totalitarianism. But on account of his hatred of democracy and on account of what constantly shines through from him as a desire to fix the things in the city into place, to put a halt to the evolution of history, to stop self-institution, to suppress self-institution—on this account, Plato obviously becomes, in a certain way, the inspirer of and arsenal for everything in history that will represent this attitude. To put it simplistically: of everything reactionary and pro-establishment; everything opposed to the democratic movement. This is found again among the Romans, among the first Christians, during the Middle Ages, and in modern times. I won't and I can't—it would be an immense task—truly go through the history of all that.

Finally, one must, of course, keep in mind the enormous element of authentic creation that exists in Plato, creation of an incontestably trans-historical value that is attached to his work, that is also another kernel of his work, or the other pole. I don't like to speak too much of a *pole*, because it isn't in opposition; the relations between Plato's philosophical and literary—artistic—creation and what that creation carries along with it, what it bears within it, in the way of a political and, of course, philosophical imaginary are quite strange. There is this other element, Plato's creation, his incomparable genius linking at once philosophical depth, logical-dialectical power, literary artistry, and a savoir faire in the politics of ideas of which I spoke a moment ago. This has played a big role in the influence he has had; the result is that, while we are discussing Plato here and when we discuss the *Statesman*, the *Republic*, and the *Laws*, we shall not be able to speak of him as if he were simply some "ideological" author with regard to whom it would suffice to point out his sophisms. At each step, one runs up against—one becomes enraptured [*on s'extasie*] because one discovers—some philosophical nugget or other; one discovers, in the end, yet another of the roots of what we think today, of our modes of thought.

~

Before getting to the positive points, it must be added that with Plato, and for the first time, we have what later on was called the partisan spirit in philosophy. It is sustained by his rhetoric and his staging. Before Plato, and even afterward, the philosophers expound their opinions. Rarely, as with Heraclitus, do they have some disdainful remark to make regarding other philosophers. Starting with Plato, they discuss the ideas of their adversaries, as Aristotle also did later on. Plato, however, is the first and perhaps the last philosopher to transform this discussion into a veritable combat—and in this sense, he comes close to reminding us of Marx; or, rather, Marx reminds us of him. Plato really wants to polarize his readers, to summon them to choose between them and us, between the bad guys and the good guys. The bad guys are those who are mistaken [*se trompent*] and who want to deceive [*tromper*] the world; and the rest of us are those who are in the truth and in the good, in justice. Or he sometimes, in extreme cases, stops arguing altogether in order simply to heap ridicule on them.

But Plato doesn't limit himself to that. As Aristotle would also later do, he doesn't limit himself to these attacks against them and these refutations. He is also the first one—and here again we see the ambiguity of his creation—who used the weapon Paul Ricœur later called *suspicion*, which has indeed loomed so large in modern times, with Marx, Nietzsche, and Freud. He doesn't say: What you are saying is false and I am going to prove it to you. He asks, rather: Why are you saying what you're saying? And the *Why* refers not to logical reasons but to subjective reasons in the largest sense: You are saying it because it suits you to do so; you are making up sophisms because you're a Sophist. And that isn't a tautology. *You are a Sophist* means: You are a merchant of falsehoods, a trader in fallacies, a *kapēlos*, and it is your ontological and social position as a Sophist that makes you say what you are saying. Logical refutation is complemented by, if I may put it thus, ontological, social, and political assignment: You are saying what you are saying because you are an enemy of the proletariat (Marx). You are saying what you are saying because your neurosis leads you to say it (Freud). You are saying what you are saying because truth is a poison for the weak and because you cannot bear it (Nietzsche).

In Plato, it goes as follows: You are saying what you are saying because you make a living off of lies. And you are making a living not only in the sense that you are getting paid for your lessons—a point Plato insists upon a great deal—but because you make a living in this way ontologically. The being of the Sophist is a being that relies upon not-being. This is because there is not-being and the possibility of making not-being pass for being and being for not-being—which leads to the famous ontological revision made in the *Sophist*, to the murder of the father, of Parmenides. It is therefore because one can mix one with the other, being and not-being. And that means, in a certain fashion, that being is not and that not-being is. And moreover, this qualification *in a certain fashion* is too much. As Plato himself says in the *Sophist* {259b}, "Ten thousand times ten thousand, being is not . . . and not-being is." And it's because there is this ontological connection that you, the Sophists, can exist.

And it is, moreover, from this standpoint that one can make the distinction—even if that's not our principal interest—between two groups of Platonic dialogues. On the one hand, there are the basically staged and polemical dialogues, which are designed to refute one or two Sophists: the *Euthydemus*, the *Menexenus*, the *Gorgias*, with the series Polus, Callicles, and Gorgias. These dialogues take place before an audience, a public, which is like a chorus that prevents the Sophist from persisting in his sophisms by using a kind of silent disapproval that mobilizes an ultimate residue of shame. Even a Sophist, even Thrasymachus, has some of that in his soul.

And then there are the dialogues involving real research, the zetetic dialogues, for which no public is necessary and from which the public is in fact entirely absent. Thus, in the *Parmenides* some very profoundly outrageous things are said there, but there is no public. One is among people of good faith—Young Socrates, Parmenides—and one has no need for a chorus, for a silent and reproachful judge.

~

As for the properly philosophical creation, one must simply recall a certain number of points. And already, first of all, there's the fact that Plato is the creator of the interpretation of the positions taken and not only of the refutation thereof. It's the fact that he is constantly resuming his research. Plato is the first person to have tried to fix in place the aporias, and perhaps the ways out of these aporias, that for us surround the question of knowledge and truth. And also the limits of rationality in this world. This is basically the theme of the *Timaeus*, and it comes back all the time. He's the first to attack vigorously the problem that still today remains the *pons asinorum* of philosophy and logic: on the one hand, the relationship between the universal and the singular (among other texts, this is found in the *Parmenides*)—to what extent we can say that there is one dog and that there is one society and that there is one God and that there is one French language and that there is *one* number one. In what sense all that is one, and what the relationship of this Form or Idea or *eidos* of the one is with, on the other hand, the concrete realities (as we shall say as Moderns, as post-Kantians), which we can think only with the aid of—or more exactly, by means of—this category of the one. Can we think by means of this category of the one only, as Kant says, because such is the structure of our mind? Because we cannot think otherwise, and that, allegedly, is something that could be demonstrated? Or is it that we cannot think without the category of the one because there is the one? There is the one, if I may say so, but where? And we still haven't exited from all that because, obviously, the form of the one couldn't be imposed upon the phenomena or upon objects if something didn't lend itself thereto, if something therein didn't permit the propping up [*l'étayage*] and instrumentation of our categories. Therefore, we cannot simply affirm that the one is a category. But on the other hand, the idea that the one belongs to the things, or that causality belongs to the things, appears, indeed, to be completely enigmatic and seems to open a gulf about what that can really mean. In a sense, we have hardly advanced since these in-vestigations [*interrogations*] were laid down and worked out the way they were in the *Parmenides*, in the *Theaetetus*, or, in another fashion, in the *Philebus* and in certain passages from the *Republic*. We shall see some examples of this while speaking about the *Statesman*.

Plato's *Statesman*

And so, without further delay, we can now turn to hand-to-hand wrestling with this dialogue. But here again, there'll be some preliminar-ies, and this is going to seem complex and disordered to you because I don't know the means whereby I could speak of an important work or an important subject in a manner that would be both true and linear, well-ordered. I don't know how to speak about it other than by taking it by one end, coming back, going further, turning the thing over, making di-gressions, and so on. There will therefore be a lot of back and forth in this discussion—as there is, moreover, in the text of the *Statesman* itself.

A second point: Why chose to begin with the *Statesman*? For three rea-sons, basically. And first of all, for a reason that is relatively contingent to our work this year. Given our object in this seminar, we cannot make an in-depth and detailed analysis of all the texts that interest us. During the past two years, we did this work around a phrase from Anaximander, a chorus from *Antigone*, one or two speeches in Thucydides, but this year it's impossible to make a genuine analysis of the *Republic*, of the *Statesman*, and of the *Laws*, then of Aristotle's *Politics* and of the other texts that come afterward. And on the other hand, I want us to do some work together that, though far from exhaustive, will be an in-depth work upon a determinate text. Let's grapple with a text to see what it means to work genuinely on a text. And the only one available from the standpoint of size is the *Statesman*. The *Republic* is too long. The *Laws*, like Aristotle's *Politics*, is huge.

The second reason is that the *Statesman* belongs to what I shall in a minute be calling Plato's fourth and last period. It's a text in which, in a sense, and without being too Hegelian about it, the results of his entire prior development are implicitly found sedimented. And there's not much more to come. From this standpoint, the *Statesman* virtually contains Plato's philosophical trajectory—the problematic, the aporias, and the antinomies of this trajectory. They can be drawn out of the *Statesman* and out of what appear to be the incoherencies in this dialogue and its strange goings-on [*étrangétés*]. This impression of incoherency and strangeness [*étrangété*] comes in a second moment. In the first moment, one tells oneself while reading through this dialogue that things are going quite well, that it's just Plato or Plato's idiosyncrasies. In the second place, things don't go at all. And then, in a third place, a sort of structure is salvaged. And, at a fourth level, one gets a glimpse that this structure itself contains some very deep faults and that these faults are no accident; these are the faults of Plato's thought, and perhaps of all thought.

A third reason: this fourth period of Plato's is embodied and manifested in the *Statesman* via a basic change relating to a point that in appearance is minor but that goes very far, because, here again, given the magmatic structure of thought, one can take off from it to find nearly everything. The change that is there in the *Statesman* is the change relative to the definition of he who is suitable [*propre*] to govern, that is to say, the statesman [*le politique*], the political man, or the royal man. In the *Republic*'s definition, he who is suitable to govern is identified with the philosopher, once he has undergone adequate training. In the *Statesman*, no direct mention is made of him, but the royal man—to whom we shall return later on—appears not as a shepherd [*berger*]—that's the first definition, which is later abandoned—but as a royal weaver. What he weaves, as we shall see later on, isn't very coherent, either. It's disparate, not so much because the things woven together are disparate but because they are situated at different levels: on the one hand, they're the different individuals of the *polis*; on the other hand, they're the different parts of the souls of individuals. And no one-to-one correspondence can be made from one term to the other.

And then, even this royal weaver turns out not to be the true definition of the statesman. There is a third, subjacent definition of him, which is not the philosopher and doesn't lead to him either. And this definition, in fact, prepares the way for the type of regime and government Plato described later on in the *Laws*. And in the latter dialogue, while the members of the much talked-about nocturnal council are philosophers, educated as such and endowed with a curriculum vitae that reminds one of the philosophers of the *Republic*, in a sense they are not—not formally, at least—the ones who govern. The true governors in the city of the *Laws* are magistrates, and these magistrates are elected. And the *Statesman* is this passage, this ford, the place where the waters become shallower and where one can pass from one bank to the other. One can pass from the regime defined absolutely in the *Republic* as the power of the philosophers to the regime of the *Laws*, where there are elective magistrates whose strings—to speak coarsely—are pulled in a sense by the nocturnal council. That situates the *Statesman* at quite an important point in Plato's overall development.

I would like to say now how I intend to speak about this dialogue. There are six points:

1. a few words about the date and historical situation of the *Statesman* in Plato's oeuvre, then about its general problematic;
2. the *Statesman's* structure as such and its strangeness, this jumble [*enchevêtrement*] of definitions, incidental points, and digressions;
3. the two definitions;
4. the eight incidental points;
5. the three digressions;
6. the problem of composition: Is there or is there not a structure hidden behind what appears to be an entirely baroque edifice, with two main towers, three adjoining towers, and eight secondary buildings?

And, finally, if we have the time, we shall take the opportunity to make a sort of critical inventory of everything there is in it—unless we do so along the way.

I. Date and Historical Situation of the *Statesman*

Almost all authors are agreed that the *Statesman* is to be situated between 367 and 360 B.C.E. Some, including myself, would opt for a later date. Why this dating? This is connected with the whole story of Plato's voyages to Sicily. Born in 428, Plato was at least thirty years old when Socrates was condemned to death (in 399). After Socrates' death, Plato—like, moreover, Socrates' other disciples—perhaps fearing that this sentence might have legal consequences for the rest of his disciples, left Athens. Plato himself withdrew for some time to Megara, where he very soon founded a school of Megarites that continued a certain side of Socrates' teaching. Then he undoubtedly made a series of voyages, including certainly one to Egypt, between 399 and 387. Around 387–386, he founded the Academy at Athens. Before that, in 388–387—and we have here testimony independent of Plato's *Letters*—there was the first voyage to Sicily. There he met the tyrant Dionysius I and struck up friendships, which later proved to be important, with Archytas, one of the last great Pythagoreans (who were then very active in southern Italy, in Magna Graecia), and with Dion of Syracuse, son-in-law of Dionysius.

Legend has it that, during his trip home, Plato was taken prisoner by pirates and sold either at Aegina or at Corinth. A more elaborate legend even reports that a number of philosophers were meeting at that very moment in Corinth and that, when they saw Plato on the slave block, they chipped in together right away to buy him back! One may think that this is too *ben trovato* to be true. I myself have many doubts.

Following the tradition, both of the *Letters* and that of the doxographers, there would have been two other voyages in Sicily that were tied to the twists and turns of Sicilian politics. Dionysius I, a very astute and very powerful politician, had died. His son Dionysius II then acceded to power. Dion, who was the son-in-law of the two Dionysiuses—Dionysius's family affairs were very complicated, mixing polygamy, incest, and so forth—was also a very brilliant young man, probably Plato's *erōmenos*, not necessarily in the physical sense but in the form of an amorous friendship like the one described in the *Symposium*. Plato considered him the one who might be able to put his philosopher ideas into political practice. And according to this tradition, Plato is said to have returned to Sicily in 367, in response to an appeal from Dion, in order to transform the young Dionysius into a philosopher-king. This he failed to do. Dionysius broke with Dion and exiled him but sought to retain Plato at Syracuse. Plato is said to have refused.

Three years later, still according to the same tradition of the *Letters* and the doxographers, Plato made a third voyage to Sicily, Dionysius having promised him a number of things, including the recall of Dion. But Dionysius failed to keep his promises, held Plato prisoner, and finally released him only after the intervention of the Pythagorean Archytas of Tarentum. Four years afterward, Dion landed in Sicily and expelled Dionysius from power. A few years of cruel and sordid civil war ensued. And finally Dion was assassinated by another student of the Academy, Callippus.

There would therefore have been, according to this tradition and the *Letters*, especially the seventh one, three voyages to Sicily. That in 387 is certain. The two others, in 367 and 362, are the subject of polemics. Why do the "dogged minority" of scholars, as M. I. Finley calls them, refuse to accept these two other voyages? (I'm not a "scholar," but I belong to this minority.)[2] There are two reasons at least. First, neither Diodorus Siculus—who speaks *in extenso*, however, of Sicilian affairs, of the fall of Dionysius, and of Dion's campaign—nor Aristotle utters a word about them. And yet Aristotle was at the Academy in 367 as well as in 362; and in the *Politics*, he talks about Dion. It is unclear why he would not have mentioned Plato's going to Sicily.

The second reason is that, in any case, for him to have undertaken a third voyage—that is to say, to have believed Dionysius's promises a second time and returned to Sicily—would show in Plato a sort of radical and incurable inability to judge human beings that is really too hard to impute to him. Whatever Plato's desire to influence a king or a tyrant or a holder of power might have been, it cannot be believed that he could have been mistaken on this point a *second* time apropos of an individual like Dionysius.

This impossible gullibility is also, thereby, a contributing factor in rejecting the authenticity of the *Letters*. And there are good reasons that allow us to understand why at the Academy, very early on, these *Letters* would have been fabricated: to reinforce, first off, the legend of a Plato attempting by every means to test out, to realize his ideas; and, secondarily, to try to redeem the behavior of two students of the Academy, Dion (the pretender and then quasi tyrant; see Finley)[3] and Callippus (the assassin). There are so many unpleasant things in the affair that it would be very convenient to cover them over with the great figure of Plato, who, himself, made a try, risked his life for his ideas, and then came back.

However, what stands in the way of the *athetēsis*, as the philologists say, of the refusal to accept the authenticity of the *Letters*, is, however, the quality of the *Seventh Letter*, which is quite beautiful and very profound. From the outset, the justification for Plato's no longer getting mixed up in politics after Socrates' conviction is entirely convincing. Then there's the extraordinary passage about language's relationship with ordinary knowledge, with the knowledge of the things themselves and of the Ideas, and with the much talked-about *exaiphnēs*. It's here that he says that all the other forms of knowledge are preparatory for true knowledge. One must be trained in those forms, but they aren't what bring true knowledge. They are like the preliminary "rubbing" that eventually, at an indeterminate and unexpected—surprising (*exaiphnēs*: sudden)—moment, makes the flame shoot up, the flame that lights up at once the object and the subject and that permits one to see. That's what all logic, all discussion, all mathematics, all dialectics serve to foster. It is preparatory. And this recalls what mystics said later on about the fact that mystical asceticism is there to prepare for a moment of clairvoyance that cannot be forced or wrung out. Knowledge—true knowledge, ultimate knowledge—is described in this *Seventh Letter*. And this description corresponds well enough to what is said in the *Symposium*, in the *Phaedrus*, and in the *Republic* itself about the soul's relationship with knowledge to think that, if this *Seventh Letter* is not authentic in the literal sense—is not authentic for the facts of the third voyage—it is authentic for the philosophical treatment it provides on the question of knowledge's relationship with its object.

Anyhow, the *Statesman* can be catalogued as having been written only after the date of the alleged second voyage. And if there were second and third voyages, it would perhaps be between those two, perhaps after the third. If you've read the *Statesman*, you may recall that it comes in the wake of the *Sophist*, which is supposed to come after the *Theaetetus*. And at the same time, there's the promise of a fourth dialogue, which wasn't written and which would have been the *Philosopher*.

The three existing dialogues and the fourth, the promised dialogue, the *Philosopher*, are linked by a sort of round of characters, a circular dance of the protagonists. In the *Theaetetus*, it's Socrates who asks the questions and it's the young Theaetetus who answers. In the second dialogue, the *Sophist*, it's still Theaetetus who answers, but the questioner is the Stranger from Elea, the *xenos*. A remark: in Greek, *xenos* doesn't mean only *stranger*, *foreigner*, but also and especially he who receives the treatment reserved for foreigners, that is to say, hospitality. There is a Zeus Xenios, protector of foreigners; and *xenia* is hospitality. *Xenos eleatēs* is therefore both the stranger as well as the guest, the invited visitor from Elea. Nevertheless, we shall say *the Stranger from Elea*—even though *the Eleatic friend* would be more faithful—since that's how he is known and since the Moderns adopt it because it's chic: he's a stranger who enters into the game.

In the third dialogue, the *Statesman*, the Stranger from Elea remains the questioner. That's the point that remains fixed with regard to the *Sophist*. And this is foretold explicitly: the person being questioned is Young Socrates, a young Athenian at the end of his adolescence, like Theaetetus, who happens to have the name of Socrates—at one point, moreover, Socrates plays on this, saying that Theaetetus looks like him, that he is ugly like Socrates, and that Young Socrates has his name. One can assume that the latter, like Theaetetus, is very intelligent. In the promised but never written fourth dialogue, the *Philosopher*, the person questioned would again have been, for reasons of symmetry, Young Socrates, and the questioner should have been Socrates.

If we belonged to the structuralo-deconstructionist school, we could ramble on about the fact that Theaetetus, like Socrates, is very intelligent and very ugly; that in the end, when it comes to defining the true philosopher, we'll have the true philosopher questioning Young Socrates; we'll have a return of *logos* into its identity, including from the standpoint of the speakers [*des énonciateurs*] and not only from that of their utterances [*des énoncés*]; and that, as by chance this fourth dialogue was not written, it lies within the margin of the Platonic text. Under this form, all that stuff doesn't interest us. What interests us is the content and the developmental process of Platonic thought.

This tetralogy with a part missing—the *Theaetetus*, the *Sophist*, the *Statesman*, and the *Philosopher* (which wasn't written)—is artificial, in my opinion, as a tetralogy. The three existing dialogues really do belong to what I am calling the fourth period, but the *Theaetetus* is nevertheless rather different from the other two. Its object is as follows: What is called knowledge or knowing? It is an essentially aporetic dialogue: it doesn't arrive anywhere [*n'aboutit pas*], and that, too, is the genius of Plato. The *Theaetetus* is an enormous, extraordinarily rich dialogue that asks what knowledge is and ends up admitting: For the moment, we don't know! We'll see each other again tomorrow. What daring! The Moderns don't do things like that! When they do, it's a bit rotten.

The *Theaetetus* proceeds dialogically. And as in most of the Platonic dialogues, the dialogic form is both false and true. But in the end the dialoguing form isn't superfluous, whereas it is entirely so in the *Sophist* and the *Statesman*. There, the dialogue is a pure artifice, which irritates adolescents who come across these dialogues in high school and can't help but ask themselves what these goings on [*procédés*] are all about.[4] Above all, the logical instrumentation of the *Sophist* and the *Statesman* isn't in the form of a dialogue but is to be found, rather, in its diaeretic tool, in logical division and those interminable divisions the much talked-about Stranger from Elea deploys both in the *Sophist*—Plato deploys six levels of division in order to try to capture the sophist, who always escapes, never letting himself be caught within a division—and in the *Statesman*, where there are two consecutive definitions, which, as we shall see, don't in fact succeed [*n'aboutissent pas*] in capturing the statesman.

From this standpoint, then, there is no clear unity between the *Theaetetus*, on the one hand, and the *Sophist* and the *Statesman*, on the other, whereas the latter two dialogues are actually all in one piece. This is so not only because of the presence of the Stranger from Elea but also because of the devices [*procédés*] he employs. For, this *xenos*, this guest-friend, has in dramatically quite correct and convincing fashion an identical style of discussion in the two dialogues: his mania for diaeresis, his obsession with division, an obsession successfully handled in both dialogues.

And they are all in one piece also because of their content. For—and here again, one could amuse oneself by doing some structuralo-deconstructionism—there's a link and an opposition in the content; there's a joint articulation. The *Sophist* talks about falsehood and not-being; it talks about the corruption of the philosopher that the sophist is; it talks about the fabrication of falsehood; and it doesn't talk, or talks only very incidentally, about the philosopher, which is understandable since there should have been a fourth dialogue, the *Philosopher*. And the *Statesman* talks about the true statesman and talks only incidentally about the false statesman. Well, structuralism being basically a mnemotechnical procedure, this gives us the following diagram:

T	F
φ	σ
π	?

T = true; F = false. One has true knowledge—well, one should have
had it; that's the *Philosopher* (φ). One has false knowledge, too; that's the
Sophist (σ). One has true praxis; that's the *Statesman* {*Politikos* in Greek}
(π). But we're missing something; there's a blank (?). And that's how one
gets oneself elected to the Académie française! Why is there a blank here?
Obviously, this blank isn't completely a blank, because in the *Statesman*
there's a moment when, between the lines, indirectly, one can see what
the false statesman, the demagogue, is. He's talked about a little at the
end. But the subject would have merited a real treatment of its own. And
then the true tetralogy would have been: the *Philosopher*, the *Statesman*,
the *Sophist*, and the *Demagogue*. The demagogue was treated, but always
very indirectly. Whenever he can, Plato takes potshots at the politicians;
in the *Statesman*, he has some very disparaging words for Themistocles.
But there is no dialogue that attacks the demagogue head-on and that
would be the *Sophist*'s counterpart.

Yet we still have, in this whole story, a unity of content—that is to say,
the concepts, the great themes that connect together [*articulent*] these
two dialogues. But this in fact concerns four dialogues, two of which are
not written, even if the end of the *Statesman* talks a bit about alleged
statesmen, people who pretend to be so without truly being so. And we
should have had:

• The *Philosopher*: Socrates would there be questioning Young Socrates;
• the *Statesman*: the Stranger from Elea questioning Young Socrates;
• the *Sophist*: the Stranger from Elea questioning Theaetetus;
• the *Demagogue*: Socrates would there be questioning Theaetetus.

As for the most important philosophical presuppositions, it must be
noted that the *Sophist* and the *Statesman* belong par excellence to that series of dialogues where new points of view are put in place. There still are
aporias; but whereas in the early dialogues, these aporias were above all
verbal and notional, here they are entirely real. And these are dialogues
that grant and place at the center of their preoccupations the mixed and
no longer the pure ideas. To speak in more facile terms: no longer the ab-

solute but the mixed, the real, the approximate, the relative. On the political plane, this is expressed through what in the *Statesman* is called the *second navigation, deuteros plous*. There's a first navigation, that of the *Republic*, which yields the true truth and the good city. Only, we can't claim to be realizing this idea; or else, such a realization could only be the result of chance. We therefore have to be content with a second choice, which is described later on, in the *Laws* (739e), where it is also said that this city, in relation to the city of the *Republic*, is, according to the reading of the manuscripts, either *mia deuterōs*, second according to the deep-seated internal unity, or *timia deuterōs*, second in dignity. *Timia deuterōs* is Otto Apelt's correction, I believe, but I am in agreement with Pierre Vidal-Naquet in saying that *mia deuterōs* would be the right reading.[5] It is really much more profound as an expression to say that the city of the *Laws* is second in unity, in the intensity of the articulations of its parts, in relation to the city of the *Republic*.

If, therefore, contravening all the most respected contemporary rules, we address ourselves to the content of the dialogues and to the evolution of Plato's philosophical thought in order to group the dialogues—this is a general digression, but an indispensable one if one wants to talk about Plato—we see that, in adopting the right criteria—which I am going to explain—this grouping pretty much coincides, on the one hand, with the classifications made according to so-called external criteria—dates, references to characters present or mentioned in the dialogues—and, on the other hand, with the much talked-about stylometric analysis, that is to say, the chronological layout of the dialogues according to indices of style, statistics relating to particles and expressions Plato uses. There are, then, four groups of dialogues:

1. First, the Socratic dialogues, which are his youthful dialogues. Without wanting to enter into the much talked-about and insoluble problem—Who is the true Socrates? Who is the true Plato? Where does Socrates end and where does Plato begin?—we have some dialogues that quite certainly continue, perhaps in giving a more thorough look to it, the Socratic teaching: the *Apology, Crito*, the first *Alcibiades, Euthyphro, Laches, Lysis, Charmides*, the two *Hippias*, and *Ion*.

2. Then we have a second phase, which hasn't until now been separated out as a phase, but I think that it must be separated out. It is a transitional phase and a phase of attacks against the Sophists. During this period, we have some dialogues that are in a sense purely polemical, con-

trary to those of the last period, which are interrogatory without great polemics. These as well as those of the third period are among the most beautiful: this is Plato's mature phase, when he was in full possession of his poetic powers. Here we have the *Protagoras*, the *Euthydemus*, the *Menexenus*, the *Gorgias*, and the first book of the *Republic*—which is often called *Thrasymachus* after the Sophist who is Socrates' principal interlocutor there.

It is obvious that the *Protagoras*, the *Euthydemus* (the dialogue that ridicules the Sophists the most), and the *Gorgias* thoroughly attack the Sophists. The "*Thrasymachus*," too. The *Menexenus* plays a bit the role of the piece that could furnish the material for illustrating the empty box here, because, with its parody of the Athenian funeral oration, it's a kind of charge lodged against the politicians or the demagogues (in Plato's sense) who go around telling stories. What they were recounting, as presented in the *Menexenus*, is so improbable that, for serious readers, it can only backfire against the orator.

3. The third phase involves the discovery, affirmation, and deployment of the theory of Ideas. One can begin this phase with the *Meno*, and it includes the four great "idealist" dialogues: the *Phaedo*, the *Phaedrus*, the *Symposium*, and the bulk of the *Republic*.

4. Finally, there's the fourth phase, which extends from the height of Plato's maturity to his old age, and which I begin with the *Cratylus*, a deeply aporetic dialogue. It is absurd to say, as many commentators do, that Plato upholds the theory that some words are naturally correct [*justes*] and that others are not so. The *Cratylus* is absolutely aporetic and sows enormous confusion, because it investigates our relationship to language and language's relationship to things and poses the question: Since what we state as truth goes by way of language (to formulate it in modern terms), how must language be in order that we might be able to state a truth? It's taken hold of at one end, the correspondence of the terms of language with things, but that's the problem that is being taken up.

There are, then, the *Cratylus*, the *Theaetetus*, the *Parmenides*, three highly aporetic dialogues, and the results of this *aporia* and *aporēsis*, which are given in the *Sophist*, the *Statesman*, the *Timaeus* plus the *Critias*, and the *Philebus*—and the *Laws* in quite coherent fashion come at the end. And it's in these last dialogues that the theory of the mixed is posited and expounded upon to the furthest extent possible:

• The *Sophist* begins by dissolving the absolutism of Parmenidean being while imposing the truth that not-being is and being is not always or not under all aspects;

• then the *Statesman*, we shall see, opens the way to the abandonment of the *Republic*'s absolutism in the matter of political regimes;

• the *Timaeus* establishes the mixed on the ontological and cosmological plane and makes the god himself, the demiurge, incapable of doing more than is possible according to the nature of things, namely, according to the nature of the matter he fashions, on the one hand, and according to the nature of the numbers by means of which he fashions nature since these numbers don't allow one to do as one wishes;

• and, finally, there's the *Philebus*, which, under the pretext of talking about pleasure, states a number of extremely important theses about the fact that all that is is a mixture of one and several as well as of determination and indetermination, of *peras* and *apeiron*. And the *Laws* come at the end of this fourth and last period in entirely coherent fashion.

II. The Object and Structure of the *Statesman*

The manifest object of the dialogue is given by its title and by the discussion: to find a definition of the statesman. Nevertheless, Plato explicitly states the opposite in the dialogue itself, and this has to be taken seriously. At a given moment (285d), the Stranger from Elea says: It is obvious that we are not seeking the statesman for his own sake; we don't have that much to do with him. All this is for us an exercise in dialectic. We learn to divide as we should by adopting the criteria we should adopt. But it is quite evident that this second level is only a pretext; and that, in a third stage, it really is the statesman who is Plato's preoccupation here; and that the title of the *Statesman* is perfectly justified. What interests Plato, as in the *Sophist*, is to define the sophist and the statesman, that is to say, this kind of grid-mapping of the highest human activities: on the one hand, those concerning knowledge; praxis, on the other. When he tells us that all that is only a pretext to learn to divide correctly [*comme il faut*], we could say, coarsely: Tell that to the marines! That isn't true; he doesn't choose the division of lice or cockroaches to show us how to learn to divide. In psychoanalytic jargon, it isn't just by chance that he chooses the sophist and the statesman; he chooses two objects that are of passionate interest to him as such, and it's these two objects that are going to bear the brunt of diaeretic analysis. But if they're going to bear the brunt of it, that's because Plato has some negative or positive accounts to settle with the question of the sophist and the statesman in general. So much for the object of the dialogue.

The structure of the *Statesman*, as one can glimpse quite immediately while reading through it, is quite strange. The *Sophist*, too, is constructed very bizarrely, but the strangeness there, however, is much less pronounced. Briefly speaking, in the *Sophist*, there are six successive attempts at definition: after the sixth, one returns to the fifth, which constitutes an anomaly. But all these definitions serve a certain purpose, presenting the Sophist in the guise of various disreputable practitioners; all these definitions are attempts to compose a portrait of the Sophist that is as disparaging as possible. And there is only one lengthy digression—which apparently comes about by accident but had, in reality, long been in preparation—that of being and not-being. This is a rather complex feature in the development of Plato's work, and it's difficult to pronounce on the matter with certainty. But in the *Parmenides*, where both Parmenides and his enthusiastic student Zeno—his *erōmenos* (it's obvious that in the dialogue Zeno was Parmenides' *paidika*, his young beloved)—are present, the old master Parmenides' very own teaching—that is to say, that being is and that not-being is not, and that there is, moreover, only the one—is put to a very severe test. It is made clear that this teaching cannot but lead to a series of impasses. In my opinion, that is the teaching of the *Parmenides*. One is left with this negative conclusion.

The *Sophist* furnishes, therefore, its positive complement by way of the much talked-about parricide {241d}, that is, the moment when the Stranger from Elea says: Our father Parmenides must now be killed; this horrible thing must be said, that being is not and that not-being is. He works this out positively, if I may put it so; he gives an entirely new version of the theory of Ideas, which he himself calls the *supreme kinds* {254c}. And he gives the five forms of supreme kinds—being, the same, the other, rest, movement—as always being; today, we would perhaps say: the ontological transcendentals from which all that is is made. (Parenthetically, we may note that this is clearly so for being, the same, and the other. But for rest and movement, the term *movement* obviously shouldn't be taken in the Galilean or post-Galilean sense: until Galileo, and in any case among the Greeks, movement doesn't mean only local movement.

Movement is change; it's alteration. In Aristotle, this is quite clear; and it is so in Plato, too. When it is said that rest and movement appertain to the supreme kinds, that means immutability, on the one hand, and the possibility and the effective actuality of alteration, on the other. And that's what the *Sophist* says.)[6]

This digression in the *Sophist* comes naturally in relationship to the definition of the Sophist, because the latter has to be defined as a trafficker in not-being. But how can one be a trafficker in not-being if not-being is not? Not-being must be, in a certain fashion; and it must be possible to present being as not-being and vice versa. Therefore, in this apparently trivial, not to say derisory, way, one of the greatest theorems of philosophy from its beginnings to the present day—that not-being is and that being is not—is introduced on the basis of the definition of this manufacturer of false images. Behind this, there is, as is immediately clear, a whole series of interrogations that the Sophists and then the Megarians were already raising: How is the false possible if the false is defined as stating what is not? But Parmenides says: What is not is not, period. One can't even say it—which, in the end, would reduce Parmenides himself to silence. One had to get out of all that. And one gets out of it with the *Sophist*, with its unique, central ontological digression.

In the *Statesman*, things are quite different. The structure is quirky [*bis-cornue*]: it includes two definitions of the statesman, neither of which is the correct one [*la bonne*] from Plato's point of view. The right [*bonne*] definition is hidden within the dialogue; it's played like a charade. There are, in addition, three digressions and eight incidental points. And if one were Pythagorean, one might say that eight is two to the third power! So, it's normal that there are eight incidental points, since there are two definitions and three digressions.

The *Statesman* begins with a short preamble (257a–258b). Then comes the first definition: that of the statesman as pastor [*pasteur*]. This first definition goes from 258b to 277c, where it will be abandoned. But along the way, there's the exposition properly speaking (258b–267), along with the critique of the definition, which is made in several places (267c–268d, 274a–275a, 275b–c). The first definition is expounded through a kind of downward division, of dichotomy with the different species of knowledge (theoretical knowledge/practical knowledge), and finally one arrives at this idea of the pastor.

In there we have two incidental points, both of which are very impor-

tant from the philosophical point of view. First (262a–263b), there's the
distinction between species and part—and, if one is the slightest bit a
philosopher, one sees right away that this is an absolutely enormous question. What is a part and what is a species? The human species is a part of
the animal kingdom! Well, well! And then the legs are a part of man but
aren't a species. What's going on?

The second incidental point (263c–264e) is just as important. If one
doesn't pay attention, the point of view of the person who is dividing can
be fatally determinative for the content of the division being performed.
That's the content of this second incidental point: Watch out for the subjective point of view in the divisions one performs.

Next, after a recapitulation of the first definition, there's the critique of
this first definition: The statesman cannot be the pastor. Why? First of all,
because there are other arts also that attend to [*s'occupent*] the raising of
men. Next, because a pastor properly speaking attends to everything,
whereas the statesman doesn't. And here, all of a sudden, and before going further into his criticisms, there is a first major digression: the extraordinary myth of the reign of Cronus. It's really brought in like a free
association; for, in Greek, a pastor is *nomeus*, from the verb *nemein*, which
means at least two things: to divide, on the one hand; and then to tend
and pasture [*faire paître*], to attend to a flock [*troupeau*] or something
else. The pastor is by his essence superior to the beings he tends and pastures; he is superior to the goats, to the sheep. He is of another species, as
a matter of fact. Therefore, had there been a pastor of men, this pastor
ought to have been a god. And as a matter of fact, there was—in the time
of Cronus, actually—a divine pastor! It's under this ultrathin pretext that
this extraordinary digression about the reign of Cronus is introduced; it
runs from 268a to 274. We shall talk about it at length.

Back, then, to the supposedly principal purpose, so as to continue the
critique of the statesman as pastor by saying that, as a matter of fact, there
might have been a confusion of the human pastor and the divine pastor.
It is recalled that the definition is too broad. And so it is partially revised:
it must be said not only that he is pastor but that he is *agelaiokomos*, that
is to say, that in a certain fashion he cares for [*soigne*] the flocks
(275c–276e). And then in unexplained fashion, in 277a–c, the Stranger
says: None of that will do; this definition has to be abandoned. But he
doesn't say why. And therefore the flock and the entire pastorale are
dropped.

The Stranger then introduces a third incidental point, which is a new methodological principle. The first two incidental points have already methodologically grounded the device of diaeresis that follows with the stories of the pastor, the herdsman [*pasteur*] of horned and nonhorned animals, and so on and so forth. Treated there were the still-to-be-made distinction between part and element and the fact that one must be careful not to introduce subjective elements into the basis and criteria for division—for, in that case, cranes would divide animals into cranes and noncranes the way the Greeks divide humans into Greeks and non-Greeks, barbarians. And that won't do: there, one isn't dividing according to what is objective but instead according to a subjective point of view. Like, therefore, these first two incidental points, incidental point number three is the methodological preamble for what follows. That is to say, the whole definition given on the basis of weaving, the definition of the statesman as weaver. The third incidental point concerns the paradigm and its elements. It concerns the absolutely fundamental problem that we still face today: How is one to think one thing on the basis of another thing? Do I encounter difficulties thinking one thing by attacking it head-on, or do I not know how to take it? What I can do is find a paradigm, find something else that presents enough of a kinship or that in any case allows itself to be articulated and deployed in a sufficiently fecund fashion for me then to be able to come back to the first thing and say: OK, now I can broach it like that.

Of course, this incidental point skirts the previous question: How do I know that weaving is a good paradigm for the statesman's art? This is only a variant of the problem previously mentioned by Plato in the *Phaedo* and in the *Phaedrus*: How is it that I know what a human being is before having seen a human being? And how is it that I could glean the idea of a human being, saying, "All those are human beings," if I didn't already have the idea of a human being? Or, for that matter, how can I seek something if I don't know what I am seeking already? Plato's metaphysical response in the previous dialogues was the theory of anamnesis: it's that I have in fact always known it, but this knowledge is buried, hidden; someone has to awaken it. Whence Socrates' gnosioanalysis, his maieutic, which delivers what is nonconscious in the human being, even in the slave from the *Meno*; it delivers the truths he possesses because he has already seen them in another life.

This third incidental point—and taking into account the fact that the

Statesman belongs to the period of the mixed in Plato's thought—offers, if I may say so, a human way of solving this aporia. Better still: not a solution but a way of governing this aporia. Why? Because the third incidental point has meaning only upon the presupposition that, in the things themselves, there are intrinsic kinships that are more than just formal, or are formal but in the very strong sense of the term, in the sense that the form would very heavily determine the content. There are kinships among things that allow one in a fruitful and valid way to pass from one category of things to another, to pass from weaving to the statesman. This is not for Plato simply an easy way of expounding upon the matter: his whole development here can be valid only if there effectively is something from both sides that is sufficiently close, in a sufficiently adequate manner, for something about the statesman to be able to be thought once one has elucidated the paradigm of weaving, once that leads toward the statesman, if one has a preoccupation of that type.

And therefore, on the basis of this third incidental point, one arrives at the second definition of the statesman as weaver, which takes up the entire end of the dialogue. And it begins with an exposition (279b–280a) that delights historians of technical inventions [*historiens de la technique*] about weaving itself and the various ways of weaving. As Ulrich von Wilamowitz-Moellendorff said, it is obvious when reading these passages that Plato knew even more about weaving, materials to be woven, ways of weaving, and so on, than what he says about it. He had fully mastered the features of this technical occupation.

In 281d–e, however, there is a fourth incidental point, which—anticipating Aristotle here—distinguishes the arts of the proper cause from those of the composite or accompanying or comitant cause, as he puts it.

(An Aristotelian digression apropos of this fourth incidental point: the Greek word *sumbainein*, an Aristotelian word par excellence, signifies "to go together." In Aristotle, the idea of *sumbainein*, of *sumbebēkos*, of things that go together with other things, is all over the place. They can go together by pure chance or they can go together with other things quite essentially but without appertaining to the definition, properly speaking, of the thing. Here's an example: The sum of the angles of every triangle is equal to two right angles. Aristotle says, in an astonishing phrase: That *sumbainei* with the essence of the triangle; it is concomitant to it. It happens that the fact that the sum of the angles of every triangle is equal to two right angles is the object of a rigorous mathematical proof. But that is of little matter: it doesn't appertain to the essence of the triangle, which is to be a plane figure bounded by three straight lines. And in no way is it a question therein of what the sum of the three angles yields. Only, "it happens that" doesn't mean that it's by pure chance: it goes together.

The problem for us comes from an unhappy translation of *sumbebēkos* by *accident* in French, or its equivalent in other European languages. *Akzidenz*, for example, in German. For, semantically speaking, in all Latin tongues the accident is obviously the accident of chance. Now, if one keeps this unfortunate translation, young students of philosophy will have to be subjected to an intensive training, wherein they are told: Beware, *accident* in Aristotle has nothing to do with road traffic or with any other kind of accident; it can be something entirely essential. Thus, the heart doesn't enter into the definition of man, and it's by accident that you have, that we have, hearts. I have proposed, and I insist upon it, that one translate *sumbainein* and *sumbebēkos* by *comitant*—which is the translation of *cumeo, comitans*, going together. One can then have essential comitants and accidental comitants. And this is the same word one finds again, with a redundancy, and often a misspelling, in *concomitant*. It's spelled with one *t*, since in French it doesn't derive from *mettre* but from the participle of *cumeo*. And concomitant variations are variations that go together.)

Incidental point number five is a very important one. It is made before returning to the definition and it concerns the measure of things. There are, for Plato, relative measures and absolute measures, measures that have their meaning only though comparisons and absolute measures, norms of things. A very strange idea, to which we shall return.

Then comes the sixth incidental point, Plato's trickery about the true object of the dialogue: It isn't the statesman, about whom one more or less doesn't care, but dialectic, dialectical exercise (285d). The discussion's been going on for a good while apropos of the statesman, OK, but that's only a pretext; only dialectical gain interests us.

And yet one returns to weaving. In order to define it. Then, a return to the city in order to define the plurality of the arts of life in common in the *polis* (287c–289c). Plato first enumerates the seven arts of life in common, then, as a third part of this definition, the auxiliary and subaltern arts (289–291a). And here appears, in a detour, as if hitched onto the 291a passage, the most magician-like of all the sophists, the democratic politician. It is then that the two other huge digressions come in:

A. Digression two, on the forms of political regimes (291d–292a), taken up again as digression two and a half between 300d and 303b, where Plato says that democracy is both the least good and the "least bad" of regimes. B. Digression three, of capital importance, wedged in between the two parts of digression two, where he develops the idea that science alone is the basis for the definition of the statesman. This third digression is articulated in five points:

1. 292 gives the basis for the definition;
2. in 293a–e, the absoluteness of the power of he who knows is affirmed;
3. then, in 294a–c, there's the development about the essential deficiency of all written law;
4. the fourth point is the first navigation (294e–297d), where Plato reaffirms the absolute power of he who knows, whose mere appearance of its own right abrogates all laws;
5. finally, from 297d to 300c, there's the second navigation, where it is said that in the genuine statesman's absence, one may content oneself with these deficient and inadequate regulations that are the written laws.

And it is indeed in terms of this second navigation and of what is said there that, in digression two and a half, the theme of the forms, the types, of regimes can be taken up again, since here, contrary to what was the case in the *Republic*, the existence of a rights-based State [*l'État de droit*] or one ruled by laws [*ou un État de lois*] becomes a trait that enables one to discriminate between regimes. The least corrupt regimes are those that, even though they are not governed by the statesman, have laws and obey them, whether one is talking about monarchy, aristocracy, or democracy. And the most corrupt regimes are those in which there aren't even any laws.

After digressions two, three, and two and a half, there's a return to the status of false statesmen, which had been dropped (303b–c), then something on the auxiliary and elementary arts (303d–305d). The seventh incidental point concerns the arts that serve other arts. The existence of a hierarchy among the arts is affirmed at 304b–d. Therefore, the definition of the statesman as weaver is given again (305e). And we thought our troubles were over, but no: for, suddenly, one can very well ask oneself in the end regarding this story about the statesman as weaver: A weaver, yeah, OK; but what does he weave, this royal weaver? What are the materials he must blend together [*méler*], interlace, in order to perform his job? Now, of course, the first reference to the object of this weaving relates to these different arts, the seven principal arts and then the auxiliary arts that are indispensable for life in common. But here, all of a sudden, Plato, after an incidental point number eight about the diversity of the virtues (306a–308c), or at the same time as this eighth incidental point, introduces a new object of weaving that has no relationship with the preceding one. Whereas, until now, one might have understood—and it wouldn't be wrong—that the statesman is the royal weaver who weaves together all the arts necessary to the life of the city, even if he doesn't so much weave them personally but permits, rather, the coexistence of these different arts in the city, here we have something entirely different; we have the fact that the human being's virtue includes parts, that these parts are diverse, that they constitute a diversity, that they can even be opposed to each other, in a certain fashion. That's a theme Plato had already more or less sketched out in the *Republic*: for example, if one is brave, and merely brave, that can border on being opposed to a certain *phronēsis*. One can be simply reckless, absurdly brave. And Aristotle took up this theme later on in his theory of virtue.

Being introduced here, therefore, is a new distinction, one that is psychological in the sense that the term *psychology* has in Plato. The counterpart of ontology is psychology in its great dignity and with its grand dimensions. Starting from this, the statesman weaves together these different parts of virtue, the psychical parts of virtue in individuals; and thus starting from there, one returns anew to the statesman as someone weaving together those aspects, those dimensions of virtue. And along the way, there really also is something that is like a kind of addition. The statesman doesn't simply weave together the arts and then the parts of the soul; rather, he also weaves genetically the inhabitants of the city. He tries to ensure a blending [*mélange*] of the most daredevil families with the families that are the most prudent, so that their descendants will display a blending of these qualities that would be the right blending, and we arrive finally at the final definition (311b–c).

I'll stop here. Next time, we'll attack the discussion of the two definitions, the eight incidental points, and the three digressions, in that order.

Summary of the Carving Up of the *Statesman*

Seminar of February 26, 1986

Resumption and Anticipation

You will recall that I carved up this dialogue—I hope like a "good butcher," to use Plato's expression from the *Phaedrus* {265e}—into many parts. And more specifically, into two definitions, eight incidental points, and three digressions, the second of these being able, moreover, also to be divided in two.

I remind you that the first digression is that of the myth of Cronus (268e–277c), that the second digression concerns the forms of regimes (291d–e), and that it is complemented by digression two and a half (300d–303b), which is an evaluation of the bad regimes, of regimes that aren't the absolute regime. Finally, from 292a to 300c, there's the third and most important digression, the one that justifies our speaking here of the *Statesman*, which contains the much talked-about thesis that it's science alone that defines the statesman. It is explained in a first part, which furnishes its basis; a second part demonstrates the absolute character of a political power that would be grounded upon science; and a third part, finally, criticizes the law on account of its essential deficiency. This is the much talked-about idea that the law never speaks but of the universal, whereas in reality one is always dealing with the singular. The conclusion of all this is thus that if the royal man, the political man, is there, everything else must give way. There no longer are any laws; the law is the will of this royal man. Such is the result of what can be called the first navigation.

Only, at the end of this first navigation, Plato says that all that isn't pos-

sible in the context of existing cities: There is no royal man; and if there
were one, the others wouldn't recognize him. Consequently, a second
navigation is required; one has to return to the problem as a whole, which
will lead us to the discovery of the power of the law as lesser evil. The city
ruled by laws will therefore be second on the scale of values, but it will
take precedence over all the cities in which law is not mistress.

Thus, we have in this third digression the two pivotal ideas that regulate the movements of Plato's thought at this stage in his evolution.
Namely, first of all, the Plato of the theory of the Ideas, the "absolutist"
Plato—though not only in the political sense—the Plato who thinks that
there is a genuine science of things in general and of human things in particular, and that, by way of consequence, it is up to the trustee of this science to settle, to regulate, to govern human things. And then there's the
other aspect, which characterizes all the great dialogues of the final period: a philosophy of the mixed, at the ontological and cosmological level
as well as at the anthropological and psychological level. Plato is recognizing here that, by the very nature of things, there can be neither perfect
knowledge nor perfect regulation of things that are real, and that, by way
of consequence, one must have recourse to a second series of measures, or
provisions—to this lesser evil that the law effectively is.

Let us make a retrospective incidental point in order to underscore how
extraordinary and ever-valid this part of the third digression, which concerns the law and its essential deficiency, truly is. For, what Plato is formulating in this passage for the first time—the gap between the universal
rule and the particular reality—is, of course, a constituent element of the
human world. This constituent element is a cleavage of its being. And it's
this same observation that later bolstered Aristotle's reflection in the
Nichomachean Ethics, the one on the much talked-about problem of equity (book 5). But above all, it's this observation that—contrary to what
Plato himself thinks and what he wants—quite obviously and directly
leads, at a deeper level, to the abandonment of any idea of a perfect city
defined once and for all. There can be no law that embraces all aspects of
human activities once and for all. For, the gap between the law and reality isn't accidental; it's essential.

And if you draw the conclusions that follow from this idea—which,
once again, immediately and massively imposes itself on you—you see
right away that it implicitly contains a condemnation of Plato's prior attempts in the *Republic*, as well as of the subsequent attempt of the *Laws*.

In the *Laws*, it is true, there are a few provisions for revising the laws from time to time. But they're very weak, marginal, and the essential aim of the *Laws* is, there again, to freeze history, to freeze the institution of society.

And beyond Plato's critique—which, after all, is relatively secondary to our interests—you end up, of course, with a radical and entirely justified condemnation of every utopia, that is to say, of every attempt to define and fix in place the perfect society. There can be no such definitions. And we should already have known this since the *Statesman*. No regulation will ever be able to get a tight grip upon the perpetual alteration of social and historical reality. At the very most, such a regulation can try to kill this alteration. But then, in killing it, it kills the social-historical; it kills its subject and its object. By way of consequence, if we are seeking the way toward a better constitution, we cannot want to fix this constitution in place; rather, we have to aim at finding the constitution that each time best allows self-altering social-historical reality to give itself the legislation that corresponds to it. That is to say, adopting my terminology: We can aim only at changing the relationship between the instituting society and the instituted society. We can therefore want only a society that once and for all condemns the reign of the instituted and seeks the correct relationship, the just relationship between the instituting and the instituted. We have to aim for a Constitution of society that would permit society itself to fulfill this role, which even the royal man, if ever he were to exist and to be accepted by all the citizens, would never be able to fulfill, that of the correct government, therefore of self-government at all echelons.

I offer here and now these anticipations of what is to come. I do so because, if we don't have in sight this central kernel of the dialogue—the positions developed there and the problematic to which they give birth—we cannot understand the genuine stakes that are there during the discussion of the two definitions. This discussion I therefore now undertake.

III. The Two Definitions

And the first observation to be made, here again at the outset, is that these two definitions are perfectly superfluous. They are useless; they serve no purpose; they teach us nothing. They aren't what Plato is intending; that's not what interests him. Not because, as he says elsewhere, what interests him would be the exemplification of the dialectic, dialectical exercise. No, that's a misleading confession [*un aveu trompeur*], for

what interests him is another definition of the statesman, which is not
stated in the two definitions but is implicitly contained in the third major digression: The statesman is the *epistēmōn*, he who knows, and he who
knows what each is to do because he possesses true knowledge. And his
extraordinary task—once again, I'm anticipating what is to come—is to
prescribe for each—each individual who participates in society, each citizen—to follow what is the just thing to do and not do (295a–b). The
term used by Plato is extraordinarily strong; it's *prostattein*, to order, to
prescribe. And elsewhere, further on, he says: to order *parakathēmenos*,
while being seated beside him, while being at his bedside, at his side so as
to tell him at each instant: "Now, you get married, now you buy leeks,
now you fire your servants," and so on and so forth.

Here I'm talking in banalities. But Plato has taught us, with his much
talked-about story of the lice in the *Parmenides*, not to neglect these:
everywhere and always, the royal man has to prescribe to each what he is
to do. And you see what this means, both as a crazily impossible thought
and as a denial of the capacity of the individuals who make up society to
run their own lives [*se diriger*].

And not to stray too far from our contemporary reality, we may observe, moreover, that in modern times there have been attempts to realize
this idea of prescribing what each individual is to do and not do at each
instant—not under the form of the royal man but through the whole totalitarian tendency of bureaucratic regulation. This is evident at the point
of production, in the factory, where in principle everything the executant,
the worker—and even an upper-level executant—is to do is supposed to
be defined, down to the tiniest details, so that the person to whom the
regulation is addressed is present in this regulation only as a pure physical
principle setting things into motion. Every managerial feature [*Tout l'éle-
ment de direction*], the entire meaning of his act is snatched away from
him in order for it to be deposited in the bureaucratic regulation of production—or in the bureaucratic regulation of the very life of the citizen,
in the case of a totalitarian regime. He then is no longer anyone but the
one who moves his hand so that, at the moment set for him, the part may
be presented to the machine, then removed; or else, he is no longer anyone but the one who applauds when the leader utters the term that calls
for applause and who jeers when this same leader utters the terms that
herald jeers.

One must therefore have it in one's head that this third definition of the statesman is what Plato is intending when the first two definitions are discussed. When you bear that in mind, you will be convinced of their superfluousness—and, in a way, of their pointlessness, if one takes them for their own sake. But this will also help to underscore for you the existence of the aporia created by the second navigation, both in relation to this definition—which according to Plato, in his heart of hearts, is the true one—and in relation to the two definitions explicitly stated, especially the second one. For, you ask yourself what this statesman, this royal man, this weaver really is doing in a city where there are laws like the ones Plato ultimately accepts at the end of the second navigation.

First Definition: The Statesman as Pastor of Human Flocks

Following a short preamble, the explanation of this first definition commences. This definition claims to be in a sense a true, a direct, and not an analogical definition, whereas in the second definition—of the statesman as weaver in the city—weaving is explicitly posited as an *analogon*, as a paradigm, as another case sufficiently akin, according to the essence of things, to the art of the statesman that one might be able to use it in order to understand what the statesman does. The definition of the pastor isn't given as analogical but as a genuine definition: an attempt is made to insert the statesman into an exhaustive series of divisions, that is to say, of definitions of species and of specific differences, as Aristotle was later to say in his theory of definition in the *Analytics*. And the idea of the pastor, in this part running from 258b to 267c, is apparently taken seriously. At least, one affects to take it seriously, as one affects to take seriously the successive divisions, at the end of which an attempt will be made to get a tight grip upon the statesman.

As you will remember, one begins with the sciences. Some of these are theoretical, others aren't. Among the theoretical ones, the directive and self-directive ones are distinguished. The raising of animals belongs among these self-directive sciences. Therein, there are animals that live in flocks, and that are tame, and that walk instead of fly, that don't interbreed (unlike, for example, horses, mules, donkeys, etc.). And, finally, we arrive at men. Statesmanship is then the science that *nemei*, that tends and pastures, that nourishes, that attends to the life of human beings living in common; it's the science whose object is the raising of men in common.

Even if it isn't of much importance, let's make a first remark in order to underscore right away Plato's rhetorical dishonesty. For, starting from 258e, there is what could be called a change in the basis for the division, something that isn't permitted in logic. At the outset, the dividing was done according to the form of activities, according to what is intrinsic to these activities; sciences/nonsciences, theoretical sciences/practical sciences, directive sciences/executive sciences,[1] and so on. And then, starting at a certain moment, the criterion changes and the dividing is done according to the matter of the object and no longer according to the form and the meaning of the activity. This is a remark of technical, secondary importance, no doubt, but it is one that allows us, here again, to underscore how much Plato is often more of a sophist than his Sophist adversaries.

In the second place, all the divisions the Stranger performs are till the end basically dichotomous. But—as Plato himself points out later on, without being entirely comfortable with this observation—there is no intrinsic reason for these divisions to be dichotomous, for one always to be dividing in two. Of course, there's a formal reason: division in two corresponds to a/non-a, p is true/p is not true. One can therefore always divide any set whatsoever by picking out a property and by regrouping the objects that have it and those that don't have it. Therefore, one can always operate by dichotomy. But that doesn't mean that this dichotomy is pertinent, that it corresponds to something real in what one is dividing. And here we have one of the problems of formal logic qua binary logic. One would think that the binary character of this logic—yes/no; true/not true; a/non-a—its exhaustion of every universe of discourse via contradictories, should have led to some sort of postulate about a binary structure of what is (which is still there, more or less, in contemporary physics). Now, that isn't possible. But we shall talk about it again when we discuss the species/part question in the first incidental point.

I would like to pause here over two *petitio principii* Plato imposes upon us. He imposes them upon us so skillfully, so "in passing," that most commentators don't even flinch. Such is the strength of the hold of the Platonic text, as well as of ideology.

The first one, which appears very early on, involves the identification statesman = royal man. At no point is this identification discussed; it is posited as going without saying. And yet this is unheard of, monstrous, for Greeks especially and for Athenians in particular. In the age when Plato was writing, there was no king in Greece. At Sparta, there were indeed two "kings," but they had no power; true power was shared between the ephors and the *gerousia*. In addition, while there were some tyrants in Sicily, unless I'm mistaken they didn't get themselves called *king*. Dionysius, for example. Or if they did, other Greeks looked down upon them as upstarts [*parvenus*]. Of course, there were kings in Macedonia, but Macedonia had a very bizarre status: a few years after the *Statesman*, when Demosthenes was trying to mobilize the Athenians to fight Philip, he exhorted them not to "let themselves be subjugated by barbarians." Well, the Macedonians spoke in a Greek idiom, but they didn't truly belong to what the cities considered to be the Greek world—precisely, among other reasons, because they had kings and Macedonia didn't consist of cities. Finally, when one spoke in Greece during the fifth and fourth centuries of the "king," that noun designated only one, very specific character—"the Great King," the king of the Persians, who was the incarnation of despotism. And yet Plato quite coolly identifies the statesman with the royal man, which for Greece in the fifth and fourth centuries, and in any case at Athens, was pretty much a monstrosity.

A second *petitio principii*, but of much greater import, is the following: as early as 258b, we are told that the statesman is *tōn epistēmonōn tis*, "one of those who possesses a science." This will be confirmed by the third digression. But who says so? And with what arguments? It could very well be said that statesmanship is an empirical form of know-how [*savoir-faire*]. And that's what should be said, moreover. By *empirical* I don't mean a bonesetter's art, but, well, it's something that cannot under any heading be called a science. Yet the Stranger says that the statesman is *tōn epistēmonōn tis*, one among the scientists [*les savants*]—but the knowers of a certain knowledge [*les savants d'un savoir certain*]. "How could it not be?" answers Young Socrates. And off we go. Statesmanship is a science; and the statesman is he who possesses this science.

This fallacious subsumption of the statesman under science is going to allow Plato to make the rest of his argument. The French translator Auguste Diès translates *tōn epistēmonōn tis*, very badly, as "[belonging to] people who know." But *epistēmonōn* doesn't refer to the people who know: the politician isn't someone who knows that the trains for Brittany leave from the Montparnasse train station; he's someone who possesses a certain knowledge about an important object, a knowledge whose principles are grounded. Plato wouldn't call a cobbler *epistēmonōn*. And in this dialogue—as elsewhere, moreover—Plato uses *technē* and *epistēmē* without distinction—the two terms being nearly indistinguishable all the way from Homer to Aristotle. Later, Aristotle made a distinction between the two but without always sticking to it. And above all, when he did make his distinction, he placed *technē* and *epistēmē* on one side and *phronēsis* on the other. *Phronēsis*, too, was later very badly translated into Latin, as *prudentia*, whereas it is something that should belong, rather, to what Kant later called the "faculty of judgment," while at the same exceeding the latter, since the Kantian faculty of judgment, or, more generally, of ordinary logic is the capacity to recognize that a case falls under a rule. It is a primordial and irreducible capacity because, if you had a rule that told you that this case falls under that rule, the "this case falls under that rule" would again be a case that would have to be subsumed under the rule that says "this case falls under that rule." There again, therefore, you'd need a faculty of judgment. Thus, you have an infinite regression. It's impossible to break down this faculty into component parts [*décomposer cette faculté-là*].

But *phronēsis* isn't only that. Beyond this somewhat mechanical side of the faculty of judgment is also something that is indefinable a priori: it's the capacity to recognize each time what is pertinent and what isn't. So, if you remain on the mechanical side of the faculty of judgment and if you grant what in logic is called Church's theorem—if it's logical, it's formalizable and mechanizable—recognizing what's pertinent and not pertinent would mean sending in a computer to work out all the possible cases and end up, statistically speaking, halfway, saying: Yes, this is pertinent. But that's not what we call *phronēsis*. Judging a situation isn't going over billions of possible cases and saying: That one is the pertinent case. No, it's going directly to the decision: This is pertinent, that's not pertinent. And this capacity is also irreducible, even if it is liable to gradations and differs among adult individuals: some have a lot of it; others have it less. But I certainly don't want to say by that that it's genetic.

So, if statesmanship appertains to something from this point of view, it obviously isn't to *technē / epistēmē* but quite obviously to all that brings *phronēsis* into play, that is to say, the faculty of judging and of orienting oneself (another Kantian term, moreover)—for, in the end, that's what separating the pertinent from the nonpertinent is—in relation to human affairs, to the real things in society.

I have insisted upon this point. That's because, once again, this fallacious, unexplained subsumption of the statesman under *epistēmē* later becomes, of course, the explicit axiom of the third digression, the one about the absoluteness of the statesman and of his power.

Let's return to the text of the first definition. At the end of the series of divisions-dichotomies, statesmanship is defined as the science whose object is the raising of men in common. And there commence the criticisms of this definition. There are three criticisms, in fact. First of all, the first criticism (267c–e) says that this definition can't be right because there are other arts that attend to the nourishing and raising of human beings: the wet-nurse [*la nourrice*], for example, or else the doctor, the restaurateur, and so on. A second objection appears in 268a–c: The statesman cannot be a true pastor because the genuine pastor attends to everything that concerns his flock: he feeds [*nourrit*] it; he arranges crossbreedings, the beasts' nuptials; he cares for them when they are sick; he helps them give birth; he plays music on his flute for them, and so forth. Now, the statesman doesn't do all that. These two criticisms are, moreover, as you can see, quite complementary, if not two sides of the same coin. Finally, in a third criticism—which comes after the first digression, the myth of the reign of Cronus, as an apparent justification for this long detour—the Stranger convinces Young Socrates that between the pastor and the flock there is always a difference in nature. It isn't a cow that leads the other cows; it's a human being. And it isn't a sheep that leads the other sheep; it's the shepherd. Therefore, if there were a shepherd of humans, he would have to be of another nature than human beings. He would have to be the divine pastor spoken of in the myth of Cronus. And if there have been such divine pastors, they belong to another cycle of the world, the reverse cycle, the cycle defined by the reign of Cronus.

The matter therefore seems settled. These three objections Plato makes to himself radically and completely cancel out his first definition. Yet— and here again the strange goings-on in the structure of the *Statesman* intervene—the first definition is taken up again, reshuffled, from 275c to 276e. The first criticism is answered by saying that the statesman isn't a nurturer [*nourricier*] of men, isn't a true pastor, but simply a caretaker [*soigneur*] (the Greek term is *therapeutēs*, he who takes care of [*prend soin de*], a little like a boxing trainer [*soigneur de boxe*]); and he is a human caretaker, as opposed to divine pastor; finally, he is a benevolent and voluntary (*hekousios*) caretaker, as opposed to the violent (*biaios*) caretaker who would be the tyrant. So, in 276c, we are again given a sort of definition of the political or royal art, which is the art that takes care voluntarily, and with the consent of those of whom this art takes care, with the consent of human communities: "We shall call statesmanship the freely offered and freely accepted care that is exercised over a herd [*troupeau*] of bipeds; and he who exercises this care is a true king and a true statesman" {276e}.

And then, a dramatic turn of events [*coup de théâtre*]: the Stranger declares that this definition won't do, that it isn't good, that it is entirely external, that it doesn't grasp the essence of the thing. He declares in addition that another method must therefore be adopted (277a–c). And it is here that he introduces his considerations about the paradigm—which will furnish us with the object of the fourth incidental point, to be discussed later. He doesn't give any reason for abandoning this definition; he doesn't take up again any of the three preceding objections. He simply lets it drop by making a declaration—to which Young Socrates, as one might expect, subscribes right away—and he embarks upon some entirely different considerations. Here's the exchange (277a):

YOUNG SOCRATES: We very likely, Stranger, may have thus finished our demonstration as concerns the statesman.

STRANGER: That would be a great success, Socrates, but it isn't enough that you have this conviction; we both must have it. Now, in my opinion the sketch of the king is not yet finished. On the contrary, like sculptors who leave their work unfinished, we have left it unfinished. [In bringing up the myth,] we have shaped its outer lines, but there is no relief to it.

Fine, but those are all just words. No clear reason is given for abandoning the definition of the pastor. And yet it is abandoned. One could have stopped at this definition: the statesman is the caretaker-trainer (not the pastor-nurturer), the human (not divine) and voluntary and consensual (not violent) caretaker of human communities. At that point, an additional question would, quite logically, be raised: In what way would this caretaker differ from other caretakers of human beings? That would lead us directly to the considerations at the end about the different arts in the city, to everything that serves at once to subtend, to sustain, and to illustrate the second definition. And we would at that moment perhaps be led to say that there are caretakers of parts and that what is needed is something like a caretaker of the whole or of the totality. That's what we say and don't say with the weaver, because the definition of the statesman as weaver says this thing, but says it, as we shall see, in a very bizarre fashion and without attacking the problem of the caretaker of the whole head-on, and still less, moreover, that of the legislator, but I shall come to that.

On the other hand, if this first definition really had to be abandoned, why spend all that time with those stories of beasts that walk, beasts that fly, beasts that have or don't have horns, beasts that can or cannot impregnate one another? And left aside is the obviously essential thing, of which no Athenian was unaware: the constitution of the city as a whole. Plato himself knew this as early on as the *Protagoras*, even if he puts it in the mouth of Protagoras: Besides and beyond and through and above all the particular arts that are necessary to the existence of the city, there is another capacity that intends the *katholou*, the totality, the whole of the city's affairs. And this capacity, which Protagoras says is shared equally among all citizens (by which Plato means that it doesn't belong to a single individual or to rare and exceptional individuals), is defined by an object that is the *polis* as such—an idea that would be par excellence Platonic. The human being whose object is this *polis* as such would be the statesman. Only, there's no question here of all that.

We are therefore led to ask ourselves: Why this first definition? What's it doing in there? And, as for myself, I think it really has to be recognized that we have here a curious reversal [*inversion*] going on: the myth of the reign of Cronus is introduced in order to allow the first definition to be eliminated—but to be eliminated not in logic but in the rhetoric of the text. I insist upon this point because, in the logic of the text, it would suffice to say: There are pastors, who are of another nature than the animals they tend and pasture. If there were a pastor of humans, he could only be superhuman. OK. So, the statesman isn't a pastor. But there are activities that take care of human communities, and the statesman appertains to that group of activities. He's a caretaker; he's not a pastor. But instead of that, we go through the long detour of the myth of the reign of Cronus in order to eliminate the consequences of the logical approach of the first definition rhetorically. And it's abandoned. Moreover, it doesn't interest us. It's perfectly trivial. True, it belongs to the stock of Greek folklore (and without a doubt, also to a much larger stock of folklore): the king as pastor of men. Without going back to Homer, it's found in Xenophon, in his *Cyropaedia*, and especially, in the popular mind [*la représentation commune, la représentation populaire*]. And it perhaps wasn't worth the trouble of mobilizing so much dialogue in order to eliminate it.

We are therefore obliged to come to the opposite [*inverse*] conclusion:

it isn't the myth that is introduced in order to be able to eliminate the first definition; it's the first definition that is proposed falsely, rhetorically, in order to be able to introduce the myth. The point [*finalité*] of the first definition concerning the pastor was to prepare the following idea: There were pastors of human beings, but they were gods. And that took place at the time of Cronus's reign. Plato can then introduce this extraordinary fiction of a world that sometimes turns in one direction, sometimes in the other, with the reversal of the direction of all movements and the mystery of the reversal itself of the direction of time during these periods. But we'll talk again later about that in more detail.

Second Definition: The Statesman, the Royal Man, as Weaver

We pass therefore to the second definition. And, of course, it can be noted incidentally—and this has already been noted—that the dialogue itself is a weaving: Plato himself is the weaver who weaves together all these extremely heteroclite, different, even bizarrely assorted and multicolored [*bariolés*] elements in order to compose a tapestry that nevertheless holds together.

It holds together, however, in quite a strange manner. For, this second definition—for the very reasons I just mentioned—appears to be introduced in an entirely artificial way. First of all, because, once again, the first definition is dropped on the basis of a decision that is entirely unmotivated. But above all, because the way in which the Stranger, after his incidental point about paradigms, introduces the story about weaving in 279a–b is perhaps one of the most arbitrary passages in world literature. It's a total jump from one thing to another [*un coq-à-l'âne total*]: We need a paradigm. Right, says the other guy. How about weaving? the Stranger suggests. Why not? says Young Socrates compliantly. (The latter, let it be said parenthetically, is always saying: Right, yes, certainly. . . . Except, that is, at one point, which, for this reason, takes on a value of its own. And that happens when the Stranger, during the third digression, says that the true statesman reigns with laws, without laws, with *grammata*, without *grammata*, by killing, by not killing. The true statesman does what he wants. So, there, the young Socrates rebels, and his revolt takes on more plausibility and weight in light of his perpetual consent.) Weaving, then. But why weaving rather than architecture, prosody, musical composition, and so on and so forth? It's totally arbitrary.

This long story about weaving nevertheless begins, is interrupted by digressions and incidental points, and runs, in fact, from 279b until the end of the dialogue. What happens during this whole discussion? Well, some very strange things happen. First, the Stranger begins by discussing weaving as such. For, if one wants to use it as a paradigm, one must know what it is, of what it consists. But it also must be classed among human activities. And here, in passing, just like that, Plato offers us an extraordinary and remarkable universal division of human activities. I'm not going to talk about it, but I recommend that you reread 279c–e: all we create, manufacture [*fabriquons*], and acquire is organized there, divided up. The French National Institute of Statistics and Economic Studies (INSEE) didn't take this passage into account in its classification of socioprofessional activities (preferring, rather, Bourdieu), but there is indeed a basis for division here: all we can do or acquire is because of this or because of that; in order to do something or in order not to undergo something; and what is done in order not to undergo something is divided into enclosures and armor of war, and so on. Here—as for the divisions that concerned the pastor—we have a sort of dichotomous inspection and review of the totality of human activities.

After that, there are incidental points four, five, and six, about proper causes and comitant causes; relative measures and the absolute measure—with, right in the middle (this is the sixth incidental point), the following disarming affirmation that is made at that moment: The genuine object of the dialogue is obviously not the statesman, about whom one couldn't give a damn; it's learning to discuss and to divide; it's dialectical exercise. I already talked about this the last time, and I believe I've shown you that this is just an affectation, a false claim, and that in reality, at a third level, it really is the statesman who is the object of the *Statesman*.

Then, after having "boringly held forth" {cf. 286b} on weaving as such, on the thread, on the woof, we henceforth know what weaving is, how it is done, what is involved therein. And one can pass on to its application by "transferring onto the statesman's art, in order to know it well, the example of this art of weaving we previously expounded" {cf. 287b}. Weaving is going to serve as a paradigm; the statesman is a sort of weaver. That's what the Stranger says in 285d–e. But then the question immediately arises: If the statesman is a weaver, what does he weave? This is broached a bit, tangentially but not really, in 287a–d: it isn't being said that one must find what it is he weaves, but some elements of the life of the city are introduced about which it can reasonably be thought that the statesman is the weaver thereof. And those elements are all the arts necessary to the life of the city. The discussion is then going to take the form of a division of the arts that are practiced in the city. A laborious, very muddled division—and I say this without any polemical intention in mind, without any acrimony or animosity. Plato acknowledges this himself: "It's difficult, the work we are undertaking to carry out" {287d}. Here, one is truly in the material, in the empirical world, where nothing can be exhaustively divided. And then it is very difficult to know what, in human activities, is an instrument, and an instrument of what, for performing a univocal classification. This thought, moreover, is quite correct, and it is pregnant with other ideas Plato doesn't develop. But in the end he speaks of seven arts. It isn't really clear what the first of these seven arts is, but the others are known. When Plato enumerates them, he speaks of the first, then of the other six (289a–b): "We have the primitive species, then we have instruments, vessels, vehicles, shelter, diversions, and nourishments." That's it for the objects of the six possible arts, plus a first art that is not given—that is perhaps the art of manufacturing the instruments of the other ones, although that isn't said. And this enumeration precedes a second distinction between the arts that intend the thing itself and the arts that are auxiliary and subaltern arts, which is discussed between 289c and 291a.

An incidental remark. In this entire passage floats an interrogation, an implicit one. For those who have read Plato (the *Republic* and other texts) before, it is there between the lines: Which among these arts are truly necessary to the life of the city, and which are not? This matter can be taken up from the somewhat childish, normative, moralizing standpoint of the "old philosophy"—that of Plato, too, in the *Gorgias* and even in the *Republic*—according to which what the city needs is agriculture, the raising of livestock, perhaps some metalworking, but certainly not the art of the chef or of the perfumer. But that's not the point of view being adopted here; all the arts, including those that serve simply to amuse, are considered to be necessary parts of the city—this is the relative humanization of Plato about which we have spoken. And the question Plato is posing implicitly—What are the truly productive activities, and which are not productive?—was later taken up again by Aristotle and then rearose in the middle of the eighteenth century.

For the Physiocrats, for example, the sole truly productive activities were the primary ones, that is to say, agriculture and all those activities that extract something directly from nature (mines, quarries, and so on). For them, industry wasn't productive; it didn't add any value. By way of contrast, in the grand tradition of English political economy, Adam Smith, and so on, all activities having to do with a material object are productive, provided that these activities transform that object. Therefore, primary industries (agriculture, extraction, and so forth), of course, as well as manufacture, are productive. Smith very clearly made the distinction, saying in substance: "No doubt the existence of our king, or of our poets, or of our artists, or of our judges is even more essential to the nation than the existence of peasants and manufacturers. Nonetheless, as precious as those activities might be, we cannot think that they increase the national wealth." And he was excluding thereby everything we would call *services* so as to retain only that which has to do with the manufacture and transformation of material objects.

Marx's theory of value basically relies upon this distinction, too. And it is this same distinction that still today {in 1986} serves to contrast Western systems of national accounting from Russian and "socialist" systems of national accounting. For, in Western systems of national accounting, all the activities that are performed or that could be performed for pay—and that are legal; it's curious, but that's how it is—appertain to the national income. This rules out, for example, the truly clandestine and illegal activities of the Mafia, but it leaves a problem with respect to casinos and prostitution to the extent that these aren't illegal activities: Do they or do they not increase national income? But in the Eastern-bloc countries, the allegedly orthodox Marxist definition includes in national income only those activities that produce material things or transform them. There's something very Aristotelian about this, a notion of substance and of its attributes. For, among the essential attributes of substance, there is *keisthai*, being-in-a-certain-place; hence transportation, which modifies an attribute of the thing—its place—appertains, according to "Soviet" national accounting practices, to productive activities.[2] But not commerce, which in no way alters the Aristotelian categories of the thing. Obviously, Mr. Gorbachev hardly knows who Aristotle was, but that's not the issue; his national accounting works according to those categories.

This problematic also underlies the distinction the *Statesman* makes between the different species of arts, the principal arts and the auxiliary arts, the manufacture of instruments, the things used by the instruments.

In any case, this long discussion can only leave us with the impression that what the royal weaver is to weave together is precisely all those activities, the arts that form the city.

Then there is, in passing, an attack on another art that had not previously been distinguished, that of the sophist-magician, as he says—that is to say, of the statesman who is not the statesman as Plato defines him but, in fact, the democratic statesman. And it is at this place in the dialogue that the long digressions on the form of regimes and on science as the statesman's sole foundation come in. There's a return to the Sophist, that is to say, to the democratic statesman, in 303b–c, so as to eliminate him as false statesman, which doesn't interest us. Then auxiliary statesmanship arts of another type—strategy, rhetoric, and the art of the judge, for example—are introduced. But they couldn't be statesmanship itself, because they are subordinated to it. Aristotle, moreover, took up this idea again later on, at the beginning of the *Nichomachean Ethics*, when he says that politics is the most architectonic art {1094a27}.

And in 305e, it may be thought that our troubles are over. All the fakes have been eliminated, all the auxiliaries have been subordinated, and the Stranger concludes:

> As to this activity that commands all the others, that is concerned with the laws and with all the affairs of the *polis* and that unites all these things in a fabric in the most perfect way possible, we shall be right, it seems to me, to choose for it a rather simple name for the universality of its function, and we should call it *statesmanship*.
> YOUNG SOCRATES: Absolutely; I agree completely.

It might therefore be thought that we have found the elements that the statesman weaves together, that they are these various arts, and that the definition of the statesman has been found. But no, not at all. For, now the Stranger undertakes an initiative that is unrelated to what has preceded. And as if nothing had been said before, or as if everything that has been said had nothing to do with the weaving materials the royal man weaves, he launches into the following:

> —Since we have spoken of weaving, we must now determine what things are woven and in what way, in order for us to produce the fabric statesmanship weaves.
> —Evidently, says Young Socrates {cf. 306a}.

There's a new twist in the plot, therefore, and we start again—but now for the last time—with an entirely new idea, the idea of the parts of virtue. There are parts to virtue, which differ according to their species, according to their *eidos*. And a variety of examples are gone through. In doing so, Plato is abandoning—this is very important, and it's undoubtedly also the deep-seated reason for this new twist—his cardinal doctrine concerning virtue, namely, that virtue is in fact essentially one and that in any case it has a unitary relationship to knowledge; and that, without knowledge, there is no virtue. At this spot in the *Statesman*, we have a rather different conception: there are parts to virtue, and these parts are opposed. Bravery, for example, is opposed to prudence. And the fact that there might be different virtues can have very deleterious effects upon the city, some pushing too far toward war and the others too far toward peace. We therefore arrive, on account of this, at a sort of new definition in 308e–309e, which concerns the capacity to put these virtues together [*composer ensemble ces vertus*]. Then it is discovered in 309 that these different virtues have, so to speak, bioanthropological embodiments, that is to say, that there are indeed men who possess sometimes more of one, sometimes more of the other; that, therefore, the art of the royal weaver—who becomes a species of pastor again here without it being said, or a gardener who crosses good lines in order to obtain the results he requires [*qu'il lui faut*]—is to cross the appropriate lines in the city in order that there might not be too much recklessness or too much circumspection. And thus there suddenly reappears the absolutism of the genuine political man [*véritable homme politique*] who, in order to fit [*ajuster*] together the different lines, must have the right to expel from the city or to put to death those who don't correspond to the good materials from which the city is to be woven and to educate the others. And this culminates finally in 311c with the following definition:

> Let us say then that here is achieved in straight weaving the stuff that political activity interweaves when, taking the human characters of energy and temperance, the royal science assembles and unites their two lives through concord and friendship and, thus producing the most excellent and most magnificent of all fabrics, envelops therein, in each city, all the people, slaves and free men, draws them together in its weft and, assuring the city, without lack or failing, all the happiness it [the city] can enjoy, it commands and directs. . . .

This is in truth a quite strange definition, if one keeps in mind what, along the way, the third digression has taught us: that it is the laws that, in the end, are to direct everything in human affairs. Certainly, there's this "command and direct," but that doesn't tell us much once the task of the statesman is limited to making the reckless temperament and the circumspect temperament coexist harmoniously, the one tempering the other. This obviously involves a fantastic shrinkage. In other words, this paradigm of weaving, of the elements to be woven, is used in three ways that are neither congruent nor convergent:

1. There are the different arts that are necessary for the life of the city, and it is presumed that the statesman must know how to combine them not in himself but in the existence of the city.

2. There are auxiliary quasi political arts, like strategy and rhetoric, and the statesman must know how to subordinate them and tell them what they have to execute.

3. Finally, there are different components of virtue and human temperaments, out of which the statesman has to know how to make a harmonious blend (this third case being, moreover, something from an entirely different level than the preceding ones).

I'd like to conclude on the basic question this ultimate definition (indeed, both definitions) raises for us in its coexistence with what the second navigation teaches us. If there cannot be an absolute royal man with his absolute power, if one must therefore be satisfied with a city of laws, what can the statesman or the royal man, whether he be pastor or weaver, do therein? What is his place in a city where the laws, in the main, say what is to be done? Let's take up the question at a very radical level: here we have a city in which, suddenly, the royal man appears; so, according to the truly true discourse—the absolute discourse, the discourse of the third digression—the existing laws cease to be de jure, cease to be just, cease to have legitimacy. The royal man imposes, at that moment, what is right, what is just. And quite obviously, his task, his activity, cannot be defined as a simple weaving of the elements he finds in the city. At that moment, this royal man—whose emergence brings about the collapse of the existing legislation, the existing institution of society—creates a tabula rasa through his very appearance. This is a sort of institutional and political earthquake. The whole edifice crumbles; and he must reconstruct the city, radically reinstitute it. And *that* goes much further than any comparison with any sort of weaving. It's incommensurable. He doesn't weave anything; he constitutes. To say that he weaves is to forget the deep-seated relationship—which Plato knows very well; he talks about it at length both in the *Republic* and in the *Laws*—between the institution of the city and the composition of the human elements that are found therein. One can't take individuals as elements that are independent of the city; individuals are made by the *paideia* of the city—what I myself call the *social fabrication of the individual*. And this extends from marriage to the permissible musical modes, passing by way of the education of children. Therefore, if he's a royal man and if the laws subside, all the laws subside—even musical laws. And I'm not kidding here: the word *nomos*, in Greek, also means the types of melodies, of scales (the Dorian *nomos*, the Lydian *nomos*, and so on). And regarding precisely these *nomoi*, Plato declares in the *Republic* that some of them have to be forbidden because, being too lascivious, they corrupt morals.

Therefore, if the royal man appears, the law as such subsides, and the statesman has to radically institute everything. There can be no question for him of weaving. Or else there is no royal man. The law then remains "secondly just," and what is already given needs only to be woven together. But in both fashions, the statesman appears to be missing his goal.

One can then try to save the situation by saying that the royal weaver to which we are led at the end of the *Statesman* is not the true political man as he is defined in the third digression. Therefore, he is not a primary and radical institutor. And therefore he must live in a city of laws that are de jure, that are legitimate in a royal man's absence (even if this is a second-order legitimacy). Now, in such a city, there is a place for a *kubernētēs*, a governor, a pilot, who would be the statesman. But then this statesman is no longer an *epistēmōn*. Once again, if he were an *epistēmōn*, the laws would crumble. This statesman is something else, something that has not been defined in the dialogue, and he practices this weaving of the different arts, of the different virtues, of the auxiliary arts of the statesman and statesmanship itself, and of individuals, of bioanthropological lines that embody the virtues necessary to the city. What is presupposed for him to be able to practice this profession? We aren't told. And we won't be told anywhere in Plato's entire oeuvre—it's one of the aporias. We won't even be told in the *Laws*, where we'll have another regime: a group ruling the city, in fact, two ruling groups, the elected magistrates, as at Athens, and then that much talked-about nocturnal council, which is a sort of power that isn't hidden [*occulte*], since everyone knows that it exists, but which in a sense pulls the strings. And it is to be assumed that the people who belong, by vocation at least, to this nocturnal council—there are, indeed, provisions for this—are people who, a bit like those in the *Republic* but not to the same degree or with the same level of formality, have followed a specific kind of education and training.

There is, therefore, this hole, this blank, this gaping void in the *Statesman*: in the end, we don't know what kind of statesman is being talked about. And the implicit answer is given in the *Laws*: It's the statesman who belongs to a city whose laws are to be respected but in which, nevertheless, something is always to make up for [*suppléer à*] the laws. In dramatic fashion, at the end of long periods of time, when these laws must be reformed, this is foreseen and provided for; and undramatically, from day to day—or, rather, from night to night—this is accomplished by the nocturnal council, which constantly watches over things so that the *kubernēsis* (the "government," the "rudder") of the city hugs to the good way, follows the right path.

So, there we are. I'll stop here for today. We have finished with the definitions and a bit with the general spirit of the dialogue, the function it serves in the works of Plato's final period. Next time, we'll talk a little about the incidental points and especially about the two major digressions on the myth and on the statesman's science.

Question
On Parmenides, the creation of philosophy, and so on.

I said last time that there is something like a second creation of philosophy by Plato. Well, at what moment was philosophy created? That's difficult to say. As you know, it's traditionally set at the time of Thales, of the Ionian school, because they are supposed to have said things about the element of being. Are we entitled to tie the birth of philosophy to that? For my part, I believe that this tradition is correct, not for the reason invoked but because that is the moment when the inherited representations are called into question, destroyed. They have done with cosmogonies, theogonies, mythology, and so on, and they say: No, that isn't it. Thales says: It's water. And this water has nothing to do with Poseidon and the water of mythology. It's an element.

Of course, we don't have any texts {from that period}. Or just the fragment from Anaximander I studied {in the seminar} three years ago. But I think that with Anaximander, in any case, we already have the philosophical statement of a position. And then, afterward, I won't trace the birth of philosophy back to Parmenides. From this standpoint, its full blossoming takes place without any doubt with Heraclitus. We know that he wrote a book—as Parmenides, after him, wrote a *Poem*, of which we still have nearly 150 lines. And again three years ago, I tried in my own way to show that what Heraclitus states is a set of propositions that we would call systematic in the good sense of the term. That is to say, there is an interrogation followed by an interpretation of the being of the world, of the human being, which turns back upon itself, interrogates itself about itself in a sense, interrogates itself about the powers by which one can arrive at this knowledge. This is, if you will, the moment of reflection, there, with Heraclitus.

In what sense, then, can it be said that there is a second foundation of philosophy with Plato? First point: perpetual "interrogativity." When I speak of *interrogativity* apropos of Plato, I am not intending simply the moment of reflection, which is already there with Heraclitus: Is what I am saying true? What means do I have in order to state the truth? Are my senses deceiving me? Is discourse adequate? No, I am intending something very different, which is very difficult to define, moreover, but which is found in the dialogues, and in the *Statesman*, of course: the constant reopening of the question, the fact that in a sense, constantly, the result matters less than the path that allowed one to get there. Once posed, the question brings up another question, which touches off a third one, and so on. So, one could ask oneself, as in the much talked-about dialogue between Cineas and Pyrrhus: But why, ultimately, does one do all that? Why didn't one just sleep peacefully from the outset? Whereas, as Plato says explicitly in the *Statesman*, this is the very path of research, which is philosophy. And it's not so much the fact of reaching a conclusion, such as: Being is fire. Or: Being is water. Or else: Being is and not-being is not. What matters is this kind of movement, of process, of progression.

And in relation to the pre-Socratics, it really must seen that it's one thing to try to give a set of positions that somehow or other are grounded and mutually coherent and it's something else entirely to introduce precisely this perpetual interrogativity, the idea that, ultimately, there is no statement alongside which one can lie down and rest. It is in this sense that we really have a second creation of philosophy. I know that in saying this I am irritating many historians of philosophy, for whom there are one or several Platonic systems. But the difference between the pre-Socratics and Plato—Socrates himself being the enigma—is that for the pre-Socratics there are statements upon which one can set or rest the truth. Now, for Plato, there are and there are not. There are, for at each moment one goes through phases, positions, or else one could no longer say anything. Even in order to refute an idea, one must posit the possibility of that idea and the possibility of its refutation as provisionally incontestable. But ultimately, what is created by Plato—and perhaps unconsciously—is this endless movement. I say *perhaps* or *in part unconsciously*, for here one cannot speak of unconscious creation when it comes to a writer like Plato, who wrote a dialogue on knowledge, the *Theaetetus*, which doesn't lead anywhere, except to three theses about knowledge, all three of which are refuted, and who wrote the *Parmenides* and its enigmas on being. And, moreover, the *Sophist*'s very own ontological thesis shows that that's the way things are. If you will, there's a sort of prolongation—which he doesn't make and which is perhaps a bit audacious, if not reckless, to make—a prolongation that is gnosiological, about the theory of knowledge of the *Sophist*'s ontology. In Greece—and, in my opinion, in all thought—being and truth are correlative. To say *being* means: It's true. And to say: *It's true* means: It's like that. And similarly for falsehood and nonbeing.

Now, what does Plato say in the *Sophist*? He says that "ten thousand times ten thousand, being is not . . . and not-being is" {259b}. In order that something might be said, there is a *sumplokē*, a "complexion," of being and nonbeing at the narrowly logical level of affirmations and negations. But in the same way it can be said that there is always in discourse a complexion of the true and the nontrue. At least, a complexion of what is true and of what is missing from what is true in order for it to be the definitive, final truth, after which everything stops, the world stops. It is because there is always this moment of nonbeing in being, this moment of lack of trueness in the true, of still something else that can arise, and that will arise at a detour in the dialogue, or in another dialogue, or in the next philosopher, because there is this movement of philosophical discourse in order to "correspond" thereto.

Plato isn't just simply explicating the source from which statements shoot up; he has a specific attitude in relation to this interrogativity. And the statements don't just shoot up like that. But those who think—the philosophers, or the alleged philosophers—have always wanted, once a point has been reached, to go to sleep near this point, to lie down and rest upon it. That wasn't the case with Plato. Nor was it the case with Aristotle, either, who was the most interrogative philosopher conceivable. His case is thus a fantastic historical aberration: for centuries upon centuries, people spent their lives turning Aristotle into a dogma *ne varietur*, the source of all truth: *Ipse dixit. . . .*

There is, therefore, this interrogativity that is created by Plato in the movement of being, and it is continued by Aristotle. And then comes reasoning with another meaning. And here—while talking to you, I was reflecting—I'm taking up Parmenides and Heraclitus again. Parmenides is, therefore: Being is, not-being is not. The Parmenidean "gesture" is therefore the ontological gesture. That is to say, it's not finding a general equivalent of all beings [*étants*], as could be said of the pre-Socratics (in an interpretation that is, moreover, somewhat hasty and superficial). Rather, it's reflecting being [*l'être*] as such. This reflection, moreover, in the fragments of the *Poem* we have, doesn't go much further than tautology, since it consists first of all in affirming that, if one reflects being as such and if there is one being as such, then it must really be concluded that if being is, well, being is. We have this kind of "starting from which" foundation, but it comes to an abrupt end, for afterward not much is said. Nevertheless, there really is an attempt here to try to consider not whether one can impute to being this or that other equivalent property but what one can think of being as such. In this sense, I would not say that philosophy is born with Parmenides but rather that he undoubtedly marks a very important turning point, one that can, moreover, be called the ontological turning point as such, a break with the very highly cosmogonical and psychological aspect discourse has, for example, in Heraclitus.

In relation to that, Plato creates something new—in terms, once again, of this interrogativity, of the parricide we were talking about, and of the introduction of what I call philosophical reasoning. That's something that was unknown among the great pre-Socratics. Once again, Parmenides' *Poem* is an expository presentation [*une exposition*]; and the "fragments" of Heraclitus are plausible statements, which sometimes offer justifications for themselves, their reasons, a *gar* (a "for" or a "since"), but they don't form a reasoned expository account [*un exposé raisonné*].

So, the correction I'd like to make to what I said to you the last time on this matter is in one sense minor, in another sense not. It's that on this point Plato is not quite the first. The first were obviously the Sophists. And we still have the remains of something written by Gorgias, *On Not-Being*.[3] (Until then, all philosophers had written about being, about the nature of being. Their works are lost, but we still have the titles, of the sort *Peri phuseōs tou ontos* {*On the nature of being*}.) The audacious, even provocative Gorgias took the opposite stand from Parmenides and from all the philosophers and made it his task to prove that nothing exists. He manages this by means of the following threefold stunt:

1. Nothing is.
2. If something were, it couldn't be known.
3. If it could be known, it couldn't be communicated.[4]

He is therefore attacking philosophy on three levels: at the level of being itself, at the level of the knowability of being, and at the level of the validity of philosophical discourse. We may well be able, strictly speaking, to have an intuition of being, but we cannot say it. And Plato later says something equivalent: As concerns genuine knowledge, we can have something like a view, like a flame that shoots up, but we cannot truly say it. And he makes a thorough critique of discourse, and especially of written discourse, saying that it's a sorry image, a very deformed image of what genuine knowledge is.

Thus, in Gorgias we have an employment of syllogisms—a negative one, of course, since it's a matter of demonstrating that being is not. There's dialectical reasoning, polemical and pinpoint [*ponctuel*] reasoning: Gorgias has three theses, and he proves them. It's like a lawyer standing before a court—the Sophists were also quasi lawyers—who proves the innocence or guilt of a defendant: first, he was at the scene of the crime; next, he had blood on his hands; finally, he had every interest in eliminating the victim. And so this wasn't something Plato invented. Nor even Gorgias. This is just reasoned discourse. And philosophical reasoning is really something else: it's a kind of reasoning that, as in Plato, is constantly examining its presuppositions—and that is how this point is connected with the question of interrogativity. It's a kind of reasoning that asks itself whether it's right [*s'il a raison*] to posit such and such premises. Or it is so at least when it is well conducted. And today we have underscored Plato's negligence or his logical dishonesty when he fallaciously posits the following outrageous premise in the *Statesman*: The statesman is an *epistēmōn*, a man of science. But in the end, at his best—in the *Theaetetus*, for example—he keeps coming back to his presuppositions, calls them into question, and asks himself whether he has the right [*s'il a le droit*] to use this mode of reasoning. And on top of that, all this is no longer just sporadic [*ponctuel*]; it's really—please excuse this military metaphor—like the movement of an army during a great well-ordered campaign being directed by a great leader [*chef*], where all the army corps converge, by apparently the most disparate paths, toward the same objective at the opportune moment. It's clear that, behind these reasonings, there is a conductor [*chef d'orchestre*] who conducts the dialogue toward an objective that isn't isolated [*ponctuel*] but instead quite essential. That's Plato's huge innovation. And under both these headings—reflectiveness as well as philosophical reasoning—it can be said that we really are witnessing with Plato a second creation of philosophy.

Now to the question of whether Parmenidean not-being is the same as the not-being of the *Sophist*. No one, in the absence of the two main protagonists, can give an answer. We don't know what Parmenidean not-being is. Is it a pure negation of this being that is posited as one, as identical to itself? If one rereads the Platonic dialogue that is called the *Parmenides*, one sees precisely why for Plato this "being one" is unacceptable, since it leads to absurdities. This will take us to the *Sophist* and to the theory of blending, of the mixed, of being and not-being.

I would like to end by underscoring something strange going on in Parmenides. It has undoubtedly not escaped your attention, and it is something quite basic. From the very beginning of the *Poem*, Parmenides says to us:

> There are two ways; you will take the way of truth and you will avoid the way of *doxa*. On the way of truth you will know that being is, that not-being is not. That you are not to say that not-being is and that what is is the same thing as that of which it is thought.[5]

That's the Parmenidean position, which one encounters on "the way of truth." But Parmenides begins by saying that "there are two ways"! And on "the way of *doxa*" there is this proliferation of "X"s, which can be called neither "beings" nor "not-beings," but which are sunbeams, this room, this watch, you, me . . . so many "elements" belonging to the *doxa* group. Well, the question isn't even whether all that is or is not, and in what way. The question is that a discourse is being introduced in which it is said that being is one and that the one alone is, and that, in order to introduce this discourse, the world and what is being said about it have previously been duplicated. Two ways have been spoken of, that of truth and that of *doxa*. And ultimately this is what the two Platonic dialogues of the *Parmenides* and the *Sophist* play on: such a position is untenable.

For the radicals of the Eleatic School, and Zeno above all, it is in that spirit that, according to tradition, they have conducted their various arguments. If you take them literally, it's as follows: Multiplicity doesn't exist, diversity doesn't exist, alteration doesn't exist, movement doesn't exist. I would remind you of what I was saying about movement: notwithstanding the examples of Achilles, the turtle, and the arrow, it's not just movement according to place, but it's alteration, that doesn't exist. All the arguments where Zeno proves that local movement is impossible can be transposed to show that alteration is impossible. Taking all that seriously, then, one is bound to conclude: We live in a world of illusions, of ghosts, and we ourselves belong among these ghosts, and this statement that we are ghosts living in a world of ghosts is itself ghostlike. And to say that it is ghostlike is in turn ghostlike. And so on and so forth.

So, once again, the culmination of this absolute ontology is a sort of absolute skepticism. We can no longer speak. Or else, one really has to commit parricide, as Plato did in the *Parmenides*, and say: No, it's not like that; there isn't this one, absolute, immobile being. There is a being that is determined also by negations, which *are* in a certain fashion.

Seminar of March 5, 1986

I shall begin by reading you an excerpt from the *Statesman* by way of an epigraph to our discussion:

> I say then that it is your duty and mine to recall the observations now made when it comes for us to blame or to praise the brevity or length of our comments on any subject, so as to think not at all of judging their dimensions by the relationship they have to each other but really by this part of the art of measure we were just recommending that we remember, suitability. . . . Still, let us not at all bend everything to this rule. For, it isn't the need to please that will impose on us this concern with proportions, except in an accessory way; and finding in the easiest and swiftest way possible the solution to the problem being raised ought to be but a secondary preoccupation and not a primary end, if we believe in the reason that prescribes that we indeed rather bestow our esteem upon and accord the very top rank to the method that teaches how to divide by species, and that, even when a discourse might be quite long, we pursue it resolutely if it renders more inventive he who listens to it, without making us any more angry today about its length than another time about its brevity. Moreover, we mustn't so quickly and so suddenly let off the hook this judge who criticizes the length of discourses in talks such as ours and condemns digressions that are roundabout, after making the following simple criticism: "These comments are too long"; rather, we must make him have to show us, in addition, that, if briefer, they would have made the listeners more suited to dialectics and more skillful at finding the arguments that bring the truth into its full light and, as to all other blamings and all other praisings, on whatever point they may bear, we must treat them absolutely with disdain and not even look as though we are hearing judgments of such a nature. (*Statesman* 286c–287a, Diès translation {translated into English})

55

In other words, we can go on speaking without concerning ourselves with the length of what we say or worrying about the criticisms of those who judge that our comments [*propos*] are too long or too detailed. We don't worry about these criticisms. Rather, we go on with our comments, concerned simply with the basic issue, that is to say, the question of whether this discussion renders those who hear it more inventive or less inventive and makes them think further or less far.

∿

I would remind you that we have in the *Statesman* two definitions, eight incidental points, and three digressions. Also, that we talked last time about the two definitions: that of the pastor, first, then that of the weaver. And, finally, that we have found them to be strange, to be conducted in a strange manner, and to be ultimately deficient.

We also noted that these two definitions were leading to a true definition, which is not posited as such, though we shall come to it again at the end of our discussion, and that this other definition has nothing to do with either the pastor or the weaver but concerns in fact the *epistēmōn*, he who possesses science. The objects of this science are to be determined, but in the end this science is concerned with the acts of human beings. And more specifically—here again there is a problem, a heterogeneity—it is a science that concerns the "complexion" of the different arts that make up [*composent*] the city.

∿

Before entering now into the discussion of the incidental points, I would like to underscore in passing that, at the very outset of the first of these points, in 261e, the Stranger gives Young Socrates some encouragement, saying to him, "If you persevere in this detachment with regard to words, you will show yourself to be richer in wisdom as you advance in age." And this proclaimed detachment from terminology, from words as such, is interesting to note, for it sheds some definitive light, settling the problems raised by the *Cratylus*. Indeed, in that dialogue, two positions appear: according to one of them, words are what they are by nature, and they correspond by nature to the objects they designate; and according to the other conception, words are by *nomos*, that is to say, by convention. In the *Cratylus*, Socrates demonstrates in a certain fashion that both conceptions are untenable. But this effectively is an aporetic and problematic dialogue. And the *Statesman*, which is undoubtedly a dialogue that comes afterward, squarely gives the answer when the Stranger says to Young Socrates, "You will be much wiser if, as you grow older, you continue not to grant too great an importance to words as such, *mē spoudazein epi tois onomasin*."

IV. The Eight Incidental Points

The first incidental point begins in 262a and concerns the question of whether one is to divide according to species or according to parts.

And quite obviously the Stranger says that a good division, a correct division, doesn't cut up the parts just any which way but follows natural articulations. The part must possess a Form, an *eidos, to meros hama eidos echetō* {262b}. The same idea returns later in the *Statesman*, in 287c, where it's a matter of dividing according to the closest number. It is to be found again in the *Philebus* and elsewhere,[1] and this basic problematic is also found in incidental point number three, to which I shall return. What's at issue is the opposition: arbitrary division according to quantities / division according to species. Now, this of course points to a fundamental problem: Can we establish distinctions solely on the basis of quantities? Or else are there Forms, species, *eidē*, on the basis of which one can establish divisions, the articulations of masses, of multiples, of things that present themselves in number?

And what Plato is saying here is quite literally: When you divide, divide according to the right properties. That is to say, according to properties that constitute Forms, *eidē*. And we end up in a sense with the following statement, which in itself is very problematic: Every property (as we would say nowadays) defines a class; and every class defines a property. Now, that is indeed what occurs in the logic of the living being [*du vivant*], in the logic of the human. And it's something that, when pushed to the limit, leads to paradoxes and aporias. For, indeed, from the absolute and abstract point of view, we cannot say that there is an equivalence between property and class. There exist properties that do not define a class—more exactly, that do not define a set. That's what Russell's paradox, for example, says: The property "set that does not belong to itself" is a property, but it does not define a set; for, if one posits "Let there be a set A of all sets that do not belong to themselves," we end up in a contradiction—this set has to belong, by definition, to itself and at the same time, contrarily, it must not so belong.

In the case of Plato, we aren't going to go to the limit of abstraction; we are interested simply in the Forms, in the *eidē*, which form classes. And this opens up another question, to which the *Statesman* does not respond and which also appears in other dialogues of Plato, the *Parmenides*, for example, and in the *Philebus*, too: How can an *eidos* belong to another *eidos*, and what does that mean? And one can even go much further: What place must be given to properties? Are properties sufficient for classifying, or is an *eidos* much more than just properties? That is only touched upon lightly in 263a, and there is no answer; there are simply some exemplifications of good divisions. Like, for example, divisions into two, symmetrical divisions: male and female, or even and odd. But can one generalize? We also have nonsymmetrical divisions, as in the *Philebus*, where there are divisions into three, or into even more than that.

And all that raises a very important question that is not resolved in the *Statesman*. I emphasize it because we see here how problems that still remain problems for us today were raised and provisionally resolved. For example, in the *Statesman* and in the *Sophist*, we have a division apparently through *a*/ non-*a*. One begins by establishing a sort of hierarchy: a science, a very general art. Is this science theoretical or not? One then takes the nontheoretical branch, within which one establishes a property and leaves aside that which is not characterized by this property. That is to say, the descending order, the specification, the branches that go toward the details each time go by way of a positive *a*, the rest being non-*a*. Now, that of course appears to be artificial. Let us say I begin by performing divisions by saying: Property *a*, OK; property non-*a*, no, that appertains to what doesn't interest me. And I continue: *a'*, yes; non-*a'*, no; *a''*, yes, non-*a''*, no, and so on. And I have here a dichotomy that sometimes appears to be natural but sometimes to be entirely artificial. And that remains a problem; Plato offers no answer. But he makes one see the interrogation that is always there in a division. I can always, for example, divide into *a*/ non-*a*, black / non-black. But to the extent that any object has several characteristics, I can take any one of them; and what possesses this characteristic is *a*, what doesn't possess it is non-*a*. That's all. And on the one hand, Plato is criticizing that. And this is connected up, moreover, with the second incidental point, which we'll come to in a minute. That is to say, it isn't reasonable to say: I am dividing humanity, as the

Greeks do, into Greeks and non-Greeks, that is to say barbarians (or, as initially meant, individuals who do not speak Greek or any comprehensible language). So, that's being criticized.

But at the same time, the examples Plato gives of a correct division—male/female, even / odd—give us a division that is at once a dichotomy (division in two and not into three or more) and a good division. For, it does indeed correspond to something that is a natural *eidos*, a natural Form. We therefore have here a sort of tangling up [*enchevêtrement*] of one procedure for division—which consists in positing a property, a characteristic, and in dividing according to whether the objects do or do not possess this characteristic—with another manner of going about things that consists in finding properties that are relative, of course, to one another but not necessarily in contradictory polarity, in *a*/non-*a* exclusivity—it can be, for example, a plurality—and that as properties also allow one to divide, to establish a hierarchy. This is what, for example, botany and biology do when they classify plants or animals: there are ten orders, some of which have four classes, others six classes; then there are genuses, families, and so on.

Here we encounter a problem: How is one to split up and share out [*répartir*] what is? And in this "How is one split up and share out what is?" we have two bases that are not identical: one being the yes / no—that is to say, a property and the contradictory of this property—the other being properties, characteristics of objects that can be 2, 3, 6, *n*. . . . And how from then on is one to divide?

We cannot go any further; I don't want to go any further. We must simply recall on the one hand that, for example, in Hegel—and already in Kant—the two becomes three. That is to say, what is is always presented as belonging consecutively to a thesis, an antithesis, and a synthesis; therefore, three does indeed become not only a privileged number but also a number that categorizes, that articulates, what exists. And we can also turn to contemporary physics and to its unanswered questions [*ses points d'interrogation*]: Can the ultimate elements, the search for the final elements be made by means of an *a*/non-*a*, that is to say, by means of a property and the contradictory of this property? And this is apparent also in the importance the category of symmetry has for all that is physical, that is to say, for the tendency in research in general, in physics research, to establish symmetrical entities and counterentities; the tendency, therefore, to perform, in a certain way, divisions by two, dichotomies—the

privilege of dichotomies!—but at the same time without ever culminating in the effective possibility of a division by dichotomy.

I don't want to go any further. I don't know if you see the importance
of this matter, what it means, but ultimately the question is why and how
there are several things and not one. If there isn't a single one altogether,
there are several of them; and these several things, we class them, we classify them. Why isn't there one fundamental property that would allow us
to split up and share out everything that is into that which possesses this
fundamental property and that which doesn't possess it within an internal, intrinsic organization? The strange thing in reality is that this dichotomous or dichotomizing procedure is at once valid and not valid.
That is to say, it is dependable and valid in a very great number of cases—
including once again, on the elementary level, in the realm of physics.
Here's an example: everything that is elementary, like a molecule—well,
it's actually particles that obey either Fermi-Dirac statistics or Bose-Ein-
stein statistics. There are fermions and bosons. That's a division in two,
and here we find ourselves facing a dichotomy of all conceivable particles.
In addition, at levels that are almost as basic, what we encounter are not
dichotomies, or even trichotomies à la Hegel, but "polytomies." We live
with both of these as well as an unanswered question: How and why does
one divide what is into classes, and into two classes or more than two—
and why?

*The second incidental point (263c–264c) is, of course, tied to this. In any
case, the Stranger criticizes dichotomies that have subjective bases.*

So it is with the Greeks' division between Greeks and non-Greeks. And
the same goes, he says ironically, if one takes the wisest animals: the *gera-
noi*, cranes. They'd divide up all living beings into cranes and noncranes.
Well, that won't do. And there is here even an implicit criticism of the act
of taking something subjective as a basis for division.

We have here, of course, a bit of an echo of Xenophanes' very old criticism in the *Fragments* of his that we still have. We spoke about this three
years ago. That is to say, Xenophanes' criticism of all anthropomorphic
constructions of the world, his much talked-about statement that "if the
Ethiopians [the Blacks] have gods, obviously these gods are black. But if
horses had gods, well, these gods would be horses."[2] Therefore, it's purely
anthropocentric if the human beings we know give a human form to the

gods or to God, who do not possess this form. Likewise, Plato is saying here that divisions based solely upon subjective criteria, or upon what the subjectivity that divides is, must be dismissed, and one must try to make the distinction according to the thing itself—the primary point, the point of departure being the intrinsic properties and not the properties that depend upon the one who is making the division or upon that one's point of view.

The third incidental point—by far the most important one—concerns paradigms.

In fact, this incidental point is rather closely connected with the others, both with the first one and with other ones that follow, in particular the fifth, which concerns the genuine object of the dialogue (dialectic). So, what does this third incidental point say? It is preceded by a sort of abandonment, neither very comprehensible nor very well justified, of the definition of the statesman or of the royal man as pastor. That won't do, says the Stranger; we must start over again. How is one to start over again? A paradigm must be found starting from which one can try to understand the statesman. All that begins in 277d, where the Stranger says, "It is difficult to show something important while doing without paradigms."

What follows then is a sort of avalanche of extremely important ideas, which are much more important than what is said in the rest of the dialogue. First of all, says the Stranger, one must use paradigms, since each of us, even though we know everything in dreams, risks not being aware of [*ignorant*] these things in a waking state. (This is, of course, one of Plato's essential central ideas, and I shall come back to it, but it isn't clear why it appears here). Young Socrates doesn't get it, and so the Stranger makes, if I might say, a third incidental point–digression, saying: Well, to get you to understand what I mean, I have to give you a paradigm of the paradigm.

And he expounds as paradigm of the paradigm children and letters. In the shortest syllables, children can easily begin to sense, to understand, the elements, the *stoicheia*, the letters. And thereupon, children can express themselves while telling the truth. And then, when it comes to complicated syllables, children at first become tongue-tied [*s'embrouillent*], but in understanding the simple ones they can establish similarities and an identical nature from the complexions they encounter, the *sumplokai*, and on that basis, they little by little come to recognize in a confident way what is the same and what is other. Therefore, we have this learning process [*apprentissage*] by children of the elements and of the complexes of these elements, which when they are short are relatively accessible in an easy way, but are much more difficult when they get bigger. And therein, it is by analogy, by similarity, that children will come to see the truth concerning more "complicated" complexions of letters.

Well, says the Stranger, that's what is to be understood by *paradigm*. That's a paradigm of the paradigm in general. That is to say, when one tries to see something, to comprehend something, to think something by means of a paradigm, one is intending one and the same thing found in something else that is disordered or that is not connected. One tries to intend this one and the same thing in a correct way; and precisely by means of the paradigm, one ultimately ends up intending it in a correct way and in a collected fashion by rediscovering it in both of them.

~

Therefore, what is supposed by the theory of the paradigm is that we possess the truth, or that we can possess the truth, or in any case that we can reach the truth more easily when it is a matter of certain simple elements, but that we are in trouble, confused, when faced with the totality of complex objects. By way of consequence, we have to come back to the understanding of the limited paradigm about a relatively small object, as was just done with letters. And that's also what we'll do, says the Stranger, in trying to find a paradigm concerning the statesman or the royal man. And that will be done in order to come back, next, after this paradigm, to the statesman or to the royal man. And without further ado, and using some expressions that, when one reads the text, seem truly astonishing, the Stranger thereupon introduces weaving as a paradigm (279a–b):

> What could we take then as a paradigm that would be bound by the
> same operations as statesmanship and, although very small, would suffice
> to make us find through comparison the object we are seeking? By Zeus,
> O Socrates, if we don't have anything else at hand, would you like us for
> want of anything better to take weaving? . . . For perhaps that will show
> us the way toward statesmanship.

It's as if this has fallen from the sky or been drawn at random. And, of course, Young Socrates acquiesces: "Why not?" he says.

Here we have a completely arbitrary imposition of weaving, but I shan't dwell upon it now. What interests us is that weaving is introduced here, imposed, after which time it becomes necessary to find a common participation in the forms that are the same in both weaving and the activity of the statesman or the royal man. Perhaps it's that in weaving one has a relational form, a form of composition that will help us to find what the statesman or the royal man is about.

But at bottom, what's happening in the third incidental point is that Plato is raising, without resolving, two key problems that are also encountered in the rest of his work. For him, both of these problems are quite fundamental.

1. The first one—which is, moreover, the more weighty—is raised by Plato in the form of an incidental point inside the incidental point, in passing. It's the phrase I just read to you, that it is difficult to show something important, since "each of us risks finding that we know everything in dreams and are ignorant of everything in a waking state" (277d). That's the first problem.

2. As for the second problem, it's the following: Upon what basis and how do elements lend themselves to complexions; and upon what basis can we discover analogous complexions of the same form across the elements that make up these complexions? And in fact, this second problem is included in the first. For the moment, I am going to concentrate on the first one.

Paradigms must therefore be used to indicate, to show, major things. And why must that be done? Because each of us knows all these things as in a dream but doesn't know [*ignore*] them in a waking state. The phrase is there, and it comes back in 278e. That is to say that, in order to advance, it is necessary to pass from sleep to being awake. Now, we know that this is Plato's fundamental theory. It is expounded at length in the *Meno*, in the *Phaedo*, and elsewhere: Each of us knows [*connaît*]—potentially, virtually, as will be said anachronistically—and knows everything he can know. Only, he doesn't know [*sait*] it. That's Plato's conception: It's not known; it's sleeping in us. Each of us is like someone who is sleeping with this knowledge. Let us recall the analogous expression that comes from Heraclitus—not that Heraclitus would have had the same idea, but, well, the expression is already there. Each of us knows [*connaît*] but does not know [*sait*] that he knows [*connaît*]; and each of us can be helped to understand what he knows [*sait*] already. That's what Socrates does in the

Meno: he takes an illiterate young slave and, both apparently and in reality, gets him to prove the most advanced, the most mysterious, the most incomprehensible theorem, the most paradoxical one for that age, namely, the theorem establishing that the ratio of the hypotenuse to the sides of an isosceles right triangle is not rational but equal to the square root of two. This theorem, discovered relatively recently at that time, was monstrous, outrageous, paradoxical, because it established that there are numbers that are not rational—*arrētoi*, as is said in Greek, that is to say, *unsayable*. It was equivalent, for that time, let us say, at least to proving that space is curved, for example—a theorem as advanced, as difficult, as that. So, Socrates takes a slave and has him prove this theorem. And the objection that "he's making him discover it through yes/no answers" doesn't hold up, since he could do the same thing with an Athenian nobleman.

A footnote can be added here: he has him prove it by asking him the right questions, ones to which the slave gives the right responses each time. One can put an ironic spin on this point: it's Plato who is making him give the right answers. That doesn't cancel out what the dialogue is trying to illustrate: that each person in truth knows, except that he doesn't know that he knows. And someone is needed to awaken this knowledge in him. Here, it's Socrates; more or less everywhere in Plato, it's the real Socrates or the supposed Socrates who asks the questions, who poses the right questions, and who allows others to arrive at the truth.

And this is connected with another aspect, one to which I alluded last time: How can one seek what one doesn't know? Or: How can something like knowledge be gained if one doesn't already possess it? In fact, what Plato says is that one cannot truly acquire it: one already possesses it. And that's the goal of this theory of anamnesis, which is tied up with the immortality of the soul: Souls know because they have seen the Ideas elsewhere, in a supracelestial place; and in becoming embodied, they are weighed down and they forget this knowledge, which nevertheless remains; it still resides within.

~

This very strange theory may seem archaic, folkloric, bizarre, wild, primitive, pagan, something we have no wish to accept. However, this theory is, in a sense, entirely justified. Why? For a very simple reason: every theory that says knowledge stems from a learning process runs into insurmountable difficulties. That is to say, we find ourselves in a situation where it is practically impossible to accept the idea that something might be learned.

And that comes back in Plato already. The question of the *Meno* is: How is it that I can seek if I don't know what I'm seeking? If I don't know what I'm seeking, I won't recognize it if I find it; I won't know that *that* was what I was searching for. What then does *seeking, searching for* mean? What is this strange and singular state of knowing/not-knowing in which I am able to seek?

But there's also learning. How can I learn? What does it mean to learn? And this is connected to the whole problem of induction—I'll come back to this later. It can be said inductively: All men are bipeds. How does one know that? One has simply looked at men. I am passing over the fact that induction is empirical; one may *not* know. OK. But how do you know that what you're observing are men? Of course, one can say: I call *man.* . . . But one is obliged to get into more elementary characteristics. On the basis of these more elementary characteristics, one is obliged to posit an individuality that is at the same time a universality and an essentiality about which you cannot say that you grasp it in reality. In any case, it doesn't go without saying. I shall come back to this point. Anyway, the problem this incidental statement is confronting, and to which Plato has responded, is the following: How can there be learning? And in principle, the answer is that there cannot be learning.

And it must be seen how little this position is folkloric, antiquated, backward, weird, for it's exactly what someone like Noam Chomsky professes today in linguistics. Linguistic structures, says Chomsky—not the surface structures but the deep structures by means of which you speak, we speak—are innate. To speak means to organize the world; it doesn't mean *blahblahblahblah*. It means: stating propositions, sentences, which have subjects, verbs, adjectives, adverbs. This—and here we are returning to Plato/Aristotle, of course—expresses in linguistic form the logical categories: If there are substantives, that's because there are substances; if there are adjectives, that's because there are attributes; if there are verbs, that's because there are processes, or actions, or states. There is an ontology behind grammar, and this grammar is innate. Not under its apparent form, where the apparent grammar of French is entirely different from Arabic or Chinese grammar, but in the deep structures, which are the same.

Well, OK, that's Chomsky's theory; it's debatable. Chomsky himself says that his linguistics is a "Cartesian" linguistics. And Descartes is someone who thinks that we have a priori ideas. And that's also what Plato says. It matters little whether you stick on it the metaphysics that this a priori was learned by looking at the Ideas in a supracelestial site or otherwise. There's an a priori.

Since we're talking about Chomsky, what can one say of the strong points and weak points of his position? (We're still at the preparatory level.) Well, Chomsky talks about syntactic structures, deep structures. That is to say, there's a subject, a verb, and so on. But the question that is being posed is obviously the following: Are these deep syntactic structures, which would be—let us suppose—the same in every tongue, radically separable from semantic magmas? And the answer is: Certainly not. It cannot be said that semantic magmas can be radically separated from syntactic structures. In other words, it cannot be said that any signification whatsoever can be poured out into any tongue whatsoever, whatever the syntactic structures of that tongue. There isn't that kind of separability. Therefore, we cannot purely and simply accept that what is a priori are fully syntactic structures.

And as we know, on the other hand, that semantic magmas, the magmas of significations that each tongue bears, are altered in and through social-historical creation, it is therefore impossible for us to grant that syntactic structures are fully innate and radically separate from semantic magmas. And we can back up this point.

As for what does hold in this Chomskian theory, we know that, as a nursling, every human being can learn any tongue, will learn any tongue to which it is exposed. But not only "will learn": *will think* according to that tongue. This means that the nursling will understand the significations that tongue carries along with itself and that it won't understand the significations that are in other tongues. Or it will have to make a special effort to learn that tongue. But anyhow, we can add that, for the great majority of human beings, this faculty of learning a tongue—like all other faculties: becoming a dancer, a pianist, and so on—is lost once one gets older. Therefore, we are dealing with an a priori faculty that consists in storing some a priori, but storing different a prioris. Storing some a priori—why? Because, when the nursling is in the process of storing, it forms its thought according to that tongue. And quite obviously one's tongue is an a priori imposition of a structure, or an organization for what is to come.

So—I'm returning to learning, and we are going to make a long circuit within this labyrinth—learning, yes, but what is this learning on the part of the child? It cannot be said that the soul knows, a priori, all tongues that ever were extant, all the less so as tongues are still in the process of being created. Nor can it be said that the soul has seen these tongues in a supracelestial site. We know then that the soul possesses a priori the faculty of learning any language whatsoever, therefore the faculty of entering into any system of thought whatsoever. And we know too that, with time, the soul loses this faculty. Therefore, we know that there is a teaching, a learning, and that this learning is not a learning; it's a learning of the forms of learning, of recipients, of molds, of articulations, but it's not a true learning. If you learn a tongue, you learn ahead of things, ahead in terms of its organization, its articulation, and ahead also in relation to the content.

But on the other hand, we are obviously incapable of accepting the idea that there might be a complete tabula rasa, that there would simply be a faculty of learning, because, as I just said, a capacity for educational formation [*une capacité de formation*] must be presupposed. If the subject were not at minimum capable of forming what it is furnished, be it just the elementary words of its tongue, the subject could say absolutely nothing; it couldn't even grasp what it is furnished.

We therefore need to think that the subject can form nothing by induction without a forming capacity [*une capacité formante*], which, itself, is certainly innate in the subject, a priori. And what is meant by this *forming capacity*? It means a capacity that on an elementary level is discriminating. This goes hand in hand, without being identical, with the fact that the subject has to possess the capacity for some kind of recognition of forms. And there's also, quite evidently, a universalizing or, if you will, a generalizing capacity. It isn't just a matter of separating, of discriminating, but also of recognizing that *a* is, anew, what had already been discriminated. And then, it's recognizing, establishing, on the basis of the object *a* that has been discriminated and of which a form has been fabricated, being able to say that there's another object *a′* that offers itself at once as separate and as presenting the same form; and it's putting *a* and *a′*, then perhaps many others, into the same class. This is to say that the subject possesses categorial or categorizing structures, a capacity for positing-classification-differentiation already almost at the sensorial level [*au niveau de la sensorialité*].

But we cannot stop there. We are obliged to grant, on the one hand, that every human subject (though this is true, too, for any subject whatsoever) has to possess a priori a subjective organization, this subjective organization being a capacity for organizing what gives itself out, what offers itself. And that capacity cannot be a slave to what offers itself, cannot give in to [*obéir à*] what offers itself: it has to possess something like considerable "degrees of freedom." And that's something we know, for example, from the following quite trivial material example. We know that our sensoriality permits us to organize colors in a certain fashion. And we know that there exist animals whose sensoriality makes them organize colors in another fashion and makes them sensitive, for example, to the polarization of light, whereas we aren't. We ourselves "noticed" the polarization of light only starting in the nineteenth century and with the aid of special apparatuses.

Therefore, subjective organization, organization as the relatively free capacity to organize what offers itself—what offers itself being at first, of course, X. But at the same time—and here is the other aspect—this subjective and relatively free organization couldn't organize just anything. It has to rely upon, to lean upon [*s'étayer*], a minimal organization of what is—which in a certain fashion is, at the ultimate level, always unknown and remains ever to be sought after.

Let me explain. There is a tree, then three trees, then a dozen trees, and it's a grove. There are five hundred of them, and it's a wood; then fifty thousand, and it's a forest. Here, then, our language (the language we are speaking) discriminates and organizes what appears in its own fashion. Another language might have a hundred words for organizing these same trees. But in the end there is this particular organization of the given, and it seems entirely arbitrary. But there are two points on which it is not arbitrary. The first is that there are trees in the plural, that we do not see *one* tree. And we see cows, human beings. That is to say, this universality, to which we accede through organization, is in another manner already subjacent in what is given. And if it were not subjacent, we wouldn't make that particular organization. Another one would be made. But in order to make another one of them, any one, we need something that is quasi universal in an immanent way. And we thereby have something that does not depend upon our a priori subjective organization, and this is the fact that there are ten trees, or one hundred trees, or fifty thousand trees. Here again, this depends upon the organization, upon our definitions, of what is called *tree*. If someone calls *tree* the branches, that makes millions of trees. All the same, it will always be a certain number. And the possibility of using this number is based upon the fact that what you encounter, what is furnished, is similar enough for it to be able to be counted. And that's something we couldn't invent absolutely.

Or rather, we would always be able to, of course, and at the same time we couldn't really. So, if you've done a bit of set theory, you can perfectly well say that all the objects, living or nonliving, in this room form a set. An arbitrary application of numbers, to be sure. But each time we attempt to know, to understand, something, we are refusing (and here, I return to incidental point number one), precisely, to apply numbers arbitrarily. It can be said, for example, that there are in this room not one set but two: human beings and the other things. That makes some sense, perhaps. But there are again two sets if one considers this part of the room and that other part. OK, but what's the interest? What knowledge, what understanding does one gain therein? No, we'll form numbered sets, when it comes to reality, on the basis of other characteristics that allow us to fortify the separation, division, and enumeration we perform. And in order to make these sets we shall be enumerating—ten trees, ten sheep— we shall rely upon something that supports [*étaye*] this enumeration and that does not depend entirely upon us.

If we take the tree, you can see clearly both sides of the issue. On the one hand, if you're a physicist, you know that this tree is shot through at every instant with millions of perfectly ungraspable neutrinos. So, what's this tree, then? Where are its boundaries? From this side, setting off this tree seems entirely arbitrary. But on the other hand, it isn't arbitrary. Why? For the very simple reason that, as a matter of fact, a tree reproduces itself as this type of tree. Aristotle says: *Anthrōpos anthrōpon gennai*, "a human engenders another human," a human can be engendered only by a human. So you can say, along with all a priori philosophers: We organize the world entirely. Everything that is observed in a laboratory, a physicist would say, depends upon the setup of the instruments. Question: Is there an instrumental setup by means of which you can make a cow be born of a crocodile? No, the cow resists, and so does the crocodile. And you are obliged, in your organization, to lean upon the articulations with which what comes forth [*ce qui vient*] already furnishes you, without it ever being possible to eliminate totally from what comes forth our point of view on what comes forth.

Well, how is this organization performed?

I'm now leaving the "leaning-on" [*étayage*] side, because the leaning-on side answers in fact to ontology, a point we'll come to later. I'm keeping to the organization side, to the subjective side. We were talking about discrimination—that is to say separation, recognition, and universalization. If you reflect upon these three terms, you'll see that they are nearly unanalyzable. One can separate out their elements, but one will be biting one's tail immediately: By means of what does one separate? By means of what does one recognize a form? By means of what does one universalize? And then, one can universalize only separate things, but recognizing a form already contains the seeds of a universalization.

OK, but setting aside the fact that a thing has been isolated, has been separated, how does one recognize it? One recognizes it because it is similar [*semblable*] to itself or to something else. But how does one know that it is similar to itself or to something else? What does it mean that a thing is similar to itself or to something else? Of course, to say *similar* doesn't mean identical. If it isn't identical, that means that it is not completely alike [*semblable*]. But it is posited as similar because one considers that a part of this thing is sufficient for one to be able to characterize the thing, for one therefore to be able—be it only provisionally—to pass from the part to the whole.

～

Generalization. When one universalizes, one passes from like [*semblable*] to like. One doesn't regroup identical things: if they were identical, they'd be unique. But if you make several copies of a thing via repetition, those copies aren't identical. They are different, be it only through their different position (see Leibniz on indiscernibles). When one passes from like to like, one is making what in rhetoric or in literature is called a *metaphor*: a hero and a lion are similar. This corresponds in psychoanalysis to what is called a *displacement*; and it corresponds, too, to what can be called *"valuing as," equivalence, exchange value* in economics. One thing can be taken for another if they are enough alike: one wheel of my car is flat, so I replace it with the spare wheel. It's not the same wheel, but they are similar enough for me to make the displacement, the metaphor from one wheel to the other. Why can I do it? Because the two wheels have a part that is more than similar, quasi identical, sufficiently identical as to need and usage. I therefore pass from the part to the whole, which presupposes that previously I had passed from the whole to the part. For, I cannot pass from the part to the whole if I don't have the part. This means that, to the extent that I discriminate things, I can discriminate in this thing some parts, and, on the basis of the kinship of these parts, pass to the similar and to the universal.

Now, passing from the whole to the part, or from the part to the whole, is what is called in rhetoric *metonymy*. Would you like to have a glass to drink? That's a metonymy and also a *synecdoche*: one drinks the contents of a glass, not the glass—that'd make your stomach feel very bad. In psychoanalysis, this is *condensation*. And the word *glass* is *valued for*. This is no longer a schema of equivalence but, rather, a schema of instrumentality, of belonging.

We therefore have these two absolutely fundamental procedures in this whole labor of recognition: separation and universalization. That is to say, on the one hand, the passage from the whole to the part and from the part to the whole; on the other, the passage from like to like. Or, metonymy and metaphor, without one being able to establish a priority of one in relation to the other. It would be tempting to say that every metaphor presupposes a metonymy. When I say, Hercules was like a lion, my metaphor relies upon a metonymy, namely, that both Hercules and the lion have a property, a part of themselves that is bravery or strength. But this capacity to discriminate and to give part and whole implies an extreme form of the similar: the capacity to maintain something in its identity.

Let us retain simply this: There can never be recognition of something similar on the basis of the exhaustive totality of its characteristics. For, if there were an exhaustive totality of characteristics, it would no longer be similar; it would be an impossibly identical thing. Every similarity is, of course, partial. That's nearly a tautology.

And we find everything we have just said again in reality when we are dealing with living beings, even before there is human consciousness. For, what does one notice at the level of the living being? It is, of course, its capacity to discriminate/separate; to recognize; and to universalize, to recognize in the categories of the universal. Once again, a dog chases game, not whales. There are classes. And that holds on the elementary level.

But how does this universalization occur in the living being? Well, we now know the answer in an entirely positive way: It occurs by means of a relation of the whole and the parts—and, more specifically, on the basis of the part, or parts. It's the parts that are recognized and that lead to the whole. And we positively know that to be true on the elementary level of biology, at the cellular level, and in particular in the recognition that takes place in immunology or in the assimilation of food: lymphocytes recognize antigens through one of the latter's parts, their stereochemical feature. An antigen has a place on its surface that the lymphocyte, like two pieces of a puzzle, will recognize, adapting itself to it, clinging to it like a glove. From then on other chemical reactions will occur, and the antigen will be destroyed—or the food will be assimilated.

There is therefore a site of attachment, which can be called the lymphocyte's leaning-on knowledge. And the antibody is capable of recognizing, according to the nature of the site in question, this or that category of antigens. It therefore has in itself the principle of belonging: All of that belongs to something. And it also has a principle of equivalence or universalization, since the antibody will recognize everything that presents itself with identical stereochemical properties and will react accordingly.

And this goes even further, because this kind of process forms the basis for some medical procedures. The invention of sulfonamides consisted in isolating a substance stereochemically so that it will cling to the bacterium exactly on the site where the latter obtains nutriment. A substance has therefore been fabricated that "deceives [*trompe*]" the bacterium. For, the bacterium, too, knows; and because it knows, it can be mistaken [*être trompé*].

This entire system of stereochemical adaptation is therefore in part mechanical. But in part only, precisely because one can deceive a bacterium as one can fool [*tromper*] a human being—whereas one cannot deceive a gravitational mass.

I come back to the more general problem. The human subject—the psychical one, let us say—recognizes objects on the basis of marks. But what marks? And how does one recognize a mark? Why does one recognize a mark? And why such and such a mark? And can it be said that in nature there might truly be parts and wholes? For example, if one considers the solar system, where does what is called *solar wind* stop? And how about the magnetic storms on Earth that go beyond the outermost planets? What about the ray of sunlight and the particles it creates? All that can be said is that what presents itself in nature offers a certain number of articulations, points on which divisions can be grafted. But they will be grafted there and not elsewhere according to what the subject does. It's the subject that chooses to posit separations at such and such a spot and at another such one. Not the subject at the primary level, obviously, not the completely singular subject: here, we're talking about the collective subject, the species.

Therefore, it's the subject that organizes a world starting from a chaos in which differences present themselves. But in themselves, these differences have no privilege in relation to one another. It's the subject that privileges some of them and not others. It's the subject that organizes its world, that organizes itself in organizing its world.

Why this huge incidental point / digression within the *Statesman*'s second incidental point? Because, ultimately, it's one of the axes of the following philosophical problematic: What is a priori and what is a posteriori? What does the subject already know before being in contact with the world? And what can the subject learn in the world? And under what conditions? Chronologically speaking, before being in contact with the world, the subject knows nothing, certainly. But it learns only in organizing the world and in organizing itself at the same time. Starting from the moment a subject is alive, it is self-organization—more exactly, self-creation of itself and of the world. And it can accomplish *that* only on the condition that the world lends itself to such an organization.

Now, here we have all of inherited philosophy, from Plato until Heidegger passing by way of Descartes and Kant, which, when it discusses knowledge or being, conducts its discussion on the basis of the individual. And this individual is an individual who comes very late in the process, too late. This is the socially fabricated individual, who speaks French, English, "Latin or Javanese," as {the surrealist poet} Robert Desnos said, who has a language, who has a way of thinking according to this language, who belongs to a social-historical world, who has a history—a heavy load of presuppositions indeed! And one would first have to think the subject in relation to what the subject inherits from the living being, next in relation to what the social sphere furnishes it. And here, on the social level, we have essentially language but also a coherent subworld that passes by way of the family, the first of the human being's artificialized environments with which the subject is furnished. And we also have a reworking [*réélaboration*], a re-creation by the singular psyche of all that, of all that the singular psyche is furnished.

Take, for example, a conception like the Kantian one on the understanding, the Kantian subject. This subject is bastard, both excessive and deficient. And this is so for four reasons:

1. First of all, because one gives oneself as going without saying a sensoriality of this subject that quite evidently itself belongs to the empirical world but is supposed to be passive. That's false: this sensoriality is, quite evidently, organizing. And inasmuch as it belongs to the empirical world, it ought itself, in the Kantian view, to belong to a chaotic manifold. Now, that's not true: the subject's sensoriality is organizing and organized. There is therefore in Kant a sensibility whose underlying organization is unknown [*ignorée*].

2. Next, Kant gives himself as going without saying a thought without language, which is absurd. Or, a language that is mysteriously innate, universal, and transcendental—which simply doesn't exist.

3. Therefore, Kant doesn't know about [*ignore*] the social-historical charge of which the understanding partakes.

4. And, finally, Kant ignores the other dimensions of psychical subjectivity, without which the subject, even the knowing subject, never functions. What Kant is describing is a sort of knowing mechanical automaton, not a knowing subject. Such a subject knows only to the extent that it cathects knowledge, only to the extent that this knowledge is a wish-object or an object of desire. And we have the immediate proof to the contrary with autistic psychosis, where the subject isn't interested in, doesn't cathect, the knowing of the external world.

This goes to show simply the fatal bad old ways into which the inherited philosophy falls when it fails to recognize the two-sidedness I was just talking about, that is to say, when it tries to make a theory of knowledge while doing without (1) an ontology of the knowing subject itself, and, at the same time, without (2) an ontology of the object itself posited as knowable. Every simply apriorist or aposteriorist theory runs up against radical impossibilities.

Now—and I'm coming back to Plato and to the story of sleep and wakefulness—in Plato as well as in Aristotle the theory of knowledge is inseparable from an ontology. And one even has at once an ontology, a cosmology, and a psychology that hold together. And it is, of course, this psychology that furnishes a theory of knowledge. Well, can the soul learn in the world? No, says Plato, in terms of the arguments already put forth: How can I learn if I don't know already? No induction can ever furnish me with solid knowledge. Therefore, if there is knowledge, it's because the soul already knew. And here Plato draws the inevitable conclusion: If it already knew, that means that it knew elsewhere and beforehand; it means that there is therefore an immortality of the soul. And this absolutely ceases being folkloric; it's nearly a consequence. When embodied, the soul falls into a kind of sleep, a sleep from which it can awaken especially if it is assisted in this awakening by a midwife like Socrates. And once awoken, it recalls the Forms, the *eidē*, which it knew as immaterial, therefore immortal.

But the world—and we're coming to cosmology—with which the soul is dealing is not immaterial but material. How then can we know it? Well, that's precisely what Plato's cosmology and his theory of the Ideas are trying to respond to: The effectively actual world is corporeal, not just material. It's *sōma echon*, as he says in the *Statesman*, in the myth we shall be commenting next time {cf. 269d–e}. As corporeal, the world cannot simply be Forms; it participates in becoming and change, but it also participates in the Forms, in the *eidē*. And as, relative to the *eidē*, the soul doesn't know but recognizes [*ne connaît pas mais reconnaît*], relative to the things of the world, relative to corporeal things, it knows something in it insofar as these corporeal things participate in the Forms; that is to say, insofar as they aren't pure matter.

Here we have a paradigm that brings us back to the incidental point about which we were speaking. And therefore it is only when one has understood, not so much Plato's theses, but the articulation of the problematic underlying them that one can see why they have remained so important—even if they may seem to us bizarre, folkloric, archaic. And one can also understand to what point Aristotle himself is deeply dependent upon Plato. And this establishes already what is called, both in the customary sense and in the mathematical sense of the term, a *hereditary transmission* of philosophers' properties. For, what takes place with Aristotle is a new version in a sense of this triad of Plato's: ontology, psychology, cosmology. And it will be transmitted later on.

In other words, for Aristotle, too, there is indeed necessarily an intimate relationship between ontology, psychology, and cosmology. For Aristotle, too, the genuine being [*l'être véritable*] of something, of a being [*d'un étant*], its essence, its *ousia*, is the *eidos*; it's the Form. Only— tremendous differences with respect to Plato—he claims first of all that this *eidos* isn't separate, that it is not elsewhere, beyond. It is in this world. Aristotle therefore eliminates as mere metaphors all of Plato's phrases about participation, communication of objects, particular beings [*étants particuliers*], with the Forms. And on the other hand, he offers an extremely deep and detailed analysis of this Form. Where Plato is content to speak of *eidē*, of Forms, Aristotle says: Every being [*étant*] includes four principles, or four causes, or four elements:

- matter;
- form in the narrow sense;
- the final, effective cause;
- and then he regroups these three elements into a general form, which is the thing's destination, its *ousia*, what it was to be.

Nor should it be forgotten that, for Aristotle, this *ousia*, if it is truly ultimate, isn't definable either (that's a bit secondary). But the *kosmos* is nothing other than these realized forms self-perpetuating themselves in sublunary nature, or these eternal forms in celestial nature. And ultimately there is only one form, only one single Being-being [*être-étant*], that is God, who is pure form without matter. But in fact this Being who is God, who is pure form without matter, cannot truly be known directly by us; we deduce this Being that is God as a necessity of the existence of nature.

How do we know? Here again, Aristotle is right in the line of descent from Plato because what he says about knowledge is that, when we speak of second-order knowledge, as can be said, or of what he himself calls *logos*, the attribution of a thing, when we say something about something, then at that very moment we are using different methods, including also induction, for example, which is justifiable up to a certain point. Aristotle knows very well what's at issue in relation to induction.

But when what's at issue is the essence of a thing, this essence cannot be said through a definition; it cannot be grasped inductively. It is known directly through thought. This is what Aristotle affirms in the celebrated passage about the psyche in *De Anima* (*On the Soul*): thought—*nous*—is always true when it knows the *ousia* of things, the *to ti ēn einai*, what they were to be. But thought can be mistaken in its attributions when it says *ti kata tinos*, something about something. This is to say that we have a secondary domain in which there is more and less, true and false—a domain where we can know more or less and where we can be mistaken. But as for the essences of things, *nous* grasps them directly. There's not even any *logos*. It doesn't reflect them discursively. It grasps them. It fixes them in place. It sees them.

That's Aristotle's position. And yet—but there, it's another problem—there are other passages in Aristotle, in the *Zoological Treatises*,[3] where he says strangely that *nous*, thought, enters from the outside into the human subject, whereas all the rest is produced by the living being [*l'être vivant*], by the human being. Aristotle never talks about the immortality of the soul, but he nevertheless says that *nous* enters *thurathen*, from the outside, "by the door," into the living being, because he cannot otherwise account for this capacity of the human subject to know the essences of things.

~

So, one can see, of course, why in Plato there is a theory of paradigms, that is to say that there are Ideas that organize being [*l'être*], that even organize being in the world. There is a kinship among beings [*étants*]; one can pass from one being [*étant*] to another since there's participation in higher *eidē*. The same thing is found in Aristotle, since Aristotle thinks that the *ousiai*, the essences, are immanent in things. This can also, by way of consequence, furnish an ontological and cosmological grounding, if I may say so, for induction.

And so what is said with Plato and Aristotle outlines the framework for what will come afterward, including also its negation in the history of philosophy. That is to say, there are some subtle elaborations well afterward; there are some attempts to break up [*casser*] this articulation of ontology-cosmology-psychology. That isn't the case, I might add, with Descartes and Leibniz, who make some modifications but who keep this unity of psychology-cosmology-ontology. But there are some attempts in modern times to break up this unity: Spinoza breaks it up while keeping only an ontology, in a sense; Kant breaks it up while keeping only a psychology and while rejecting the idea that there might be an ontology and a cosmology. Of course, he's speaking on a transcendental level, but it boils down to the same thing. And for Fichte, it's the same. As for Hegel, he returns to an Aristotelian model.

And Heidegger, to arrive at the end of this course, notes that in effect all of these philosophies belong to the same circle, that this circle had not yet been closed by the pre-Socratics—which boils down to saying, on the other hand, that with Plato there is indeed a second creation of philosophy, and this is what we truly mean by philosophy—and that there is an exhaustion of this circle. And this exhaustion—with some real consequences for the principal ideas that have emerged with the circle, like reason for example, rationality—leads to desolation and leads into the desert. It is in this sense that there is an end of philosophy; it is in this sense, too, that Nietzsche's "The desert is growing" can be taken up again. But what there also is is the fact that Heidegger cannot philosophically get out of this circle but simply can note that a circle has closed upon itself. (He finds himself enclosed in it—and proclaims that it *is* closed.)

Now—and we shall finish today on this point, before returning to the *Statesman*—what we are saying is precisely that it is the question of being [*de l'être*] that is to be taken up again, and it is to be taken up again in the threefold articulation of psychology, cosmology, and ontology. But there's something else in thought—something else that, moreover, can take in [*englober*] this inherited circle and can, up to a certain point, account for it. And this resumption can occur only on the basis of the observation that being creates itself, that it is temporality, and that the subject creates itself in being as capacity to know being; and not only that, moreover, but those are the other dimensions of subjectivity of which I spoke. This capacity to know being is based upon the capacity of the subject—and here, I am speaking of the subject in the most general sense, both psychical as well as social-historical and individual—to re-create, to create anew the originary matrices in and through which the self-creation of being has occurred.

That's what is going on, roughly speaking, in the following enigma: We cannot know anything if we don't already know it; and if we already know it, how the devil would we know it? The solution to this enigma is as follows: When we know, when we learn, we are not copying reality, because that's an absurdity. We reinvent reality, and this is a reality that proves to be congruent in us to a part of the reality that exists. Or, rather: We reinvent an imaginary schema that proves to be congruent with a part of really given being. That's the response to the problem of Plato in the *Meno* and of all philosophy. And it's upon that basis that we can recommence our philosophical efforts and can exit from the circle of inherited thought.

We shall continue next time by putting a rapid end to this story of the third incidental point about the paradigm, then by treating the other incidental points that are of relatively secondary import. And we shall launch into two {of the} digressions: (1) on the myth of Cronus and (2) on the essence of the statesman.

Seminar of March 12, 1986

IV. The Eight Incidental Points (Continued)

Incidental Point Three, on the Paradigm (continued)

I would like to take up again the idea we finished with the last time apropos of this much talked-about third incidental point from Plato's *Statesman* concerning the need for a paradigm in order to understand, in particular, objects of thought that have no materiality.

We have traveled through many labyrinths, but the important point, the reason why I insisted upon this incidental point, is the necessity it reveals in Plato's thought, and thereby in the whole of philosophical thought since Plato, up to and including Heidegger, namely, the need to set [*ordonner*] knowledge—therefore, this faculty of the soul; therefore, this activity; therefore, this nature of the soul (the psyche)—in line with being in the most abstract sense, on the one hand, and with the totality of Being-being, the cosmos, the world, on the other. This articulation of a psychology with a cosmology and an ontology is quite marked in Plato and in Aristotle, and it is marked, too, in many philosophers of modern times. Sometimes, as is in Kant, it can be the object of a denial, with consequences that are, to say the least, aporetic and, to tell the truth, absurd. I mean by this that the Kantian attempt—or, at least, that of Kant's first successor, Fichte—to say something about our knowledge while looking solely at the subject of this knowing activity and while eliminating the object—claiming that as such it plays no role and that therefore this subject could function in any world whatsoever—obviously ends in aporias.

For Plato, there is, therefore, this common positing of psychology, cosmology, and ontology. The soul knows. Why? Because, qua immaterial soul, it has already known. Once embodied, it has fallen into a kind of sleep from which it can be awakened. Once awakened, it remembers, and what it recalls are the *eidē*, the Forms, which it has known from all eternity. Next, it's to the extent that the *kosmos* itself, existing reality, the totality of beings [*étants*] is composed by participation in these Forms—that is, to the extent that there is this much talked-about participation or communication, *methexis* and *koinōnia*—that the soul can know something of this real world in which it finds itself (temporarily, moreover).

The articulation is exactly the same in Aristotle. For, although the positions, the contents of the theses, are different, the main lines are the same. Here, too, there is a soul. As seen in the treatise *De Anima* or implicitly in the *Metaphysics*, this Aristotelian soul is the faculty by which one apprehends the senses, and in that it can never be mistaken. Aristotle says this explicitly: When the soul considers the data of the senses, it always speaks truly; it possesses the truth. It is mistaken only when it is operating in *logos*, in Aristotle's sense, that is to say, in the complexion of significations, in the attribute, in what he calls the *ti kata tinos*, saying something against something, that is to say, about something, that is to say, of something. It's in this reasoning part of the soul that error can be found, if one excludes the imagination—which, for Aristotle (the first to have posited this principle) can also be a source of error: "The sensations are always true, whereas most data of the imagination are false" (*De Anima* 3.3.428).[1]

For Aristotle, the knowability of something rests upon the fact that there are *ousiai*, essences, and that these essences contain something *katholou*, something universal. That's the ontological level. And at the same time—and this is the cosmological aspect—Aristotle rejects, with a disparaging remark directed against Plato, all those stories about communication and participation; for, as he says, that's not saying anything; it's just "using poetic metaphors." The *ousiai*—the *eidos*, the Form—are not separate from real beings [*des êtres réels*], from the real beings [*des étants réels*] of which they are the forms; they are immanent. There is only one single form that would be a form without matter; this is the thought of thought, what he calls God, the thought that itself thinks itself and that contains no matter. As regards material objects, there is, for Aristotle, a possibility of induction precisely because, when the soul considers things, it isn't facing, as it does so for many Moderns (for Kant, let's say), pure unformed matter. It isn't placed opposite a chaotic diversity. It is placed in front of objects whose essences are inherent, immanent to them, so that there is a certain ontological grounding for induction, although Aristotle obviously knows that induction doesn't permit one to reach rigorous conclusions. He knows very well that every conclusion, made on the basis of a limited number of examples out of the totality of a species, can be deceptive and contains no necessity. But, if there is something that permits one to know on the basis of the real, it's the *ousia*'s immanence in the real; it permits one to begin reasoning about what is, to begin to know what is.

It is therefore this relative unity, this organized articulation among the psyche, beings [*les étants*], and what genuine Being (*to ti ēn einai*) is, that for Aristotle also permits one to know not only objects but also even, ultimately, thought. This relative unity gives us this limited but secure knowledge of the world—limited because we are forever separated from what is the supreme essence, the pure form, absolute *nous*, pure activity, the *actus purus*, which is separate from the world and considers only itself. (This is perhaps the only way of thinking a deity that would have a certain philosophical dignity. All the other gods, monotheistic or not, who busy themselves with the trivialities of this world are very bizarre, very strange gods.)

This articulation is still there in many modern philosophers. It is explicit, for example, in the thoughts of people like Leibniz and Hegel, but it is also rather marked in Descartes (passing by way, there, of a god who creates the world, of course). It is interrupted in the subjectivist current of modern philosophy, in Kant—but already beforehand in Hume—who considers only the subject but who remains caught up in this problematic that can be called the deficiencies in Kant's thought, namely, the aporias that led the German Idealists to go beyond him later on. These aporias are marked by this articulation and by this circle. In the end, Heidegger didn't do anything other than note that in effect this history of philosophy from Plato until Husserl belongs to the same circle; that this circle had not yet—this is true—been locked tight at the time of the pre-Socratics; and that it was locked tight for the first time with Plato (for my part, I was telling you that with Plato there was, in effect, a second creation of philosophy). But for Heidegger, this circle is exhausted; its historical destiny has been to bolster this modern technical approach, modern rationality, the modern scientific outlook [*cette technicité, rationalité, scientificité modernes*], that is to say, to create this desert, this absence, this eclipse of Being and of the gods. To that extent, Heidegger himself remains caught up in this circle: he cannot exit from it philosophically; he's imprisoned therein and can do nothing other than call his own imprisonment the "withdrawal of Being," the historical withdrawal of Being.

Can one exit from this circle? In my view, one can exit from it to the extent that the question of being [*de l'être*] is to be taken up again, to the extent that there is another field of thought that encompasses this inherited circle. And the condition for exiting therefrom is to smash [*casser*] this central idea that holds these major pieces together, these three arcs of the inherited circle's circumference. One must smash the idea of determinacy—that is to say, of being as being-determined—and see again that being is creation, that the psyche and the social-historical are themselves creations. One must see that the problem of induction is in a sense ill posed; the third part, the cosmological dimension, is ill posed because the question is not only to note that all empirical knowledge is uncertain but also to start from this incontestable fact—or else one must stop talking—that there is empirical knowledge. There is empirical knowledge already when I discuss with someone, for that supposes that I accept his existence. This existence is not an a priori idea; it's a fact nourished by experience, and this someone is thereby the testimony of sensoriality and has a weight that is unimpeachable. But of course, we always remain with the problem of the form of this knowledge. We cannot say that we borrow the forms of intuition, space and time, or categories from this sensoriality, from this experience, or from whatever else on the outside. We are therefore obliged to note that what we do—and not qua singular individuals, qua singular souls, but qua individuals participating in a social-historical world—is recreate as thought-form what is; we re-create as thought-form what, in a sense and already in an immanent fashion, is as formable.

We have the form of the one, and it is absurd to say, like some materialists, that we extract numbers from things. I do not see, indeed, how one can extract numbers from things; in order that we might extract anything whatsoever from a thing, one must first posit this thing as one and several, and posit that there can be one and two and three . . . , and so on. It is we who posit it, but that has some hold upon reality. Things are such that they can be counted; they are such that one can separate them. Here, we must come back to the great mind of Aristotle: Things are such that one can separate them sufficiently as to need and to usage, and sufficiently as to the perspective within which one is considering them at the moment one is speaking. We aren't separated from the Earth because at every moment billions of neutrinos are coursing through us; but, as to the need and usage of discussing, of eating, or of doing whatever else, we are sufficiently separated from the totality of the cosmos, for example, and we are sufficiently separated in certain regards relative to knowledge; that is, our lack of distinction in relation to the surrounding gravitational field or to the neutrinos that are coursing through us is not of relevant interest as soon as we come to consider, for example, the Unconscious or someone's thought.

We are therefore obliged to posit as an ontological thesis that what is is ensidizable,[2] but that it is not so in an overall way; one cannot make an overall system of it. This is what is shown in the history of our knowledge and also as we gain access to different strata of this total Being-being by means of what can be called the creative imagination of individuals and the creative imagination of societies, which reposit, reinvent—which re-create—what in a sense is already there in order to be able to think it. This goes along with the idea that these different strata of what is, for which we have need to posit, to invent, to create new schemata each time in order to be able to think them, are themselves emergences, sudden appearances [*surgissements*] of total Being-being; that Being is therefore always to-be [*à-être*], or is creation. It's a paradoxical idea that there is ultimately a truth—that is to say, that there is in a certain way a truth in the most naive, the most traditional sense of the term—qua adequation, qua a certain correspondence of what we think with what is (which doesn't mean a total and exact reproduction, an *Abbildung*, but a sufficient correspondence), and that, at the same time, in order to attain this truth, we are obliged to invent it. But that's the way it is. I was quite pleased to discover that this idea had already been formulated (I don't know whether others had already stated it) by the great William Blake in *The Marriage of Heaven and Hell*. One of the "Proverbs of Hell" says:

What is now proved was once only imagin'd.[3]

This is a dazzlingly beautiful phrase and at the same time a banal one that states an obvious truth: You can never prove anything if you haven't first imagined it as the possibility of a statement that is to be proved. Once again, the poet is prophet, as another poet said. This is, in a sense, the whole history of human knowledge: imagining things and then proving them by pure reasoning, for example, and rendering thinkable something that doesn't depend upon us, something that is real, that is to say, real in the sense of what resists, what isn't pliable at will to our schemes of thought.

~

I now come back to the *Statesman*. You will recall that, apart from the two definitions, there were eight incidental points and three major digressions. We had already spoken of the first three incidental points, the first being species and parts, the second being the viewpoint of division, the third being paradigms and elements.

The fourth incidental point, in 281d, bears upon the distinction between the arts of the proper cause and the arts of the comitant cause.

With "comitant," I'm anticipating here Aristotle's terminology, but it's a question of the "incidental" or "accidental" cause, as is said in the Latin translations, which are bad. It's the cause that happens to "go along with." That's what *sumbainei* signifies.

This distinction isn't very interesting, except that it helps us to see, here again, that, when one wants to make a distinction, what today is contemptuously called metaphysics, ontology, the problems of thought always rise up again [*resurgissent*]. Plato wants to distinguish the art of the proper adventing [*de l'advenir propre*] of the thing from that which simply aids in the production of the thing; and in order to do this he is obliged, obviously, to introduce a postulate, the postulate of substance. There is an activity that produces the thing itself, qua substance, inasmuch as it is itself and not something else; and then there's a whole series of causal links that culminate in the production of this thing. All these causal links can be separated out, carved up, so as to distinguish what produces the thing itself, and this is the principal cause concerning *to pragma auto, die Sache selbst* {the thing itself}. As a nearly exhaustive example of the second case, there are the arts that produce the instruments used for the production of a thing. We could follow him here, but there aren't, as one knows, just instruments. The object is itself a separate object; it is something. It's the horse saddle, the sword. There's the art of he who forges the sword— that's the art of the principal cause—but there is also, for example, the art of he who has manufactured the hammer with which the blacksmith works. Where does the production of means stop and where does the production of the object itself begin? If you reflect upon it a little while, you'll see that, any way you look at it, the cut is arbitrary and that, even if one posits the substance of the manufactured object, that of the sword, for example, one doesn't know where one is supposed to cut; for, in order to forge the sword, the metal has to be laid down somewhere; one needs fire and a heap of other ingredients. You'll find all these problems later on in economic theory, in the theory of value: What is the object and what contributes to adding value to the object? I mention all this in order to show you how much basic thought, the fundamental a prioris, come into play, even when it comes to relatively secondary questions.

The fifth incidental point (283c–285c) concerns the difference between relative measure and absolute measure.

It's funny to see how this incidental point crops up [*surgit*]. The Stranger asks at one point: Have we made too many detours and distinctions? Aren't we circling around the thing too much, rather than tackling it itself? Aren't we taking too many circuitous paths? Here, we're smack dab in Socratic-Platonic dialogue: Yes, but too much in relation to what? What is too much? When does one talk too much? We then immediately have the general question: When is there excess, *huperbolē*, and when is there a defect [*défaut*], *elleipsis*? And this applies not only to discourse but to anything else. Are there too many stars in the sky? Is the *Ninth Symphony* too long? Do you earn too much money or not enough? Are there too many books written by human beings, or not enough? Well, says Plato, there's an art, "metretics" (*metrētikē*), which is the art of measure. And here, immediately, he introduces the capital distinction (it's not just by chance that philosophy has been condemned to turn around the Platonic wheel for twenty-five centuries!) between two different sorts of measure: relative measure and absolute measure.

The idea of absolute measure is already a paradox. But let's begin with relative measure: there is a relative measure in the sense that I can say that this man is very tall physically in relation to an average height. But one cannot remain at this relative measure, says Plato, because, if every measure were relative, one could never say that something was too large or too small. For, as large as a thing may be, there can be a larger one; and as small as a thing may be, there can be a smaller one. The very small thing will still be very large in relation to a thing that is {much} smaller than it.

And a thing that is very large will be small in relation to something larger. Careful, now. All this is very strong, very rigorous, and if you accept it, the Platonic trap closes upon you. All these measures (one cannot live without measuring, without saying that there is the large and the small) are relative. That's obvious. But if every relative measure presupposes a measure that isn't relative, you necessarily end up with the necessity—in order to think, in order to speak—you end up with the idea that there is something that is measure of the rest, not relatively, but that is absolute measure, that is norm, that is, therefore, a Form, an *eidos*. There, you can no longer get out of it; there is necessarily, if you want to talk, something that is nonrelative measure, measure that fixes in place the true advent, the right advent, the correct advent of a thing independently of all relativity and that says: That's how such a thing is to be. And if, as is obvious in a certain fashion, we can say of a poem or of a piece of music that it is too long, we are really saying it's too long as to, relative to, something, but we don't say it in relation to the average size of musical pieces. For example, there are some symphonies of Bruckner and even of Mahler that are too long, but they aren't too long because they are longer than those of Beethoven. And they can even not be longer. They are too long for what they are. There are poems that are too long and that don't contain more than twenty lines! But the *Iliad*, with its fifteen thousand lines, is perhaps not too long (even though the Romans were already saying that good old Homer . . .). The symphonies of Bruckner and Mahler are not too long in relation to an absolute measure—we're no longer within the measurable—but in relation to the form of the symphony. But there is no absolute form of the symphony—that's the paradox of the work of art—and still less an external form/norm of the poem. A sonnet is obligatorily "4-4-3-3," but poems that aren't sonnets are written, too. We have no numerical norm for the length of a poem, but we have a norm of a beautiful poem, in a sense. Do we truly have this norm of a beautiful poem, this form of the musical piece that has exactly the right dimensions [*les dimensions qu'il faut*], as one is so often certain about with great music, whether it's a matter of classical music or a jam session? This piece itself includes its norm; it brings into the world [*il fait venir au monde*] its own norm, and it's in relation to this norm that it itself reveals to us that it is perfect, and not in relation to something from outside. This norm that it brings to the world [*qu'il apporte au monde*] is a specification of something we cannot define, which is precisely the form of the beautiful, the beautiful itself.

We are reaching this other part of Plato's reasoning. Plato therefore has to introduce the distinction between a measure that is relative and another that is not and that he calls the *metrion*. We really must see how the ideas and notions are being woven together. When we say that a poem is exactly what it should be [*ce qu'il faut*], neither too long nor too short, relative measure is being implied, but in a subordinate way, namely, I know that Beethoven's *Seventh Symphony* lasts so long. There is this dimension, and in relation to it both the composer and the listener have a position, an *Einstellung*, an *impostazione*. This is to say that the *Seventh Symphony*, for example, cannot be stretched out further. There is therefore a dimension of relative measure, but it's there only to instrument the embodiment of a form that, itself, is not relative to something else, that is relative only to beauty, to the form. That's what Plato calls the *metrion*. We therefore have two "metretic" arts, two arts of measure, of mensuration: the quantitative arts and those that concern quality, which Plato characterizes by using several terms: the *metrion*, which means quite strictly that which obeys a measure; the *metron*, that's the measure; *metrion*, that's the measured in the two senses of the term, the measured as past participle and the measured as adjective (wise, prudent). There's also {the Greek} *prepon*, what ought to be [*ce qu'il faut*], the German *Sollen*, or the {Greek} *deon* (what should be [*ce qu'il faut*], what is fitting or suitable), or *kairos*, the propitious, appropriate instant, and the instant in relation to measure. This idea of *kairos* is quite astonishing and, at the same time, very profound; an act, a thing, will be measured in this, that it comes truly in its time. Here, we must think of medicine or of war, which the Greeks never lost sight of: it's the act that comes at the moment when it is necessary [*au moment où il faut*], the part of the phalanx that advances just at the necessary moment [*juste au moment où il faut*]. Here again, one sees this sort of relativity that isn't a quantitative relativity; it is relative to a result that must be brought about [*qu'il faut faire advenir*].

There is already in this incidental point the strange affirmation— strange, because here, there's a return to something quantitative and relative—that the *metrion*, therefore something qualitative, is a midpoint [*milieu*] between two extremes. And this is what later on, in Aristotle's *Nichomachean Ethics*, yielded virtue as *metrion*, as the happy medium [*juste milieu*], an expression that has been debased with a petit-bourgeois meaning, but that isn't what was intended by Plato and Aristotle.

Plato adds, in a relatively important passage, that everything that depends upon art participates in measure. And that's so true for him that, in the *Timaeus*, the demiurge, the manufacturing god [*le dieu fabricateur*] himself can fabricate the world only by going around measuring all the time. And here one sees why the world is relatively perfect, perfect as much as is possible. On the one hand, within itself, it is made as much as is possible according to measures, and, on the other, it has the right form [*la bonne forme*] not quantitatively but because it is the most perfect imitation possible of the form of the eternal living being. There we have the absolute measure of the world; and in that sense, the world is good [*bien*], because you have this form relative to which it is perfect.

Incidental point six states that the true goal of the dialogue is dialectical exercise alone.

But this is a bit of trickery on Plato's part. We've already talked about this. It is maintained here that the genuine object of the discussion is not to define the statesman but quite rather to train oneself [*s'exercer*] in matters of dialectic. And that isn't true: there is a first level where he deals with the statesman; there is then a second level where, in effect, what really matters is the dialectic, philosophical remarks: "It's because of this that we are saying all that we are saying" (286a). But in fact, at a third level, the genuine objective of the dialogue really remains not to give a definition of the statesman—since there is, in a sense, no genuine definition of the statesman in this dialogue—but, rather, to prepare for the definition of the city later described in the *Laws* and to sketch out the governors' role in that city.

Incidental point seven (304b–d) speaks of the subservient arts of statesmanship.

Therefore, those of rhetoric, strategy, and so on. Here, moreover, Plato gives a good definition of rhetoric—good, that is, in relation to himself—when he says that it is the art that persuades the crowd, *peistikon plēthous*, by means of a mythology, *dia muthologias*, and not through *didachē*, discursive teaching, dialectic, if you will: "Well, to which science shall we attribute then the virtue of persuading the masses and crowds by recounting fables to them instead of instructing them?" (Εἶεν· τίνι τὸ πειστικὸν οὖν ἀποδώσομεν ἐπιστήμη πλήθους τε καὶ ὄχλου διὰ μυθολογίας ἀλλὰ μὴ διὰ διδαχῆς; 304d). This is quite beautiful, because that's what Plato himself is doing all the time. Thus, he's rebuking the Sophists all the time, and he's the greatest sophist. He's rebuking the rhetoricians all the time,

and he's the greatest rhetorician. He's rebuking the poets and the tragedians all the time, and he has an absolutely fantastic sense of dramaturgy.
He's defining himself here, because he is *peistikos* (persuasive) through this
extraordinary combination of *didachē*, discursive teaching, and *mutholo-
gia*, with all these myths, the myth of the cave and the myth of Er in the
Republic or Aristophanes' myth in the *Symposium*. There is this weaving
together of the poetic, mythopoietic element and the reasoning and argumentative element, which has made for Plato's political potency—
political in the sense of domination in the sphere of ideas.

Incidental point eight bears on the distinction of the kinds of virtues.

And this brings us back a bit to the story about measure. But what is
quite striking here is that the dialogue has in fact ended in 305e, that is to
say, that there is an entirely satisfactory definition of the statesman—it's
he who weaves together the city. (What there is to be woven together in
the city was already explained at length and in great detail: on the one
hand, there are the different material arts, the productive arts, which are
necessary for the life of the city; on the other, there are the arts that re-
semble statesmanship, like rhetoric and strategy, but that have to be subordinated to statesmanship.)

But at this moment the Stranger from Elea scratches his head and says
that there's still another thing. There are other things that are to be composed by statesmanship: these are the parts of virtue. We end up here
with this strange idea that Aristotle took up again in the *Nichomachean
Ethics*—that something that, in itself, participates in the nature of virtue
can, in being excessive, lead to results that aren't desirable, that don't per-
tain to virtuous action. One must know how to combine souls that have
this virtue in excess with souls that have a shortage [*défaut*] thereof, on
the one hand, as these souls are given in the individuals who live in the
city and, on the other, if this is possible, by the crossbreeding of individuals in the city, making mixed marriages between those families whose
members are noted for their crazy recklessness [*témérité folle*] and those
families whose members are noted for an excessive prudence, and so on.

This sort of appendix, which undoubtedly aims at preparing the way
for the *Philebus*, appears as the principal compositional quirk [*bizarrerie*]
of the *Statesman*, which includes a good number of them—no fewer than
fourteen! This is quite bizarre, first of all because it appears after the completion of a formal definition and secondly because it introduces a con-

sideration that it exemplifies on the case of one and only one virtue. Aristotle later tried to exemplify it on the basis of all the virtues, but that's still quite artificial. Plato cannot exemplify it on the basis of anything other than this story about an excess of temerity and an excess of reserve or prudence. It's in relation to this that there is shortage "by excess" and shortage "by lack [*par défaut*]." And it's in relation to this that he brings up his new definition of the statesman as someone weaving together not only all the rest but also the parts of the soul and the individuals who possess in excess the faculties whose nonexcessive existence would constitute a virtue.

One may ask oneself what that's doing in there. The only answer consists perhaps in trying to reconstitute, from within, the thought process of a great thinker. But here we're on highly slippery ground, a ground upon which interpreters regularly fall and smash their faces. It can be said that a minimum condition for success would be to be oneself a great thinker: indeed, how is a mere professor of philosophy or of history going to be able to grasp why Plato at some point, with all that behind him already and some new problem ahead of him, was led to think such and such a thing? One can hardly see the difference between that professor and a musical ignoramus who tried to explain why, starting in 1817, Beethoven changed tack. With these reservations, then, and the due modesty, I dare to hazard an interpretation: I believe that this addition at the end of the *Statesman* ceases to be bizarre if one sees it as a kind of bridge toward the *Philebus*, just like a series of other things in the *Statesman*. The *Philebus* is a dialogue of utmost importance. There, Plato abandons his initial theory of virtue, his identification of virtue with knowledge. He adopts therein another conception that really has a huge amount to do with this blending, the mixed, moderation, the possibility of compromising [*composer*]. In this conception, he finally grants that pleasure as such is not necessarily to be banished from a virtuous life, that in the virtuous life there also has to be a place for pleasure—upon the condition that it be put in its place.

In this train of thought of a man who must have been around seventy years old and writing his last works, who was approaching this other continent that was his final philosophy, the philosophy of the mixed, it is understandable that with the *Statesman*, Plato was preparing a kind of bridge toward the *Philebus* and a conception of life wherein virtue is no longer rigorous knowledge and pleasure doesn't come solely from the *theōria* of the Ideas but can also come quite simply from human life.

And we now broach the three digressions. These will keep us occupied no doubt for at least two seminars, in addition to the end of this one.

V. The Three Digressions

The first digression recounts the myth of the reign of Cronus, the alternation of two great cosmic periods (268d–277b). The second digression bears upon the form of political regimes. As for the third, the principal one, it aims at demonstrating that science alone defines the statesman, but at the same time it ends up abandoning this definition—this is the key moment of the paradox of the *Statesman*. Plato here demonstrates in the most absolute way that science alone defines the statesman and that, if there is a statesman who possesses this science, everything else subsides, the laws, the *patria*, and so forth. But at the same time, he is telling us that this isn't possible, that this is too absolute—that, therefore, one must undertake what he calls the "second navigation." In a sense, the second digression, on the form of the different regimes, can be considered so closely tied up with this third digression as to be a subdivision of it.

First Digression: The Myth of the Reign of Cronus

I remind you what it's about. Suddenly, the Stranger hesitates over the definition of the statesman as pastor of human flocks with which one ended up, and he asks Young Socrates whether he recalls an old story in which there were divine pastors and the world turned in the opposite direction from the one in which it turns now. In fact, Plato is reworking three old legends here:

• first of all, the myth concerning Atreus and Thyestes, according to which, at one point, Zeus, angered because Thyestes had cheated, reversed [*inverse*] the course of the sun and, everything being regulated by the sun, events began to flow backwards [*à l'envers*];
• second legend is that there was a reign of Cronus, which is generally associated in popular tradition with the idea of a golden age;
• the third legend is that human beings were in the old days not produced by each other, via sexual reproduction, but sprouted from the earth, really coming out of it, and thus were *gēgeneis* {earth-born}.

So, he starts from these three legends. The legend of a golden age is certainly universal. Legends like the one that men sprouted from the earth are certainly to be found in many spots (in the Old Testament, it's from earth that Adam is made), like, moreover, the story—found in other mythologies—of the reversal [*l'inversion*] of the course of time. These are not exclusively Greek themes; they belong to rather universal imaginary schemata in the humanity of olden times.

Here's a quick summary of the content of the myth. Plato says that the history of the universe, of all that is, always goes successively through two opposite phases. There is a phase that would be the truly direct phase. Let us not forget that philosophy truly is the world turned inside out [*à l'envers*]. Plato already says this himself: the truth of philosophy is what men do not see. And what they do see is, for the philosopher, but illusion. We are living in a phase of the history of the world in which the normal thing is for human beings—and also all other living beings—to be born small and young, grow up and grow old, and, finally, die, then disappear. And perhaps that is, in our conception of things, tied up with a certain way in which the universe turns, a direction in which the heavenly vault rotates. Now, says Plato, this is just the reverse phase, the reign of Zeus: this is what happens with the world when the god {in question} abandons it to its fate. What happens, then, when the god abandons the world to its fate? Well, at that moment the world begins to turn the way it is turning now, human beings begin to reproduce and to have young, the course of time heads in this direction, from birth toward old age, and the world runs itself [*se dirige lui-même*]. But in running itself, the world cannot help but become, little by little, unbalanced, the disorder keeps on growing, entropy increases. This is a very old idea in humanity, and it's what we call the second law of thermodynamics. When Aristotle speaks of time in the *Physics*, he states, *Pas chronos ekstatikos*, every sort of time is "ecstatic" in the sense of destructive, which makes things exit from their form.[4] In this sense, it's quite rightly, he says, that people say that every kind of time is ecstatic, corruptive, destructive. But then, with his usual rigor, Aristotle goes over the popular saying: Although in truth it has to be said that it's not time qua time that destroys things but, rather, the things themselves that arrive at their destruction, at their decomposition; and this *sumbainei* in time, it happens that this occurs in time, that it goes, that it coincides, it "comits" with time, and that's the reason why it is said that time corrupts things.

We are therefore living in the phase where the world, left to itself, is heading toward its own corruption. And when this corruption reaches a sort of maximum, a point where a god—who is no doubt other than Cronus or Zeus—thinks that things can no longer continue like that, the god then takes back his helmsman's post, goes back to steering [*reprendre la direction*] affairs, and brings the course of the world back to its true course (which for us would be a reverse course). Starting at that moment, the heavenly sphere begins to turn in the other direction; all the processes we experience unfold in the reverse direction from the one we are used to. Human beings come out of the earth as old men, with white hair—perhaps even with no hair at all—and, as time passes, their hair grows darker, they arrive at maturity, start to look younger, become adolescents, grow shorter; and when they become very small, they return to the earth. All other processes unfold in the same fashion. That period is the reign of Cronus; that is the reign of Cronus. The god himself directs [*dirige*] the course of the world and, via subaltern gods, watches over all matters and conducts things as they should be [*comme il faut*]. And this is also why people believe that, during that period, men sprouted from the earth, were *gēgeneis*, on the one hand, and that, on the other hand, life was happy. Why? Because the god was himself watching over all existence, because he had subordinate gods who acted as pastors of the different categories of beings. For men, it's the god himself who tends them—Θεὸς ἔνεμεν αὐτοὺς αὐτος ἐπιστατῶν (271e)—just as now men tend and pasture various categories of inferior animals. In the age of Cronus, there were no *politeiai* {civil polities, constitutions, forms of government}, no cities, no exclusive marriages—κτήσεις γυναικῶν καὶ παίδων (possessions of women and children, 272a)—no childbirths. Once again, this age of Cronus is a golden age; it's the myth of primitive communism but also of a period of abundance. Men sprouted from the earth and recalled nothing of what was there beforehand; they were born therefore without memory {ibid.}.

Here we see the ambiguity of the story and, once again, Plato's ambiguity, an ambiguity about which it may be asked up to what point it is voluntary or not. Indeed, this golden age is purchased nonetheless by the fact that people have no memory and recall nothing of what was there beforehand. One could live, but in a kind of jungle in which the god provided for everything. Can one think about that with nostalgia? Why don't we live under the reign of Cronus? Is that what our life should have been?

First, Plato introduced this observation that people had no memory, and then the Stranger from Elea explicitly poses the question: Is what people recount true, that life under the reign of Cronus was the happiest of all possible lives? He then makes a rather obvious fine distinction that handicaps this legend and the idea of another course of the world in which men would be happy. If Cronus's nurslings (*trophimoi* [272b]) used their time, all the leisure they had, in order to do philosophy, it can then be said that the time of Cronus was truly a time of happiness. But if they lived simply to fill their bellies like beasts and to bathe in the sun, well, it will be said that that wasn't a happy existence, and that we are now enjoying a better fate.

But, he says, let's leave that aside, because we cannot know. And he comes to a sort of anthropogony of present-day humanity. From time to time, the god gives up caring for the world, and then a catastrophe occurs; the contrary course resumes, and human beings are then as they are today: they have a sexual form of reproduction, live among savage beasts, and are obliged to pass from the state of nature to the state of culture. And, says Plato, men would have perished here had there not been gifts, divine donations, the fire of Prometheus, the arts of Hephaestus and of his companion in the arts—*suntechnos* (274d)—it's clearly Athena who is intended here. It is they who have endowed men with all that, and men have thus been able to manage to survive, to set up [*constituer*] cities, and to live as we live today. Those are the main outlines of the myth.

Plato returns upon several occasions to this golden-age story, this Cronus-age story, and to this anthropogony, this sort of "politeiogony" (creation of cities). This is the case in the *Laws* (676bff. and 713bff.), in the *Protagoras* (321aff.), in the *Republic* (369b and 378b), in the *Critias* (109bff.), and so on. Why does he come back to it? There is a tradition that was taken back up very seriously in the fifth century and countered by the great thinkers of the fifth century. Hesiod, in *Works and Days*, speaks already of the age of Cronus (lines 109–11). Upon the background of an old tradition that contained this collective phantasm of an age of abundance and happiness—a tradition recorded by Hesiod himself (lines 116–21)—Hesiod adds his own vision of times becoming harder and harder: with each new human generation, they deteriorate more and more.

To this view a different one was opposed in the fifth century. That view could perhaps be called *rational* in the good sense of the term, and it is nearly the same as ours today. This is an evolutive view and, let us say, it's practically speaking a view of humanity's self-constitution, its self-creation. The first person to whom this view can be attributed is obviously the great Democritus.[5] Protagoras, who was also from Abdera, and of whom it is said that he heard Democritus speak, was without a doubt teaching similar things, and this is also (as we saw two years ago {in the seminar}) the thesis of Thucydides in the "archaeology" from the first book of *The Peloponnesian War*.

What is the content of this thesis? It's that there was an actual "state of nature," a state of savagery, a primitive state; that, little by little, human beings invented the arts, set up communities or extended them, got organized, and so on. This view is to be found in Thucydides, in the background of the "archaeology." In Democritus, we have a long excerpt, which has been handed down to us by a Byzantine author, Johannes Tzetzes, and comes to us from Democritus's *Mikros Diakosmos* [Bv3 Diels].[6] In neither Democritus nor Thucydides is there any divine gift. When Plato has Protagoras recount, in the dialogue of the same name, a myth of the birth of humanity, he is, of course, putting the divine donations given to men, the stories of Prometheus and Epimetheus, and so on into the mouth of Protagoras (321aff.). But there's nothing like that in Democritus: humanity constitutes itself, creates itself, gives itself the arts, invents life in common, and does so progressively. I have commented at length upon the fact that in Thucydides such progress concerns uniquely technique and material reality and has nothing to do with moral or even civilizational progress. In Thucydides, it's that people know better and better how to kill; in a way, it boils down to that.

That is the fifth-century view, the *Aufklärung* {Enlightenment} view. But in the fourth century, around Plato there were loads of reflections about reviving the theme of the golden age; there was a sort of backtracking. The fourth century was a period of crisis, of decomposition of imaginary significations, and so on. Already, there were the Cynics. They talked about a sort of state of nature and called for a return to the state of nature. A well-known disciple of Aristotle, Dicaearchus, took back up the theme of the golden age, combining it with what had been found out in the fifth century—it wasn't a mere return to Hesiod. There was a golden age, he says, an age of nonwar, with no political Constitution; and it was, at the same time, an age of scarcity. Here we see a kind of ecological nostalgia: it wasn't paradise on earth in the sense of abundance, but men were better; they didn't make war; they weren't morally corrupt—this is an ecological Rousseauism—but they lived in difficult times, they ate grasses and wild fruits, and so on and so forth.

Now, Plato takes back up this material that was there around him and clearly tries to give it another meaning; he fashions it as a myth but tries to make it function, in a way. The basic function of this myth is first of all to insert anthropogony, anthropogenesis, into a process that concerns the cosmic whole. This is to say that we now live in a period in which there are cities and in which the problem of statesmanship [*la politique*] and of the statesman is raised because we belong to this cosmic period during which the world is left to its fate. It's for this reason that the question of statesmanship is posed. In the other phase, during the age of Cronus, it's the god himself who takes care of us, who tends to us; and by way of consequence, the problem of politics [*la politique*] isn't posed.

We must first of all see the extraordinary combination, once again, of the audacity of Plato's imagination in the poetic sense and of the near geometrical rigor with which, once certain postulates are made, he unfolds his story. The source elements are the three elements of the mythical tradition:

1. the reversal of the direction of cosmic processes;
2. the reign of Cronus;
3. the sprouting forth of humans from the earth.

Let's take these, then, as postulates. And let's suppose, too, that there is a god who manufactures the world. This is obvious for Plato, who thinks he has established it in the *Timaeus*. There, he explains how the god manufactures the world. Let us assume, as in the *Timaeus* and as he repeats it in the *Statesman* (269c–d), that the world is an intelligent animal, that the totality of the universe is a living being [*un être vivant*]. Let us assume again that only that which is incorporeal can be eternally identical—which is also for Plato a self-evident fact, stated in 269d of the *Statesman* and in the *Timaeus*—that is to say, genuine being is the Ideas (*eidē*), which are eternally identical to themselves, the "eternally," moreover, not meaning here omnitemporality but atemporality, absence of temporality, the fact that the very question of a time isn't posed (this *aei*, this *always*, not being simply an atemporal always but a determination that posits genuine being as that which is identical to itself in all respects; that's what this very clearly means in the *Timaeus*).

There are three principles in order that a world might be made. There is eternal being, which is the paradigm within which the world is to be made. There is eternal becoming, that is to say, that which, at every moment and in all respects, is other. Here again, one can but admire the radicality of Plato's thought: when he is searching for the opposite of genuine being, he posits the always dissimilar (the *always* not being temporal), that is to say, that in which there is not a single moment—in the philosophical sense—of universality. There are not even two points in this eternal becoming that would be alike; you need only move a millimeter for there to be dissimilarity in all respects. This is therefore the infinite of dissimilarity, and what that is is matter, that is to say, the totally arational.

In addition to these two elements, a third element is required, the demiurge who constrains eternal becoming and makes it enter into a form that participates in the eternal form. But this demiurge—and in this all Greek philosophy differs from Christian theology and even from what is implicit in the Old Testament—isn't all-powerful; he gives form to this matter *kata to dunaton*, to the extent possible.

This world has, therefore, to contain a corporeal part. It's for this reason that it is; it is like matter formed by the demiurge. Being corporeal and spatial, it can by itself only head toward disorder, the absence of regularity. It doesn't suffice therefore to say that the demiurge would have manufactured it: he manufactured it *kata to dunaton* in the likeness of the eternal living being, but this world is not the eternal living being; it contains matter and cannot, as such, but head toward the absence of regularity, disorder, destruction, and so on.

Here, Plato stays within the Greek imaginary. But he isn't within the Greek imaginary inasmuch as, within this imaginary, beginning at least with Hesiod, there is in the world formative spontaneity. For Plato, there is no formative spontaneity; formation is the work [*l'œuvre*] of the demiurge. Matter has only a deformative, destructive, or corruptive spontaneity.

There is, finally, a fourth element. It, too, is Greek. It's that there's a law, mentioned again in the *Statesman*, of rapport, of balance, between creation and destruction, between *genesis* and *phthora*. This law is a necessity, an impersonal *anankē*. That is, the demiurge can do nothing about it, because it's like that. He can make this formation only in an approximate fashion and not in an absolute fashion.

Given that there is {for Plato} no formative spontaneity of matter and that there is only a disordered alteration, a destructive movement, the external ordering principle—the demiurge—is necessary: a productive, manufacturing god is needed, and the god produces this world, which cannot be totally perfect. This was subsequently very important in the history of thought, including the history of thought about society. Indeed, it's taken up again explicitly in the *Statesman*, and it's one of the hidden pillars of the dialogue as regards both the world and things human.

There's another aspect of this whole affair. It's a sort of theodicy on the part of Plato, which consists in denying that the question of theodicy can be posed: If god has made the world and if you attribute to him these attributes—for example, omniscience, omnipotence, absolute goodness—how does it happen that there is evil? There are at this point several possible responses. There is no evil; evil is an illusion. Or there's the Leibnizian response: What appears to us as evil is a necessary part of a form that could be optimized only as . . . a geometrical surface, having bumps and dents in certain places, and that's what makes its overall perfection. It matters little which response is given. Plato himself takes the argument in reverse, and the price to be paid for denying the question of theodicy is to deny god's all-powerfulness. For him, there's the product's imperfection—this is for certain, and it's repeated in the *Statesman*—since, in the period of Zeus that we are going through, things are heading toward their corruption; this imperfection of the product is an imperfection of the raw material, the primary matter in all senses of these terms, starting from which god has constructed the world. But contrary to the Christian God, {Plato's} god has not made this raw material. He therefore isn't responsible for it, and he can't do anything about it; this is the limit of his might. The world is therefore imperfect, because it has been manufactured in the absolute only to the extent possible. This is what Aristotle was responding to already when he said that Plato's arguments don't hold up, because it's incomprehensible that god, who is supposed to be perfect himself, would have produced, engendered, something less perfect than himself. This is one of the reasons that makes Aristotle think of a god who is entirely separate, removed from the world.

But the important things, both as concerns Plato's arguments and the way in which the question is posed and as concerns the whole discussion of theodicy, are the presuppositions for this discussion. The world is perfect or the world isn't perfect; but perfect in relation to what? You see, obviously, how this entire discussion originates: one can say that saying that something is perfect has meaning when it's a question of particular beings [*étants*]—nothing's perfect in this world, of course, but, well, a car is nearly perfect or else it's imperfect, badly made—when you insert something into a system, into an articulated set of ends [*articulation de finalités*] in which that something serves some purpose, in which that something fits its goal [*correspond à son finalité*], is adequate or else corresponds to the type its species determines, and so on. But when it comes to the world, to total Being-being, what meaning can there be in discussing whether or not it is perfect? Well, the meaning is obviously the anthropomorphic projection of the following wish: The world would be perfect if it corresponded to what we desire. All arguments advanced in theodicies concern, of course, all those aspects of the world that are, that seem, that are judged by us to run contrary to what we would wish, what would make us happy—though, let it be added, no one could damned well go and say what would actually make him happy, but that's yet another story. (That's precisely part of the imperfection we can blame on the world; we have been manufactured in such a way that we don't even know what could make us happy.)

There is, then, this sort of anthropomorphic underpinning to this entire way of posing the problem. That's already subjacent in Plato's choice of the term *agathon* to designate in fact genuine being, that is to say, what is even beyond, as he says, the essences and Ideas and what sustains them. *Agathon* is translated as "good," the Latin *bonum*, but the Greek etymology of *agathon* mustn't be forgotten. *Agathon* is what can be wished for; it comes from the verb *agamai* (that pleases me, I like that), which has the same root as *agapō* (I like), *agapē*. The *agathon* is the likable, what can be wished for, the desirable. By that I mean that the anthropomorphic content of this supreme philosophical idea is given away already in the word choice: Genuine being is the desirable.

That's Plato's idea; it isn't the Greek imaginary. For the Greek imaginary such as it was beforehand, being is neither *agathon* nor not *agathon*; it's neither desirable nor detestable. It's none of all that. Being is what it is; it is generative spontaneity and destructive spontaneity; it's *genesis* and *phthora*. It's there from Homer up to and including the end of the fifth century. It's there in Democritus. And this is the view that is broken up by Plato. He breaks it up in the following way: by repelling toward the Beyond every element of activity and creative spontaneity. In fact, there

isn't any genuine creative spontaneity here, since what the demiurge manufactures is manufactured in imitation of something that is given once
and for all—namely, the Forms and, in particular, the Form, the Idea, of
the eternal living being. But in the end the former element is exported
out of this world, is separated off, and what is kept for this-here world—
as one sees with the myth from the *Statesman*—is *phthora*, that is to say,
erosion, corruption, destruction. In order that this *phthora* might be
maintained, contained within limits, it is necessary, each time it reaches a
certain point, for the god to intervene again; he must reverse the course of
things and, at the same time, set himself at the helm in order to steer the
way they evolve.

I take up again the quasi theorem contained in this myth with the postulates I stated at the outset—that is to say, the idea that one must first
make room for the three traditional elements, then that there is a god-
demiurge, that matter is not entirely formable matter and tends by itself
toward corruption. The world is corporeal; it has to move. That's a corollary. It's corporeal, that's settled. In reality, it's the *aei gignesthai*, that
which is changing in all respects—therefore also with respect to spatial
determinations. Therefore, the world has to move. As it is manufactured
by god, it is as perfect as possible; and therefore it has to move following
the movement that is—in Plato's idea, but it's an idea that isn't gratu-
itous—since it lacks the absolute perfection that is immobility, the kind
of movement that comes closest to absolute perfection. This movement
is circular movement. You can see clearly the profound—imaginary, if
you will, but even logical, mathematical—kinship the circle has with
identity: if an identity is not an immediate identity, it is mediated. This is
to say that, after having made a tour [*un certain circuit*], I come back to
my point of departure. This circular movement is identical because the
circle is, among plane figures, the only one that you could make slide over
itself: in a rotation, all the points of the circle pass through all the other
points and remain upon the same circle. You can't, by way of contrast,
make a sinusoid, or a conic section, or an ellipse, and so forth, slide over
itself. You can make a straight line slide over itself, but the basic drawback
there is that it's imaginarily infinite; it is therefore for a Greek—and for
Plato, in particular—an imperfect figure.

Therefore the world, if it does move, can move only in a circle. As the
god has made the world (here, the proof is perhaps a bit less closely argued), he hasn't made it in order to worry about it constantly. He

launches it, therefore, and leaves it to follow its own movement. At that moment, the world and humanity—a certain part, at least—try to get organized, to resist erosion and corruption, but they don't succeed. And the world becomes more and more corrupt; it therefore travels through the half circle of the great circle that leads it toward corruption—that's the present phase—and at a given moment, when one reaches the limit of this movement, the god takes back the helm, makes the world turn in the opposite direction, and the direction of time produces a rejuvenation [*rajeunissement*].

Why must there be two circles? There isn't circular movement only within each of the circles. The two circles belong to another circle, since the world periodically and unceasingly passes from the Zeus phase to the Cronus phase and from the latter phase to the former one, from movement as we see it today to the movement we would see in reverse fashion and that would be the true movement. That, too, is a circle: the two subcircles make up a great circle. Why, then, are these two circles necessary? Because the world couldn't be either eternally the same—in that case, it would be perfect—or move eternally in the same way, because that, too, would again be a world of perfection (269d–e). Therefore, there has to be a reversal of movement, the world moving in the other direction.

I shall come back the next time to some of the myth's more specific aspects. I shall end today with a few thoughts about the why of this digression, what it's doing in the *Statesman*. For, the justification given in the dialogue (in 275b–c) doesn't hold up. The justification is that, when there is a shepherd [*pâtre*] and a flock, there's a difference in nature between the shepherd and the animals he tends and pastures; therefore, the true shepherd could only be a divine shepherd. But that could have been said without introducing the myth; it could have been said that this definition didn't hold up, and one could then have gone on to another definition of the statesman. Now, that's not what's done, and one instead enters into the myth and the development of this myth. Why?

I would like to maintain that this first definition of the statesman as shepherd is in fact proposed by Plato only in order to be able to tell the story of the reign of Cronus. It isn't the myth that is introduced in order to refute the first definition; it's the first definition that is introduced in order that Plato might be able to bring up the myth, in order that there might be something onto which to hang the myth.

And why does he want to bring up the myth? Well, because he wants to destroy fifth-century thought, destroy Democritus's anthropogony, which he takes over from Democritus, for the passage from the *Mikros Diakosmos* preserved by Tzetzes shows a much more elaborate description than the one Plato is summing up here of an initial state of nature and of progress toward a better self-organization. The idea must have been truly dominant among the freethinkers [*esprits forts*] of the fifth century, such as Thucydides (who was not a philosopher but most certainly a great mind), who fastened onto it.

There is, then, among the thinkers of the fifth century, an idea of the self-constitution of humankind.[7] For Plato, the point is to destroy this idea. Indeed, in the anthropogony he gives, as if in passing, in the myth, human beings would be destroyed—and here, he's going back to the old mythology—without the intervention of Prometheus, Hephaestus, and Athena (the gods who give the arts). On the other hand, he drops the part of the divine donations that had been there in the tale of Protagoras,[8] undoubtedly a parable in which Plato is talking about Protagoras himself. There, Zeus gave the political art to human beings, sharing it out among them all. The political art is here a translation of democracy, placed in the mouth of Protagoras, and it's no doubt a historically accurate translation, as it corresponds so well to the imaginary of Greek democracy. So, he drops it; the gods are the ones who make it possible for humans to survive, and these men have fabricated everything they have fabricated—cities, and so on—not in a cycle of the history of the world that is the cycle of progress or in a cycle where processes unfold in the right direction [*dans le bon sens*]; they do so, rather, during a phase of the history of the world that runs backward [*à l'envers*] (which, obviously, to our corrupt eyes, seems to be unfolding the right way round [*à l'endroit*]).

Ultimately, then, there is in this a way of appropriating the anthropogony of the fifth century by demolishing its political and philosophical meaning, by demolishing it as a kind of anthropogony that was beginning to stammer out the idea of humanity's self-creation, so as to introduce the idea that what is there during this period of corruption that makes it possible for us to survive is not a human creation but a divine donation. Anyway, all that appertains to a series of cycles that go on repeating themselves and from which we shall never exit—so long, no doubt, as we live this earthly existence. For, there always is in Plato the reservation about the immortality of the soul and of another life.

So, that's the point [*finalité*] of the myth of Cronus, to which I shall return next time.

Seminar of March 26, 1986

We're continuing with the *Statesman*.

If we're lingering so long over this dialogue, it's because it's a transitional moment between the period when Plato was speaking on the basis of the possession of a philosophical theory, of an *epistēmē*, that is to lead to the elaboration of a model, of a city plan, that has to be far removed from reality in order to be good, and the final period of his philosophy—to which the *Statesman* fully belongs—a period that could be called the period of the mixed, where, to put it brutally, the irreducibility of total being to the Idea of being crops up more and more. Total being is not only *eidos*; it's a composition of *hulē* and *eidos*, of matter and form, as Aristotle said more clearly later on. But there Aristotle was only bringing out the consequences of this fourth manner, of this fourth period, of Plato's labor.

And this recognition of the mixed, both as a kind of category and as a central problem of his philosophy, as an obstacle that sets his philosophy to work and against which his philosophy is deployed, is bound to find a prolongation in the political domain. *Prolongation* is, moreover, a bad term, as it does not take adequate account of the central interest Plato has for the political.

It is therefore within this context that the *Statesman* is situated. And this is also what allows one to understand its extremely strange structure:

A. Two definitions and a half, none of which is truly held until the end:
   —the statesman as pastor;
   —the statesman as weaver.
B. Three digressions:
   —the first one about the myth of the age of Cronus;

—the second one about the forms of regimes and their evaluation;

—a third one, of central importance, which contains the idea that science alone defines the political man or the royal man.

C. And then the eight incidental points.

Let's leave aside the incidental points, which are frequent in Plato, as in Aristotle, moreover, neither of whom are the kind of authors who write dissertations. They write as they think, as their thought comes. Of course, they shape their thought [*la mettent en forme*], but if some consideration seems worth the effort to them, they aren't going to eliminate it under the pretext that it's outside the main topic. And this is stated explicitly, in the *Statesman*, by the Stranger from Elea to Young Socrates:

> You'll mature well, you'll age well, if you continue to have the attitude of not worrying whether one speaks with little discourse or much discourse, but measure the length of discourses and their appropriate or inappropriate character according to the content, according to the thing itself, and the rest doesn't interest us. {cf. 261e and 286e–287a}

The rest, he might have said, is good for literature, not for thought, not for philosophy.

But the digressions themselves pose a real problem. And in my opinion, the dialogue is written for them. It is, in a way, the dialogue that is itself a digression for the three digressions. And it's the two definitions of the statesman that are a pretext for the digressions. And above all for the two principal ones: the myth of Cronus and the central thesis that science alone defines the statesman.

I'd now like not to resume but to complete the remarks already made concerning a few important points in this myth of Cronus.

V. The Three Digressions (Continued)

First Digression: The Myth of the Reign of Cronus (Continued)

And I remind you, first of all, about the following very important element, which for the moment we can't do much about: Plato's will to anchor his tale in a popular tradition by weaving together—a term from the *Statesman*, and, as a matter of fact, from the second definition—three elements of this tradition:

1. the recollection that there once were men who rose up from the earth;

2. the nostalgia for a golden age, for happy times, for paradise on earth: the reign of Cronus (a nearly universal element of folklore);

3. the rather strange idea that there are moments when the movements of the heavens and of all earthly phenomena—the overall direction of phenomena—are reversed. In the Greek popular tradition, this idea is connected with Zeus's wrath at Thyestes for having committed a second transgression, which caused Zeus in his anger to reverse all the movements of the heavens.

We must stop here and reflect upon what this can mean, first in Plato's text and then in itself—a second consideration that is as important as the first one.

You recall how things happen. When a world-course reaches its end, at that moment there is a *katastrophē*, a brutal transition, a reversal, a turn-about at the same time as an upheaval. Another world-course then begins. One of these world-courses is dominated by Cronus; this is the course in which the god attends to the world. During the other course, that of Zeus, the world is abandoned to itself, and humanity is then supposed to make do [*se débrouiller*] alone, to struggle against wild beasts as well as to see to its own physical subsistence and internal organization.

But what, if we reflect upon it, does this reversal mean? Of course, in speaking in a loose way it could be said that there is a reversal of time. But no sooner is this expression uttered than it fails us [*nous trahit*], for there is no reversal of time, and it can be asked whether the expression *reversal of time* itself has any meaning. On the basis of and apropos of this Platonic text, here we are as if smack dab in the middle of the Atlantic Ocean, with no life preserver, no mast, and no islets covered with vegetation. Without anything. What does *reversal of the course of time* mean? Is it conceivable, and what are the aporias to which it leads us?

What Plato is talking about in this tale, and what all the time stimulates the idea of a reversal of the direction of time, is not the reversal of the course of time—he's careful not to claim that. It's the reversal of movements, of the direction of different movements. To show this, let's take two examples from Plato: the heavenly sphere and the generation of individuals.

1. The heavenly sphere. Instead of turning in the usual direction—for

us, from east to west—it turns in the contrary direction. This is a reversal of the direction of its movements. But after all, it could be said that this direction of rotation is entirely conventional. There is no intrinsic privilege in the Earth's direction of rotation, we would say today after Copernicus. The Earth could turn in the other direction, in which case, of course, the sun would rise above the sixteenth arrondissement in Paris and set over the twelfth. The same goes for left and right. It is obvious that spatial orientations are entirely conventional. But how do we make temporal before / after orientations? We always make them on the basis of spatial bearings: the hands of our watches turn and a direction of the path followed is defined on the basis of spatial bearings.

2. The generation of individuals. In this other example Plato provides, conventionality no longer operates. Under the reign of Cronus, men came out, sprouted from the earth as old people and then grew younger [*rajeunissaient*] until the moment when, having become small children and then babies, they disappeared. Once again, one cannot help but admire, at first, the might of the creative imagination as well as the logical elaboration that accompanies it. If one leaves aside the tales of traditional mythology, this myth of Cronus in the *Statesman* is the first *entechnos* work of science fiction, science fiction written artfully—and not a mere transcription of some popular folklore—within universal literature. There really is science fiction in mythology, in the Vedas, but, as artificial writing, Plato's tale is the first in the history of literature.[1]

We therefore have these men who are born old and die as newborns. Oldborns, it would have to be said. And here, we can no longer speak about a conventionality of the path of time. Of course, a sophist, pushing an empty logic to the extreme, could maintain that after all someone old or young, well, that's conventional. But what's conventional is the term. At least at the outset, because once it exists, it commands a whole series of links and associations. One cannot change old into young without modifying a huge quantity of terms in language. At the outset, let us say, logically, they are conventional. But the state of being old or young refers us back to a real description. And this real description seems to us to be tied to a genuine before/after that cannot be reversed arbitrarily. I am elaborating at length on what can pass for truisms, trivialities. But one must be careful precisely because these questions are always there, both in philosophy and in basic physics: Is there really time? And what is the di-

rection of time? What determines the direction of time? Is it purely conventional, like drawing axes on a blackboard? The o can be placed here,
or there, and the same theorems, the same equations, can still be written;
all one need do is invert the signs correctly.

What does this before/after, which we can get a feel for from this example—a capital one, actually—of the youth/old age reversal, refer us to?
It refers us to the fact that we cannot, despite all physics and all philosophies, prevent ourselves from thinking that for us the direction of time results from a sort of *intrinsic* interlocking [*enclenchement*] of events, some
on the basis of the others. Things seem to us to unfold in the usual way,
just as we stroke a cat in the way its fur lies. And if you stroke it in the
other direction [*à l'envers*], your hand feels it and the cat reacts. There's
something like an interlocking, sequencing [*consécution*], of events that to
us seems obvious, necessary. Think of a battery of pots and pans that re-
quire the smallest one to be placed in a larger one, and so on, in order to
stack them up. We have here, then, something like a perception of a consecution borne intrinsically by the things themselves, like an internal en-
gendering of successions. And that's what we are used to thinking of as
time.

And what the Platonic tale of the myth of Cronus reveals to us between
the lines is anything but platitudes and trivialities. For, it involves one of
the great unresolved problems of philosophy and of basic physics. When
you remain at the level of great traditional physics—that is, rational mechanics, including its most accomplished form, relativity—the direction
of time is, within the framework of these theories, entirely conventional.
The classical example from mechanics, billiard balls hitting one other, is
eloquent: assume they don't fall into a pocket—for, there are indeed here
some things that are irreversible—and film the process. What you see in
the film (1) conforms entirely to the laws of rational mechanics and (2)
won't surprise you at all. Apart, that is, from the problem of the initial
impact [*choc*]. As for the rest, nothing about the sequence [*déroulement*]
will surprise you in the least.

Now, take a film of Charlie Chaplin. It shows you sequencings of actions that occur in life, that is to say, irreversible occurrences. Look at the
film in reverse: Charlie then climbs back up the staircase backwards and
at top speed. And you laugh because you have the immediate feeling that
that's impossible, that here there's a reversal of the direction of processes
that isn't possible. Why? After all, Charlie climbing back up a staircase in

reverse, his back facing the top of the stairs, is only a billiard ball whose direction has been inverted. And if a ball can go from right to left, it can just as well go from left to right. Here we're right in the middle of the great problem of the existence of irreversible processes, which is at the heart of thermodynamics and of philosophical reflection. It's just like that much talked-about story about the egg: even if mechanically there's no absurdity, if you break an egg, it won't put itself back together again on its own as an unbroken egg.[2] Here, there's something that marks irreversibility. And the attempt to show why there is irreversibility is always present, is always open, and is always unreliable. The only thing physicists could say about it is that the reversal of the direction of events is extremely improbable.

I'm not going to linger over this because this isn't what we are discussing for the moment. But I'm going to make one remark, anyway, which is implied in the text. The *Statesman*—which, with the *Timaeus*, is the first text in which the question of time is broached in the history of philosophy—refers to the following question: Can one or can one not conceive of a time that is separate from any content? Clearly, if we can do so, the conventionality of the direction of time appears to be infinitely more plausible, if not even certain. If, on the other hand, we cannot conceive of a time separate from all content—as I, along with Aristotle, believe to be the case—if we can think, if we can live a time only at the same time as we think and we live the production of an intrinsic internal consecution of events, that is to say, the production of events or of facts, some of them starting from (*apo*) the others, then, at that moment, the direction in which events unfold also gives a direction to time. And the temporal before/after is not simply arbitrary. And that would indeed be necessary to give full value to the *Statesman* and the myth of Cronus qua myth. That is to say, in order to underscore the fact that we are talking about something that is impossible and not just unusual, something that truly challenges the constituents of being, the constituents of the universe, namely, the internal solidarity of the unfolding [*déroulement*] of time with the unfurling [*déploiement*] of being. For, that's what it's about. And it's this idea of an internal solidarity between the unfolding of time and the deployment of being—which, for me, is the central idea in this domain—that is dismissed and condemned in a radical fashion in the modern age by the Kantian position, by the idea that subjectivity produces, creates, a pure form of intuition that is time and that, as such, has a meaning independent of every event that unfolds therein.

So much for what is embryonically in the myth of the *Statesman* and is so pregnant. So much, too, for what, over historical time, over the time of thought, was later on more or less developed, more or less explicated, extracted from this text. But there are still several points about which a few words must be said.

And first of all, as to what Plato is developing in 271c, we may ask the following: What was going on during those good times, during the time of Cronus, when therefore it was the god himself who was directing the course of things? In relation to our present-day view, everything was going in reverse: people were born old and died as babies. But here we come across again what Plato said over and over, fifty times in his dialogues, about the image of the world philosophy offers. Philosophy gives the true world; and this true world is, for the common man, the world turned upside down [*à l'envers*]. In the true world, as philosophy unveils it, what really matters is nonexistent for the common man; and what is fundamental for the common man is entirely unimportant. What is truth is appearance, and what is appearance is truth. And here Plato is telling us this in another form: In the time of Cronus—which is the true time, since there the world was truly being directed by the god—everything was, from our present-day view, going in reverse [*à l'envers*].

A second point, found in 272e. One can make the following diagram:

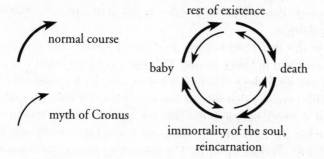

For us, this cannot change; it's time as such. And when Plato turns the contents upside down, old age equals birth and infancy equals death. Here, too, there are these two paths: men come out of the earth old, then become babies again. It isn't too clear what's happening, but it must be assumed—since, for Plato, souls are immortal—that a life continues once the child is dead, that his soul spends the time that is necessary "behind" so as to reappear by being born in an elderly person.

So, is the true world the world of Cronus? No, we don't live in a non-true world; we live in the world's bad period, the time of Zeus, when the world is abandoned to itself. But why does one pass from one world to the other? And here, Plato's response is a return to an essentially Greek way of thinking. It is to be understood that things turn round and round and round, like the way the hands on a watch or on a clock turn around, and that at the end of *n* turns, some sort of period reaches its end; starting at that point, another period, a second cosmic cycle, begins, which, at the end of *n* turns . . . and so on. And change occurs (272d) ἐπειδὴ γὰρ πάντων τούτων χρόνος ἐτελεώθη καὶ μεταβολὴν ἔδει γίγνεσθαι, "when the time assigned to all these things was accomplished, when the change had to occur," when the whole terrestrial race had been used up. But by whom was this time assigned? It's Cronus who's directing things here and who has assistant managers, shepherds who tend and pasture the different categories of beings, including human beings. Well, who then assigns to Cronus the end of his reign?

I remind you here of the kinship, if not the etymological truth, of Cronus / *chronos*: *chronos* is time itself. There is therefore a supertime that says to time: Your time's up [*ton temps est passé*]. There's a higher authority that says to Cronus: Now it's over; it's time to pass [*il faut passer*] to the other cycle. And this instance of authority is in no way a personal one. It's the things themselves, it's the necessity of the things themselves, it's an *anankē* that is superior to every personal instance of authority and to every deity.

And in this way Plato remains profoundly Greek. This conception is deeply anchored in Greek history and the Greek imaginary; it is present throughout mythology. There is an iron *anankē*, an absolutely insurmountable necessity that no god can set aside or go beyond. And this is apparent at several occasions in Plato. It's apparent in the *Timaeus*, for example, when the demiurge manufactures a world that, while as perfect as possible, isn't absolutely perfect. The same thing goes in the *Statesman*, in 273b: the world abandoned by Cronus organizes itself as well as possible, *eis dunamin*. Therefore, when the supreme deity withdraws, that deity leaves the world to its *heimarmenē*, to its destiny, and to its *sumphutos epithumia*, to the desire that is proper to it. An astonishing phrase! And the world's own desire, the desire proper to the world, is what happens then during this phase: the world and humanity try with great difficulty to get organized, but they don't succeed in doing so. Little by little, they approach catastrophe, and then it's the end of this series of cycles: the god is obliged to take back the helm, resume his post as helmsman, and set things right again [*redresser les choses*]. The *sumphutos*, co-native, desire of the world, that which sprouts with it, is at once this necessity, this attempt, this need to get itself organized and the impossibility of succeeding in doing so. For, what is most preponderant in this world, according to Plato, is the tendency toward corruption and destruction. If one wishes to be anachronistic, one can talk about the death instinct or, rather, a struggle between a tendency toward integration and a tendency toward disintegration. And as it's the second term that is the strongest, at the end of a series of cycles, the god has to intervene in order to pull the world out of it and in order to save the world.

But what is this whole story if not one huge theodicy, a huge apologia for god! If things are so bad, it's not the god's fault. He made the best possible world with the material he had at his disposal. And this matter condemns the world to a creeping [*graduelle*] corruption. Let's give thanks at least to the deity for, on the one hand, having done everything he could and for, on the other hand, his repeated interventions aimed at salvation (273b–d). For, left to itself, the world degenerates into a more and more confused organizational state, on account of the fact that it contains a corporeal element, intrinsically tied to its antique nature, which makes it lose memory of the Form the demiurge had imposed upon it. There is therefore a *lēthē*, a forgetting, of the demiurgic Forms; and, in an extraordinary phrase, it is said that the world is increasingly dominated by its passion toward the old disorder, the disorder of former times: δυναστεύει τὸ τῆς παλαιᾶς ἀναρμοστίας πάθος (273c). Abandoned to itself, in the repetition of ever more calamitous cycles, the world would end in its own catastrophe without divine intervention. Here we very much have, then, a theodicy.

There is, at the moment when the god "takes back the helm" {273e}, the following incidental phrase that goes to justify his intervention: The world is in aporia, near its ruination, and what must be avoided is that it would plunge, that it would dissolve, into "the endless ocean of dissimilarity" (εἰς τὸν τῆς ἀνομοιότητος ἄπειρον ὄντα πόντον {273d}). One could easily write four volumes about this single phrase! Dissimilarity, alterity. This "ocean of dissimilarity" is indeed *apeiros*, infinite, interminable, unexperimentable, ultimately unthinkable. Can one, in effect, imagine a group or a set of things that would all be perfectly dissimilar in all respects, each one in relation to all the others? It's unthinkable. To be is to be identical to itself first of all in time; and to be is to participate in the universal. To be is to have of itself something else that resembles itself. And this can be taken from all angles. It can be taken, for example, from the most concrete angle of humanity or of biology: one cannot be a dog all alone; that is so not only because there must be dogs but also because there must be meat hopping about in the form of hare. But it can also be taken—and this is capital—at the most philosophical level: the absolutely heterogeneous is a limit for thought. The world of the time of Zeus becomes more and more disordered, therefore more and more heterogeneous, therefore less and less thinkable; and it thereby participates less and less in being.

By intervening, Cronus saves the real, effectively actual existence of the world. He saves the universality of being, but he also saves the means for being able to tell heterogeneity. For, in order to be able to tell heterogeneity, a certain basis for heterogeneity is required. In order to be able to tell the other, there has to be the same. In order to be able to tell under what aspect alone the other is other—in order to tell, anyway, that it is other than this—it is necessary that the *b* that is other than the *a*, it is necessary that both of them, in a sense, from a certain point of view, be placed on the same level. Otherwise, it isn't possible.

The third point, 274b, relates to this new anthropogony, to the way in which the first savages were able to exit from that state and to create little by little a civilized life. I am summarizing here what I expounded at length the last time. It's that with regard to this myth of anthropogenesis or of anthropogony that we have here—we're talking here about the circle of Zeus—what was said of the individual being can be said of all humanity. Its birth is not childhood, but it is a primitive state; it marches along therein toward a sort of civilization. This idea of anthropogony and Plato's description of it are opposed to what was there as a background in the Greek tradition—that is, actually, the idea of a golden age, which is here the age of Cronus. The age of Cronus is the Greek name for the golden age, the paradisiacal time, Eden. That's the thread Plato picks up. But starting in the fifth century—and without even bothering to say: All that is just some old traditions, popular nonsense, myths—thinkers like Democritus, Protagoras, and Thucydides affirm that there had to have been a primitive state, a technically and civilizationally less advanced state than what exists today. And those are explanations that flourished in the fifth century and that also went hand in hand—this, I believe, is implicitly certain for Democritus as well as for Thucydides—with an idea that isn't formulated as such but that is very much an idea of the self-constitution of humankind. This human species really did forge itself by the sheer hard work of its own hands. Democritus and Thucydides also placed just as strong an emphasis on material inventions. From this point of view, they anticipated Marx, who after all didn't invent that much: the whole material process by which people exited from their savage state is underscored by Democritus and in Thucydides' "archaeology." There is therefore this idea, which was present in the fifth century and which was spreading at the time, of a self-constitution of humankind—even if it wasn't designated in those terms.

Now, what does Plato do with this myth? For a start, he takes back up the idea of an anthropogony and at the same time, firstly, he takes away from it the historical character it very clearly had in Democritus and especially in Thucydides, plunging it into an indefinite number of successive cycles. All that is but an eternal repetition, sometimes heading in one direction, sometimes in the other. Secondly, the best that could be done—and this we shall see in detail apropos of the central major digression—is but a miserable approximation of what could happen in the time of Cronus. But here we find again, in this deliberately ahistorical presentation, Plato's will—manifest in the *Republic* and, above all, in the *Laws*—to stop history, to freeze it, to put an end to all this change going on in the cities, this adoption of new forms. More specifically, while in the *Laws* and in the *Republic* this tendency manifests itself as a will above all not to change the city's Constitution, or else to do so in an entirely exceptional way, here, in the *Statesman*, it's simply an acknowledgment rather than a will: there is no longer even any point in putting a stop to history; in a sense, history has already stopped. And this has been so for ever, since history never unfolds except in two types of repetition that are constantly reproducing themselves, by turning either in one direction or in the other. There is no history; there are only eternal cycles that unfold in this time about which Plato himself says in the *Timaeus* that it has been created by god at the end of his demiurgia of the world as moving image of eternity.[3] This time that is only an image of eternity is thus bound to be circular, for the circle, the cycle, is the figure that best recalls identity: it can turn upon itself without anything being changed.

There is also, of course, the crudest sort of reintroduction of a completely mythical heteronomy (274c–d). Here, Plato takes over the mythological tradition to say that it wasn't men who invented tools, cities, walls, ships, as the Democritean tradition taken up again by Thucydides had taught. No, for Plato, it's once again Prometheus-Hephaestus-Athena who have given men the arts they needed in order to survive—at the moment, moreover, when they were threatened with extinction because wild beasts were much more powerful than them.

Thus, what is destroyed here is this kind of recognition—embryonic certainly, but rather assured in its inspiration—that arose during the fifth century, a recognition of a sort of self-constitution, of self-creation of humanity. Destroyed is this embryonic awareness that began to appear through efforts to reconstitute the initial phase of the history of humanity in the anthropogonies of Democritus, of Protagoras, in Thucydides' "archaeology" and also even, in a sense, in Pericles' Funeral Oration. This embryonic awareness is destroyed here by the reintroduction of a cosmological heteronomy; it is destroyed, therefore, at the mythical, cosmological level of a cosmology that has no other grounds than Plato's own imaginary. And it is going to be destroyed as well, we shall now see, in the first digression, that is to say, in the idea that what men were able to invent in order to safeguard themselves within the circle of Zeus was something quite inferior and without comparison to the art of the genuine pastor of human flocks.

A final remark on this myth before entering into the main digression. What appears to be the goal of the *Statesman*? To introduce behind Plato's political thought, behind the magistrates of the *Laws*, what could be called *strategic reserves* at the level of philosophy, at the level of ontology, at the level of cosmology. Thus, Plato's argument, his discussion in the *Laws*, is designed to show that magistrates of one kind or another are needed; and in the *Republic*, it's that it is the class of philosophers that directs things, that governs. Each time, he tries to justify all this discursively. The myth of the *Statesman* heads in the same direction, but intervenes at a much more profound level, precisely by recounting that in the true state of things, in the time of Cronus, humanity was led [*dirigée*] by divine shepherds. And it is only as "second best," a second and less good solution, that during the time of Zeus men govern themselves. But now I come to the second digression.

Second Digression: The Form of Regimes

Plato takes over the distinction between the forms of regimes already used by Herodotus, then Xenophon, and Plato himself in the *Republic* when, mixing considerations relating to political philosophy and considerations relating to sociology and anthropology, he distinguished the different types of political regimes, which have moreover remained classic within political philosophy. This discussion is resumed several times in the *Statesman*, but what interests us above all is that, apropos of this distinction between the types of regimes, there intervenes the much talked-about digression concerning the law and the fact that it's not the law but science that ought to prevail in the city. It's the statesman who possesses this science, and this science can never adequately be registered in or represented by laws.

This digression runs from 292a until 300c. It begins by setting down an initial basis in 292c, where the Stranger says: But is all this truly serious, trying to distinguish the constitutions of cities starting from the fact that it's a few who dominate, or many, or everyone [*la totalité*]; that there's freedom or compulsion; that it's the rich or the poor? Since we have posited that statesmanship is a science, isn't it in relation to this science that we ought to make our distinctions? One cannot do otherwise, Young Socrates obviously answers. The question that is raised henceforth is therefore necessarily the following: In which of these Constitutions is the science of the governance of men achieved . . . the greatest it is possible to acquire? the Stranger continues {292d}.

I would remind you that this reproduces, repeats here, the kind of *petitio principii* that was nonchalantly introduced at the beginning of the dialogue without one really being able to take notice of it at that point. This begging of the question seems to go without saying, but it's as questionable as can be: Statesmanship is a science, an *epistēmē* in the strong sense of the term. That was said at the beginning of the dialogue; one went off upon that; no one contested it; a bunch of things have been said; one then comes back to the description of the different regimes; and the way ordinary people describe them is the way they are described here. There are democracies; there are oligarchies; there are regimes where the rich dominate and others where the poor are the strongest, and so on. And suddenly, the *xenos*, a serious man, says: But what are we saying now? Hadn't we said that it's science that determines statesmanship? And if that's true, it's therefore on the basis of science that the rest, including its relationship to science, is to be determined. You are indeed right, Young Socrates, of course, responds: "We cannot not wish it" {ibid.}. And then one embarks upon the third digression, the one concerning science. But one does so only in order to leave it almost immediately, as early as 292e, and on an ultraempirical, entirely contingent, material remark, one that is of quite another nature than the a priori considerations that preceded: "Well," asks the Stranger, "do we believe that, in a city, the crowd is capable of acquiring this political science?"

Attention must be drawn here to Plato's extraordinary rhetoric—his dishonesty? Considerations like "statesmanship is a science," which appear to be logical, philosophical, a priori, go by just like that. It is, however, an idea that is situated at first sight at a very lofty level, one that seems deep—which, indeed, it is—and that raises an immense number of problems, even if it is false or questionable. Politics [*La politique*] appertains to the domain of making/doing [*faire*]; making/doing is a conscious activity. Is there a notion of "making/doing well" or of "making/doing badly"? Of course there is. If there's a conscious side to making/doing, making/doing well can only be tied to this conscious side. Therefore, the more one is conscious, the better one does. A limit is reached: Does absolute knowledge guarantee correct making/doing? Maybe. But here, how does one get to the affirmation that it's *epistēmē* alone that can yield good statesmanship [*la bonne politique*]? And to the affirmation that it's *epistēmē* alone that even defines the Idea of statesmanship? For, there is always also the tendency in Plato to slide from the norm to being: good statesmanship *is* statesmanship. Bad statesmanship *isn't* statesmanship. Likewise, bad philosophy isn't philosophy; it's sophistry. And bad statesmanship is only a variety of sophistry, that is to say, trafficking in idols, image peddling. It would have to be asked, moreover, how far this kind of confusion can go: Is a bad horse no longer a horse? OK, but here Plato's position is clear at least in the domain of the faculties.

So, this blunt affirmation with which we are being bombarded, that statesmanship is a science, is rhetorical. But also rhetorical is the way in which it is interrupted, so that the Stranger can offer the following consideration, which is of quite another nature, a perfectly empirical and material one:

—On this score, is the crowd capable of acquiring this political science?
—How would that be possible?
—But in a city of a thousand citizens, might a hundred or even fifty possess this science? {ibid.}

Here, Young Socrates steps in and utters many more than just the five or six words of agreement he usually utters:

By this count, statesmanship would be the easiest of all the arts. Out of a thousand citizens, it would already be quite difficult to find fifty or a hundred who knew how to play checkers well. So, for this art that is the most difficult of all, if there were one citizen who possessed it, that would already be miraculous! {ibid.}

Under these conditions, the Stranger continues, it falls to this rare citizen, should he truly possess the political science, to exercise the *orthē archē*, the right command {293a}. And here Plato, in a rhetorically quite beautiful yet perfectly atrocious declamation, draws out the consequences from what has just been said and justifies the absoluteness of power: "Of these individuals, it must be said that—whether they govern with or without the willingness of the other citizens, according to *grammata* or without *grammata*, whether they may be rich or whether they may be poor—it is they who are the true sovereigns" {ibid.}. Their authority conforms to an art.

And the Stranger forces his advantage by resorting at this point to a perfectly sophistical comparison with the doctor. This maneuver only reinforces the resolutely rhetorical look of the entire argument. For, Plato's rhetorical panoply is now complete; and while he knows how to use the presentation of the plausible as proof of the true, he just as well plays upon a diversionary strategy. And it's elementary: shift the listener's focus of interest and you've practically won. Try hard to prove something with arguments, figures, and so on. All your adversary then has to do is cry, "And what about Nicaragua? What about Poland? What about nationalizations?" to get the crowd to start roaring.

So, the comparison-diversion is rather obvious, since it was introduced by a "besides": "Besides, if we had a doctor, would we say that he is less a doctor because he is rich or poor? Would we say that he is more or less a doctor because he acts according to written rules or without written rules?" {cf. 293a–b}.[4] Would you say that a doctor's orders [*une ordonnance médicale*] are false because the patient refuses to follow them? Obviously not. This refers us back to the *Gorgias*, to the way in which Plato sees the relationship between medical *technē* and rhetoric. Gorgias tells us that his brother is a doctor, that he knows the right formulas to heal people, but that he doesn't know how to convince, is incapable of persuading his patient to obey him. It's therefore the role of the rhetor, of Gorgias therefore, to persuade this patient. Here, in the *Statesman*, the true doctor, whether or not he knows how to persuade and whether or not the patient is convinced, is right and reasonable [*a raison*] to purge us, to cut into our flesh, to burn, to operate, so long as he acts according to the right discourse [*le bon discours*], the *orthos logos*.

The same thing goes for the statesman, therefore. This is said without being said, and here is where all the contraband is smuggled in. "Among the political regimes, the different *politeiai*, the sole genuine and good *politeia* will be the one in which the governors authentically possess the just knowledge, are *epistēmones*, scientists in the political domain" (293c). And these governors will be right and reasonable, whether they act according to laws or against laws and whether they govern subjects who agree or don't agree to be governed, and governed thus.

Plato knows how to take care of his business. He's struck a very rich vein, and he's going to try to draw out the most extreme consequences. And when he gets there, after a discourse of apparently total rigor and several expressions of approval from Young Socrates, the latter balks once again: "All that is quite beautiful, but there is one thing that bothers me about what we've said; it's that story about according to laws or against laws" {293e}. The Stranger then resumes speaking, and this will be his occasion to offer the critique of the law. Here one may think, rightly, of Napoleon and Clausewitz, of strategy—but transposed into the domain of discourse: when a victory is won, it must be exploited to the hilt, ignoring secondary objectives and driving home one's advantage. The Stranger continues, therefore, saying: Not only against the laws, but whether he kills or banishes citizens, since he acts *ep' agathōi*, for the good of the city; since he has knowledge, he knows therefore what is good for the city. This is truly the legitimation of absolute power; it's the General Secretary of the Communist Party who knows what is good for the working class. And the tiny precautions Plato takes are rather amusing: ἕωσπερ ἄν, as long as, as far as; ἐπιστήμῃ καὶ τῷ δικαίῳ προσχρώμενοι σῴζοντες (293d–e), using science and right to save the city while making it, as bad as it was, better. So, under these conditions, we have here the true statesman, therefore the true *politeia*. And all the others are bastard imitations, bizarre, counterfeits, and so on and so forth.

No limitation can be imposed upon this absolute power, which is justified by political knowledge, other than the one limitation that results from its very own knowledge. Or else, from the nature of things. But here, nothing is specified. So, what is this nature of things? Clearly, one cannot make people walk on their heads; but beyond that, there isn't anything else. Who could say to the royal man: "You're going beyond what you can do"? In the name of what science would this be said? With what right? It is he who possesses knowledge.

And then, in 293e, Young Socrates speaks up at some length: "On all the other points, Stranger, your language looks to me to be quite judicious (*metriōs*). But the part about the obligation to govern without laws, here's a thing that one feels too uneasy to hear spoken."

And in fact, for a Greek, this is absolutely inconceivable. I remind you of the declamation, in Herodotus, of the Spartan who had deserted to Xerxes and who arrived in Greece with the Persian king's great army. Xerxes is sure of his victory, if only because the Greeks have no sovereign to lead them into battle. And Demaratus responds, "You're mistaken, O King, because they have a sovereign whom they fear infinitely more than your Persians fear you.—And who is that? asks Xerxes.—*Nomos*!" {cf. Hdt. 7.104}.

More than a century later, Young Socrates reacts the same way: This story that the statesman can govern without laws just won't do. And the Stranger says: You've done the right thing to raise this objection; I was expecting it; I was going to ask you whether you accepted all the things I've said or else whether, among the lot of them, there was some assertion that bothered you. And, "Our intention will now be to expound upon the question of the rectitude of a government without laws" {294a}. And then he launches into his much talked-about declamation, which is both very beautiful and very true. Making laws is a royal job. I remind you of this enormous abuse of language Plato commits in the *Statesman* by constantly identifying the statesman with the royal man. This is a monstrosity for Greece, even the Greece of the fourth century, because the king is the Great King of the Persians; he's the Asiatic despot. No one was a king any longer in that age, and even the Sicilian tyrants didn't dare get themselves called thus. As for Sparta, the "kings" were not truly kings. And yet Plato goes straight at it: The statesman is the king!

The Stranger says, "Since the art of the legislator is a part of the royal art, that is to say of the political art, what I am saying is that the best thing is, not that the laws be sovereign, but *andra ton meta phronēseōs basilikon*—the royal man who acts with *phronēsis*" {ibid.}. And *phronēsis* isn't at all prudence; it's the creative aspect of judgment. It is not only, as Kant would say, the capacity to place the case under the rule or even to find the common rule through a variety of cases. *Phronēsis* is finding, on the basis of a unique case, an original rule that applies to this case and perhaps to other cases that are to come. The case that arises being unique, it can't be subsumed under a law that is already there. The statesman, the *basilikos*, must govern. Why? Because the law won't do:

> —Never will the law be able, in embracing precisely the best and the most just for all, to order the most perfect, for the dissimilarities of both men and of acts, and the fact that almost no human thing is ever at rest don't permit one to state anything absolute that would be valid for all times and for all cases in any matter and in any science. Aren't we agreement upon this?
> —Incontestably!
> —Now, we see the law tends to do precisely that [that is to say, to impose everywhere and throughout all circumstances the same rule], as a presumptuous, arrogant, and ignorant man (*anthrōpon authadē kai amathē*) who wouldn't permit anyone to do anything against his own orders, or even to pose questions to him, or even, if something new arose, to do better outside the rules he has prescribed. (294b–c)

The arrogant, presumptuous, and ignorant man is the law. I said once and for all, "Put on your raincoat!" "But the sun's out," comes the reply. "I said what I said." The law has spoken once and for all, and it sticks to what it has said; it accepts neither discussion nor objections.

This passage, which condenses a whole series of other developments Plato has offered on this same subject, in particular in the *Gorgias*—and a collection of them has already been made—is also at the start of what Aristotle later developed in the fifth book of the *Nichomachean Ethics* on the concept of equity.[5] And this idea is also at the heart, at the basis, of all Hegel's criticisms of what he calls the "abstract universal." All the Hegelian criticisms of Kant, on the one hand, and of the philosophy of the abstract universal in general, on the other, are to be found therein. And all that overlaps with a very deep-seated motif of Platonic philosophy, a motif that is, moreover, contradictory—here we are, once more, in complete turbulence. This motif is contradictory because, on the one hand, we have this theme that appears here apropos of the law—that the law is always repeating the same thing—and that can be taken up again under a thousand and one different forms; the law has to at least be supplemented, completed with equity. And here this critique of the law can be given a socialist form: The law, for example, just as strictly forbids rich people from sleeping under bridges as it does poor people. Or the law prohibits stealing. Yet remember *Les Misérables*: a man is dying of hunger; he steals a loaf of bread . . . and reaps five years' hard labor.

But this critique of the law as immutable, blind, and deaf intersects with another theme very frequently found in Plato. It's a theme that entirely corresponds to what he thinks; it is, namely, his critique of the written in relation to living speech.

In this regard, the basic text is the *Phaedrus*. The *Seventh Letter*, too, which, I believe, isn't genuine but whose philosophical passages were written by someone who knew his Plato business very well. So, the written freezes thought once and for all, whereas in living speech, in dialogue, when I speak I can collect myself, go back and correct an error. Once a book is written, it's a decree. It's there once and for all; it can't be modified. In addition, the argument developed in the *Phaedrus* is perfectly just: to the Egyptian god Thoth, who, in order to aid men in their tendency to forget, invented letters and gave them to men, the Egyptian sage responds: "O so clever Thoth, you thought that you had found a medicine for men's forgetting, and you have invented a poison for their memory, because now they have letters, and they will be proud of them instead of being proud of their own recollection" {cf. *Phaedrus* 275a}. And this is entirely true: if ever you spend some time as an outlaw, you'll be astonished by your ability to remember two hundred phone numbers by heart—whereas, in normal times, you'll keep looking at your address book in order to find your girlfriend's or boyfriend's number. From the moment you know that something is written down, you trust in it, and you empty your memory. It's quite normal, and it's physiological. Another example: in court, the more illiterate a witness, the more accurately he can reconstitute what happened on August 4, 1985, between Albertville and Val-d'Isère, what color the car was, and so on.

So we have this theme of the critique of the written, of the critique of the law, of the critique of abstract and symbol-laden thought in contrast to living thought, which passes by way of speech—a theme Jacques Derrida has drawn upon a great deal in *Speech and Phenomena*,[6] and that can be connected in general with a whole way of viewing things that here anticipates some much later conceptions, that almost anticipates Saint Augustine, and that anticipates the whole Christian imaginary, as Plato does also on a bunch of other points: The truth is living subjectivity. What is true is this voice that vibrates, the labor of thought that comes about, self-correction, invention, this spark that passes between the look of one person and another when they discuss something, and so on. The rest, things written down on paper, written traces, are sorts of dead residues life has left behind it once it has passed by. I was thinking, I was truly in the truth of thought, which is a subjective activity, which is the dialogue of the soul with itself—as Plato says upon several occasions—and then I jotted down a few aspects of this now dead thought, of this dialogue of the soul with itself, on paper, on marble, on papyrus, on parchment. That's not the truth.

You see that around this theme there is a whole philosophical inspiration that continues to nourish even Kierkegaard on the truth of subjectivity as source, in contrast to every work [*œuvre*] of subjectivity and, in particular, in relation to the written, but not only that. For, this critique of the work as opposed to subjectivity is also, with the huge anachronism that this implies, a critique of the alienation included in all objectivation: The creator who produces a work alienates to it a bit of his own being, loses in it some of his substance, more than what he gains therein in the way of immortality. And this is so not only because I lose [*je perds*] my life in becoming lost [*en m'abîmant*] in my work, but also because my work is less true than what I am in the faculties of my thought, of my living thinking activity—that idea is already there both in the passage from the *Statesman* and in the *Phaedrus's* critique of the written, and it is found throughout Plato.

And when I say that we are here again in a turbulent situation and in a very deep-seated contradiction, that's because for Plato himself this idea contradicts the cornerstone of his philosophy, namely, that being is *eidos*—that being is Form, that genuine being is the Ideas. And the Ideas aren't subjects. Perhaps there is something impermissible about wanting at all costs to set these currents in Plato's thought face-to-face with each other [*en regard*] and to make them "cohere": on the other hand, there's an attenuation of the antinomy in a sort of ultimate point where the two things converge, which would as a matter of fact be that much talked-about idea from the *Republic* that is the *agathon*, the good—which is not an *ousia*, an essence, which is not an Idea, either, but which is beyond *ousia* or beyond the Idea and about which it could be said that it is that which grants at once the essence and the knowability of the Ideas; it's a meta-Idea or a metasubject in which the two combine. All that remains a purely enigmatic analysis; it yields nothing. Immediately beneath that, we have a split expressed in the following fact, that, on the one hand, every

subject [*tout sujet*]—even the highest, like the demiurge of the *Timaeus*—
is impotent in relation to the materiality of the given, but that, on the
other hand, it is itself subjected [*soumis*] to the rules to which the *eidē*, the
Ideas, the Forms give shape [*forment*]. Therefore, genuine being is as follows: it's what is always identical to itself; it's the Form. And there's the
other aspect—at least when it comes to the human domain, and it is perhaps here too that the antinomies are attenuated a bit—where Plato is
constantly affirming that the truth is on the side of the living and speaking subject and not on the side of what the subject has produced. The
truth is in discourse and not in the written; the truth is in the knowledge
and the will [*le savoir et le vouloir*] of the royal man and not in the laws.
Why, then, is it necessary, for want of the royal man, to support some
laws? We'll see next time.

From this standpoint, we see once again how right Alfred North
Whitehead was when he said that the whole of Western philosophy can
be understood as a series of marginal annotations drawn from Plato's
text.[7] It's true that I, Castoriadis, wouldn't be capable of drawing these
conclusions from Plato if others hadn't done so before me—and drawn
them in their own follies, drawn them in certain directions. And like
Plato himself in going to the utmost consequences of this thing or of
some other thing, the fact remains that it's nonetheless there that this
whole movement finds its point of departure, an infinity of germs that
were able to develop in such fashion.

Question
On spoken discourse: What's the real truth '[la vraie vérité]'?

Your question is quite clear, but you are repeating what I said when I
was talking about "moments of turbulence." There are two things in
Plato, and I don't see how one can decide between them. Plato says of
every law that it isn't false but inadequate, improper with regard to what
is at issue, that is to say, the issue of regulating human life. We shall see
the absurdities that lead to his critique of the law. What's at issue in this
whole story? Obviously, it's me who's talking here. It's that Plato doesn't
see the problem of the institution—and neither does Derrida, indeed, in
Speech and Phenomena. He doesn't see the relationship of the play between subjectivity and its works. This person who is talking, this living
voice, this animated thought is really possible only because there are

works, that is to say, because there are institutions. These institutions are
the product of instituting activities. It's true that there's an alienation that
is there all the time in history, that involves getting lost outside [*devant*]
one's works—and {that alienation is there} not for the personal subject
alone but for humanity in its entirety. That is to say, alienating oneself to
one's institutions. Forgetting that one is instituting, and for very profound reasons. It's very troubling, moreover.

More generally, we can say that what Plato doesn't see, any more than
Derrida does in his critique of phonocentrism, is the relationship between
the living subject or the collectivity of living subjects or instituting society, on the one hand, and the work or the institution on the other.

Seminar of April 23, 1986

Recall the strange structure of the *Statesman*—so strange that without really pushing things, as they say, we were able to distinguish three, or at least two and a half, definitions of the statesman in the dialogue, of which the first two are manifest. Plato first offers a definition of the statesman as a pastor of flocks. He then abandons it on the basis of the argument—which is obvious, however, even before the outset—that between a herdsman and the animals he tends and pastures, there is a difference in nature, and that the same thing cannot be said of the political man and the "flock" he looks after. This could be said at the very most of a god, which leads to the first digression.

Plato then offers a second definition. More exactly, he pulls out of his hat a paradigm, that of weaving, and beseeches Young Socrates to examine this paradigm with him on the off chance that it will shed light on what the statesman is. Off they go, then, into the analysis of weaving, concluding in the end that the statesman is indeed a weaver. One would be led to believe, given the distinction of the different activities and of the different arts that make up [*composent*] the city, that what the weaver weaves are precisely the weft and the warp threads of society. Now, in fact, there's nothing of the sort, because here, at the very moment when one thought that one's troubles were over, it is discovered that what matters is not the distinction between the city's different occupations but that between the soul's different faculties. These faculties of the soul are, moreover, expressed anthropologically and sociopsychologically, if it can be put in that way, and are presented to us as being by nature in opposition to one another: extreme courage/extreme prudence, for example. Therefore, the statesman qua weaver has to weave together these different varieties of virtues—or, rather, of potentialities of virtues, these *dunameis* of virtues.

It may be observed incidentally that the sole example that is thus composed in antithetical fashion by opposing potentialities is that of bravery. This definition of the vices and the virtues then draws to a conclusion, and it's left at that. In the meantime, however, we're treated to at least eight incidental points, including some very important ones concerning the division into species and parts, the importance of the viewpoint from which a division is made, the theme of the paradigm and the elements, and, finally, relative measure and absolute measure.

To what might all this be compared? Perhaps to a theatrical play, to one of those tragedies where spoken parts and singing parts alternate. Or to an opera in which recitatives, arias, duets, ballets, and so on, succeed one another.

So, there are the two and a half definitions, then the eight incidental points and the three digressions, which I have distinguished arbitrarily, speaking of a *digression* when the argument is much longer and of an *incidental point* when it's relatively short in length, if not less important as a subject.

V. The Three Digressions (Continued)

The first digression is the one concerning the myth of the reign of Cronus (continued).

This is the only era during which one could have really talked about a divine pastor, the god of that era, a god in the form of Cronus, with the face of Cronus, who himself would then really have taken care of human beings, as well as of all the rest. He would have cared for, tended, and pastured everyone—all of creation, as is said today. Here, there's a difference in quality and nature that would allow one to speak of the ruler [*dirigeant*], of the statesman, as a pastor of flocks.

It's in this tale that the astounding idea of the reversal of time processes comes up: during the reign of Cronus, for no clear reason, the god at some set point abandons the world to its fate. And then there's that huge reversal of processes that makes things go backward [*à l'envers*]; they go in the direction that seems *to us* the right direction—children grow up, plants grow taller, the sun goes from east to west—but that is the reverse [*l'envers*] of the true order of things. This is a clear allusion to the fact that the verities philosophy discovers are, from the point of view of common sense, absolutely mad; it's the world turned upside down [*le monde à l'envers*]. That's a theme that has been constant among the philosophers since Heraclitus at least, and one that Plato takes up again here. Then, the world, being left to its fate, tries to get organized the best it can, but everything goes less and less well; things head toward corruption—undoubtedly because, among other reasons, humans aren't capable of self-governing themselves—until the moment when, with total dissolution threatening the universe, the god takes matters back in hand, steps up to the helmsman's post again, and, with a firm hand, reverses the course of things anew, actively looks after the governance of the universe, and sets it on the straight path [*le droit chemin*].

I said a few words last time about the motivations that made Plato introduce this myth. My hypothesis is that it's not the myth that is introduced in order to justify what is said in the dialogue but rather the dialogue that is introduced in order to justify the myth. We'll come back to this point when we talk about the overall structure of the dialogue, at the end of our discussion.

The second digression concerns the form of regimes (continued).

This digression comes in two fragments: 291d–e, then at much greater length from 300d to 303b. A division of regimes is established there, and political regimes, at least the least bad ones, are evaluated. Here again, the organization of the text is neither square nor round, it isn't linear; but here it's more understandable. First, historically speaking, the question of a typology of political regimes wasn't highly worked out in Plato's time. The Greeks empirically contrasted royalty or monarchy with regimes they in general called aristocratic—without further distinction—and with democracy. Moreover, for them, monarchy remained a recollection from the epic poems. And it existed for them essentially as the barbarians' form of government. It's the barbarians who had monarchies or other forms of kingship. There were indeed kings at Sparta, but that was quite another thing than real kings. Spartan kings had a few institutional powers and were above all commanders-in-chief of the army—permanent, hereditary *stratēgoi* in a way.

I have already told you that the first formal [*en règle*] division of regimes was made by Herodotus, around 440–430 B.C.E., in the much talked-about discussion between the three Persian satraps about the best regime to bestow on Persia after the assassination of the usurper Smerdis. There, Otanes defends democracy against Megabyzus (partisan of oligarchy) and Darius (partisan of monarchy), but with some very bizarre arguments. Then, there's the flowering of Sophistry, then Thucydides, and so on. A discussion about the different political regimes, about their form, their classification, was beginning to be sketched out, but the outlines were still quite rough.

Plato himself, in the *Republic*, had provided his own account of the form of regimes. He resumes that exposition here, but from another angle. Recall what happens: at the outset, he begins by distinguishing, rather strangely, five regimes, so as to yield, at the end, seven. This was, indeed, what was to be expected after the distinctions he had made in this dialogue. From his point of view, this is the right division [*la bonne division*], the correct typology. Why seven? Because there's one regime that is the only good one, the sole true one: it's the one in which a genuine political man rules, governs. As will be seen at length and *ad nauseam*, it doesn't really matter whether he governs with or without laws, with *grammata* or without. He knows what is to be decided, he orders it, and it's done. That's the absolute—which, like every absolute, is one. There aren't several of them.

Next come the less good regimes, which are the conventional regimes, those that had already been distinguished in Herodotus. But here it's done with a supplementary distinction. For, in the huge third digression that intervenes in 292a–300c, which could be entitled "Science Alone Defines the Statesman," Plato has already established that what's needed first is the statesman's science, therefore a regime governed absolutely by the statesman or the royal man (this adjective *royal* being, moreover, a terrible abuse of language, very anti-Greek). Inasmuch as he has already established this, though at the same time he has ascertained that no such regime ever exists in practice, he's driven to what he calls the "second navigation," the second best: in the absence of this "royal" man, we can have written laws. But this makeshift solution [*pis-aller*], this lesser evil, is accepted after a devastating critique of the very idea of written laws, this critique—I draw your attention to this point—being in the main entirely just. This marks Plato's genius. The use toward which he shifts this idea is obviously another matter.

If, therefore, we have, as a second solution—a "less bad" one—a regime with laws, then we can resume the traditional typology: one, several, all. But this is done with the criteria of *according to laws or without laws*. And that yields:

• one governor, according to laws, is the true monarchy; without laws, it's tyranny;
• several governors, according to laws, is a well-regulated oligarchy; without laws, it's a tyrannical oligarchy;
• the crowd governing with laws will be a tolerable democracy; without laws, it will be a deplorable democracy. (Here Plato somewhat anticipates Tocqueville's idea of despotic democracy.)[1]

Such, then, is the division with which Plato ends up. Later on, I'll take up a few more subtle points. But this second digression on the form of regimes and their evaluation is interrupted by what is, with the myth of Cronus, the other major, central, and genuine point, the *Statesman's* other large digression: Science, the sole definition of the statesman.

Third digression: Science alone defines the statesman.

The way in which this third digression unfolds—and this third digression is also, in a sense, like a third definition of the statesman—can be reconstructed in five stages:

1. In 292e, Plato lays down the basis for this discussion.
2. In 293, he then indicates this definition's absolute character.
3. In 294a–c, the lengthy development on the law and its essential deficiency follows.
4. In 294e–297d, the conclusion that follows therefrom is drawn in what may be called the first navigation; there, Plato defines the absolute power of the royal man.
5. In 297d–300c, there's the second navigation, which offers as lesser evil law-related power and no longer absolute power.

For the discussion that follows, I would like to go very quickly back through the principal articulations of this passage, this third digression.

This is how it begins in 292: suddenly, after having discussed a bit what was said in the second digression on the forms of regimes, the Stranger from Elea collects himself, strikes his forehead, and says: But what have we been doing here? What had been said at the outset has been forgotten: that the true *politeia*, the true city, cannot be defined in terms of its wealth or poverty, or according to the one or the several; rather, something else defines it. And this other thing is the *archē basilikē*: royal, political government. Let us observe once again, in passing, that the interchangeability of the two terms, *political* and *royal*, persists throughout the text. This ought to have been very striking at the time. And it remains so for us today, moreover: the statesman cannot be called "royal." It's a metaphor still found in the expression "royal road," or when we speak of a "royal flush" in poker, but it isn't clear why politics would be the royal art.

So, the Stranger pulls himself together and says: What defines the royal art, evidently, is *epistēmē*; and if we want to be consistent with what we have said, that's what must be set at the base. Young Socrates is, of course, in agreement, and the fundamental postulate of the dialogue and of all Plato's thinking as concerns the statesman follows immediately. The Stranger questions Young Socrates:

—Well, do you believe that in a city the crowd would be capable of acquiring this science?
—How could one believe that?
—Would, in a city of a thousand men, a hundred be capable of arriving at possessing it in a sufficient fashion? (292e)

And Young Socrates responds that, if such were the case, politics would be the easiest of all the sciences, since "one wouldn't find such a proportion of champions among a thousand Greeks" {ibid.} even in the game of checkers! Therefore, whether it is a matter of a government of several or of all, all that really matters to us is that this government be straight and upright [*droit*], *orthē*, that is to say, according to science.

And therefore it doesn't matter whether those who govern according to science do so "with or against the will of their subjects, whether or not they are inspired by written laws, whether they are rich or poor" {293a}, and so on. The formulations in Greek are atrocious, but from the rhetorical, literary point of view, they are splendid: *eante hekontōn eant' akontōn*—these are the sort of rhymes that began to be introduced with Gorgias—*eante kata grammata eante aneu grammatōn, {...} ean ploutountes ē penomenoi*; if they govern according to science, they are good governors.

Here we must admire Platonic sophistry and rhetoric, for it's rhetoric pure and simple. And it garners one's allegiance when one doesn't reflect too much. For, this rhetorical and sophistical side is covered over—in the context of the Platonic dialogues, and in particular in the *Statesman*—by the extraordinary audacity, by the radicality, of what is said. We're in Greece, in the country where the traitor king from Sparta responds to Xerxes, in Herodotus, that the Greeks perhaps don't have chiefs in the way he, Xerxes, envisages them, but that they have one whom they fear much more: *nomos*, the law! And here Plato has just said: No matter whether the statesman governs with or without *nomos*, with or without consent, as long as he has *epistēmē* . . . It's outrageous!

Then, with the listener pretty much dumbstruck, there follows the sophism with the doctor example. For, the Stranger says, how do you behave with doctors? If they have medical knowledge [*la science médicale*], whether they cut, prick, or burn, whether the patient protests or whether he is in agreement, whether they follow Hippocrates, a medical dictionary, or prescribe from memory, whether they are rich or poor, if they're doctors, they act according to medicine. And the patient obeys! We're in full tautology, A = A. He's a doctor if he's a doctor. And that's what we call medicine, says Plato. "Of course," answers Young Socrates. So, the same thing goes for cities, which will be able to be called *correct* only to the extent that they're ruled by *archontas alēthōs epistēmonas* {293c}, chiefs endowed with a genuine science, true scientists. But not in the sense of the natural sciences; scientists, rather, of political affairs and, moreover, in everything. And not only seeming to be scientists, *ou dokountas monon* {ibid.}. And it is of no importance whether the rulers are rich or poor, or whether people want or not to be governed by them!

"Certainly," Young Socrates again acquiesces. But here, he speaks a bit quickly, and he will later of his own accord retract the overall consent he granted as early as 293e.

Nevertheless, the Stranger, coasting on this rhetorical groundswell that inundates the listener, the reader, and garners their agreement [*raison*] and their allegiance, proceeds to exploit his advantage thoroughly. Here again, one must be Clausewitzian: as soon as there's an opening, one must send in the maximum number of troops and crush all resistance. So, the royal man can punish, kill, or banish people so long as it's to tidy up, to purify, to cleanse the city. He can send out colonies of citizens like swarms of bees in order to reduce the size of the city; or conversely, he may "import people from abroad and create new citizens" (293d) because the city has to expand in size. Everywhere and always, so long as he acts while using science and right, he saves the city by improving it as much as possible in comparison to its previously less good state. And such a city is then what we shall call the true city; and, by implication, these rulers alone are those whom we shall call true statesmen. And the others won't interest us for the moment.

But here Young Socrates pulls himself together and says: Everything you've said until now, Stranger, is excellent, save for one thing that seems to me to be difficult to hear. To "swallow," we would say. And it's that one might govern even without laws. To which the Stranger responds: You've gotten a bit ahead of me, because I was going to ask you precisely whether you really approved of all these reflections. And so let's now examine the following question: Can there be a just government with or without laws? But in order to do that, continues the Stranger, one must first posit that the art of establishing laws is, in a certain fashion, a part of the royal art, *tēs basilikēs esti tropon tina hē nomothetikē* {cf. 294a}. And the best thing is that it is not the laws that govern but rather the royal man endowed with prudence, *andra ton meta phronēseōs basilikon* {ibid.}. That seems to be a redundancy, because one really wonders what a royal man without *phronēsis* would be; *phronēsis* appears to be an absolutely key ingredient of the royal art. Let's leave that aside. But why must one prefer the royal man to a regime of laws? And here follows that passage that I told you is splendid and entirely true. I'll read you my translation:

> Never will the law be able, in embracing exactly what is the best and the most just for all, to order what is the most perfect, for the dissimilarities of both men and acts and the fact that almost no human thing is ever at rest don't permit one to state anything absolute going for all cases and for all times in any matter and for any science. [. . .] Now, we see that that's the very thing law wants to achieve, that is to say, to state absolutes valid for everyone and for all cases, like an arrogant and ignorant man who wouldn't permit anyone to do anything against his orders or to pose questions to him, or even, if something new arose, to do better than what the law postulates outside its prescriptions. (294a–b)

You see that this passage is extremely strong and, at first glance, devoid of sophistry. Quite simply, it is in a sense the opposition, stated for the first time in Plato with such force, between the abstract universal and the concrete. The abstract universal cannot, quite evidently, cover, correspond, be congruent with, be lacking in distance in relation to what is concrete, what is real. And Plato uses this splendid metaphor, *anthrōpon authadē kai amathē*, an arrogant and ignorant man who, whatever is said, always gives the same answer: "Don't do that." "But children are dying!" "But the enemy is already in the town!" "But the house is on fire!" "No, no," he repeats, "do this, not that." The law is like a broken record.

Plato also offers another quite lovely formulation: Isn't it impossible for what is always simple and absolute to find itself in a right relationship [*un bon rapport*] to what is never simple or absolute? This is another formulation of the necessity of law. Why, then, is it necessary under these conditions to make laws, since law isn't the most correct thing one might conceive? "We have to find out the reason for that" (294d). After various examples that don't interest us much here, the Stranger offers that of gymnastics teachers: they cannot *leptourgein*, enter into "the minutiae of individual cases" {ibid.}, but rather give the general principles of training, write them down even, without going into details. "They impose upon an entire group of pupils [*sujets*] the same exertions . . . or all other exercises" (294d–e), without formulating individual instructions [*prescriptions*]. A principle of economy, therefore: envisaging the best rule for the majority of cases and the majority of subjects. The abstract universal as economy. This theme, which will loom large in the history of philosophy and in epistemology, is almost everywhere when we try to think ensidically: one tries to arrive at fewer laws, to reduce theorems to a small number of axioms, and so on.

Therefore, a general rule is given to all those who are training in the gymnasium. And the same thing goes in relation to the law, he says. For, how could a royal man, a governor, rigorously prescribe for his subjects what is to be done, everywhere and always? He would have to spend his time seated by the bedside of each of them, *parakathēmenos* {295a}, and prescribe to them what they are to do. For, that's how one is to understand what the royal man ought to do. And as remedy for this impossibility, one must lay down laws.

One can already see the many leaf-covered traps that have to be avoided in order for one to traverse this passage. There's the comparison with the gymnasium, of course, but above all the predefinition of the royal man as he who has *epistēmē*. From that point on, it doesn't work, because this royal man would have to remain constantly at the bedside, or

seated at the side, of each person. The Greek word *parakathēmenos*, however, evokes the image of the patient [*du malade*] lying on his bed. The
doctor arrives, sits down by his side, takes his pulse, looks at his tongue,
and so on. He is seated at the side: there isn't any other clear usage of the
term *parakathēmenos*. But what does this comparison mean if not that
each one of the human beings who make up the city is sick [*malade*]!
Who told us he's sick? This just slips in among the text's implicit as-
sumptions. And out comes the need for a doctor who would be seated at
his bedside all the time. As one cannot have a doctor seated at one's bedside all the time, out comes a medical prescription: four aspirins a day.
That's it. It's the second best, the second navigation, *ho deuteros plous*.

There then follows a working out of this comparison where Plato really
"pushes" things, since he makes a long comparison to reinforce his idea
that the laws are truly only a less bad (and never good) solution, yet also
to say that, though only less bad, this is nonetheless a solution. Suppose a
doctor or a gymnastics teacher has to go abroad. Fearing that what he has
said to his patients or to his trainees [*sujets d'entrainement*] might be forgotten, neglected, he writes to tell them what they have to do. There's
nothing else he can do. Suppose again, says the Stranger, that things had
turned out against expectations and that the doctor comes home more
quickly than he thought he would. He has left doctor's orders for six
months, but he comes home at the end of three months. He goes to see
his patient and says to him: Your situation has changed; your treatment
has to be changed. What would we think of the sick man who would say:
Oh, no! Nothing doing! Since these "letters" have been written out for six
months, I'm going to follow them for six months. "That would be absolutely ridiculous," Young Socrates replies reassuringly {295e}. So, if that
is so, the same judgment must be made regarding the just and the unjust,
the beautiful and the ugly, the good and the bad, once they are defined,
written down for human flocks. If he who has laid down these laws wants
to change them, he can legitimately impose new rules without bothering
to convince the inhabitants of the city. And the same thing goes if, a century later, another great man, another *basilikos*, similar to the first, appears. And *similar to him* not according to appearances but de jure, by
right. He will have the right and even the duty to prescribe other rules.
"Of course," Young Socrates confirms {296a}.

And the Stranger again exploits his advantage. Under these conditions, we have to refute what is commonly said among the Greeks, namely, that, if someone knows of better laws than those that exist, he has to try to persuade his city to adopt them; but if he doesn't succeed in doing so, he has to abstain. This is truly quite lovely: Plato is constantly repeating, but in a negative and as if mocking tone, what were the true principles of the democratic practice, which was commonly known [*conscience commune*] and went without saying. And indeed, Young Socrates is a bit surprised: Isn't what people say true then?

—Aren't they right?
—Perhaps, says the Stranger. But if someone, in forcing another and doing without his consent, imposes upon him what is correct, what would you call this violence? (296a–b)

For example, when a child is forced to do what he's supposed to do even though he doesn't know that he is supposed to do it. Or when a patient is obliged to follow a treatment, and so on. So Young Socrates is obliged to agree that that would be correct. Well, it's the same for statesmanship: it would be completely ridiculous to complain about someone who violently compels a city, despite what is written and in spite of the *patria*, that is to say, in spite of the traditions that come from the ancestors—I'll have a word to say about the *patria* in a moment—if this person who violently compels it does so in order to oblige the citizens to do something else that is more just, better, more beautiful. And whether he is rich or poor, whether or not he worries about being persuasive, wouldn't really have any importance.

The same thing for the captain of a ship. In this passage, too, there is a very beautiful and atrocious phrase—atrocious? well, all this is very ambiguous, and I shall come back to the interpretation. What, as a good sailor, does the captain of a ship do? Let's dramatize things a bit: a ship in the midst of a storm and subject to imbecilic regulations. He gives orders that may end up contravening those regulations, orders that, at any rate, neither implement these regulations nor respect them; and in doing so "he offers his art as law," *tēn technēn nomon parechomenos* {297a}. This is a very beautiful phrase that anticipates, in a sense—though all this remains implicit and hasn't been explicated by anyone—Kant's third *Critique*. For, what Kant says in the *Critique of Judgment* is precisely that, *tēn technēn nomon parechomenos*. That is to say, the work of genius furnishes a law solely on the basis of its art, *art* here meaning the capacity to connect imagination and understanding. And it's already here.

I remind you what Whitehead said about the whole of Western philosophy as commentary in the margins of Plato's text. And not only commentary in the margins, because here, it's rather like Proust's rolls of paper: there's a phrase about a party that might take place at Madame Verdurin's at the end of the book; and as the galley proofs came back from the printer, it became volumes. And it's the same thing for philosophy: something is pulled out here and then it swells up like that because that's the potentiality of the text.

So, it goes for the city the way it goes for the ship, says the Stranger. Here, moreover, mere repetition fills in for the weakness of the argument: Never could the crowd participate in this science and therefore govern a ship or a city *meta nou* {297a, 297b}, with intelligence, mindfully. And therefore, this city governed by a political man, a royal man, is the sole just city, the sole correct one, all the others being only *mimēmata* {297c}, imitations. That's a big theme that's always there in Plato, an ontological theme: The world is an imitation of the eternal living being; the other cities are imitations.

If that's the way it is in the case of other cities, it follows therefrom that, since they don't have this royal man, they are well advised to protect themselves with written laws and not permit anyone to infringe upon those laws. That's a second-order way of doing well. Then follows a sort of digression within the digression, an incidental point within the digression, which makes a kind of charge, clearly an ironic one, against democracy, and against the Athenian democracy in particular.

But I said that a commentary is in order about the notion of *patria*, about those laws of our fathers (see Finley).[2] For, in the fourth century and already at the end of the fifth century, contrary to what one might have believed, the *patria* at Athens was the democracy. It wasn't an ancien régime before the revolution; it wasn't something aristocratic predating Cleisthenes or even Solon. When the *dēmos* revolted against the oligarchic regime in 411 or, later on, against the Thirty Tyrants, it restored the *patrios politeia*, the regime of our fathers, that is to say, the democracy. OK. And when Plato attacks the idea that the regime of our fathers, qua regime of our fathers, is something untouchable, he's entirely right: it's not because it's the regime of our fathers that it's untouchable. Only, what he intends here by "the regime of our fathers" is in fact the democracy. But then at the same time it is clear how much Plato, all the while being authoritarian, absolutist—the term *totalitarian* would be anachronistic and ridiculous in this context—is radical and is absolutely not conservative. Not only because the *patria* is the democracy, but also because he absolutely does not want to restore the aristocratic regime at Athens. Any well-bred, well-educated aristocrat of sound constitution belonging to the right club at Athens would have recoiled in horror at Plato's political proposals. Plato is a radical, and his project bears no relation to the "reactionary utopia" spoken of by {the German sociologist Karl} Mannheim. He doesn't want to restore past time, if only because he knows that this past time contained—and this is very important—the seeds of its own destruction. And that's the lesson of the passage in the *Republic* that gives the succession of regimes {cf. books 8 and 9}. One starts with a regime that is approximately good, but that regime becomes corrupt; one passes on to oligarchy, to democracy, then to tyranny, and the cycles repeat themselves. Plato's effort—and in this he is simultaneously radical and something quite other than reactionary—is to find and to fix in place a regime that will stop history, that will stop the passage of time, that will stop as far as possible the self-corruption immanent in human regimes. That's the regime of the *Republic*; that's also the regime of the *Laws*, with a few concessions to make it more flexible, enabling it to survive better, to adapt itself without changing within the flux of historical movement.

~

I return to the passage that begins in 298a, to this ironic charge lodged against the Athenian democracy. It begins by a "Let us suppose." And here the Stranger from Elea takes up again his two images of the captain and the doctor. Let's suppose, therefore, that people assemble and decide all together what is to be done both in navigation and in medicine, without necessarily paying greater attention to what is said by those among the crowd who happen to be doctors or captains. A decision is made, a vote is taken, and what has been voted is written on steles. These are called ancestral customs; and it is required, under penalty of death perhaps, that doctors or navigators henceforth conform to what the *ekklēsia* {assembly} has decided. Young Socrates is astounded: "You're really spouting absurdities" {298e}. But the Stranger keeps at it: All that's still nothing, for a magistrate is going to be chosen each year by lot, and he is going to oversee the execution of what has been decided in this way. Young Socrates: "More and more absurd!" {ibid.}. But look what comes next, continues the Stranger:

> So when each magistrate has completed his year in office, a tribunal of judges (*dikastai*) drawn by lot, either from among the rich, or from a list drawn up in advance, or directly from among the whole people, must be empanelled to bring before them the outgoing heads in order for them to render there their accounts; and whoever wishes to will accuse them of not having, over the course of the year, governed the vessels according to the written letter or following the old customs of the ancestors. The same license will be given to those who heal the sick, and the same judges will assess the penalty to be inflicted on or the fine to be paid by those who are convicted. ({298e–}299a)

An ironic Young Socrates says that one would truly have to be mad to accept a magistrate's office under those conditions. And it goes on like that for almost three pages in the Budé edition: a long declamation (298a–300a) in which Plato grotesquely caricatures the Athenian democracy, comparing it to a regime that decides in every particular scientific-technical domain according to the procedures reserved for political debate. As if the Athenians had ever dreamed of deciding by majority vote about how to make medical diagnoses, the "governance" of boats, the way to conduct a battle, or the verticality of the columns of the Parthenon! They never made decisions like that. Phidias and Ictinus built the Parthenon, and that was that. It wasn't discussed, and Plato knows that very well: this is the whole discussion from the *Protagoras*. And it's the argument made by Protagoras himself, the great Sophist, who distinguishes as a matter of fact between affairs of general interest and specific, technical forms of knowledge, the *technai*, for which there is a particular competence. And if someone who knew nothing about it stepped up to the tribune and spoke in order to counsel the Athenians about the construction of ships, they'd laugh him down in such a way that the guy would stop, because everyone knew that he wasn't a specialist. Whereas, if a shipbuilding engineer [*technicien*] were to step up to the tribune and speak, he would be listened to respectfully.

On the other hand, when it came to general political affairs, anyone could talk and everyone would listen to him because there wasn't any particular, specific *technē* involved there. Protagoras says this in the marvelous myth in which Zeus hands out *technē politikē* to everyone equally.[3] And Plato, of course, knows all that. He knows at least that there's a problem. And he has to know all the more that there's a problem because his critique of the law potentially bears upon this problem. That critique also means that there is no universal knowledge; there is no discursive knowledge concerning human affairs. But then, what is this *epistēmōn* who always knows what is to be done in each particular case, whatever the domain in question might be? There's a problem.

Anyway, here this problem is skated over; this is, all at once, Plato's theatricality, his rhetoric, and his sophistic. The problem isn't truly examined. And the Athenian democracy is presented to us a bit the way the late {military aviation businessman and Gaullist politician} Marcel Dassault would have presented self-management [*autogestion*] to us at the beginning of the 1970s. Thank God, no one is talking about self-management any more! Each person has gone back to his place, and everyone has come to his senses. But for Dassault, self-management is the following: They want the hospital's cleaning ladies to operate on us! And it's these general assemblies of surgeons, nurses, the cashier, the social worker, and the women who wash the floors that will decide by vote whether the patient has an appendicitis rather than bronchitis! That's exactly what Plato is saying about the Athenian democracy, because it decides by vote. As to the domain where that vote takes place, that's covered over.

~

Once this charge has been made, we do get to the justification of his second navigation, of his *deuteros plous*. It's to say that the situation would nevertheless be even worse if, when there are *grammata*, written laws in the city, elected magistrates or magistrates drawn by lot would be permitted to do whatever suits each one: "He who dared to do that would commit a wrong one hundred times worse [than the enslavement of medical, naval, etc., and political practice to the written letter] and would annihilate all activity more surely still than the written letter was doing" (300b). Thus, as long and detailed as the critique and the charge have been, suddenly, the justification for the second choice, for the least bad of the solutions, is short, arriving unexpectedly without truly being grounded or worked out. What does the Stranger say? That there are "laws that result from multiple trials and errors, each article of which has been laid down by the people upon the counsel and exhortation of well-intentioned counselors" (ibid.); that these laws are "imitations of the truth, traced out as perfectly as possible under the inspiration of those who know" (300c).

Here's the first new thing in relation to all that has just been read: laws laid down on the basis of great experience and after numerous trials and errors! This law has therefore not been written by chance or because it was liked a lot in 506 B.C.E., in the time of Cleisthenes. No, it's on the basis of multiple trials and errors and of great experience, *ek peiras pollēs* {300b}. Of course, we nevertheless find here another nasty remark: It's not the crowd, the mob, that was able to establish these laws all by itself; skillful, learned [*savants*], and well-intentioned counselors had to know how to convince it. And, after much exertion and persuasion, the people finally laid down some good laws.

Parenthetically, let us observe that this strange combination of long experience and good counseling nonetheless assumes: (1) that the crowd is capable of distinguishing bad advice from good advice; and (2) that, after trials and errors and a number of experiences, it is capable of learning. Both these things go entirely against what was said previously. But let's pass over that.

It being understood that laying down laws enslaves reality, that it's therefore an error, transgressing these very laws would be an error squared, *hamartēmatos hamartēma pollaplasion* {ibid.}. It's for that reason therefore that this second navigation must be accepted. When the laws are laid down, no one is to act against them, even if, in all domains, they are but an imitation of reality. That's why we said that the genuine statesman, who himself is not satisfied with imitations but who is in direct touch with the truth, won't worry about laws; rather, he will lay them down according to what he thinks is good.

Plato concludes this passage and then comes to the typology of regimes, saying that each of them will be all the better after the laws, the *grammata*, have been laid down by true knowers of statesmanship and of human affairs. Here's a reminder that I think is completely indispensable for understanding the basic argument being presented in this passage. But first we have to explicate the implicit postulates that underlie everything and that are outrageous. There are at least two of them.

First postulate: There exists one and only one *orthē politeia*. That goes so much without saying that it is never discussed anywhere in Plato. And it is practically never discussed among political philosophers: none of them discuss the fact that there exists one and only one *orthē politeia* yet each puts forward his own *orthē politeia*. Exceptions can be made, of course: a little bit in Aristotle, a good deal in Montesquieu (correspondence of the best regime with "geographical" conditions, and so on). But ultimately, for most of them and for the most prominent, there exists a just and correct *orthē politeia*, and only one.

Second postulate in Plato: This *orthē politeia* is defined by a single characteristic, a single trait, the *epistēmē* of he who rules. This is knowledge, sapience, wisdom, but not wisdom in the loose sense of the term; it's the knowledge of he who rules.

These two postulates are, of course, quite connected and end in the same paradox: If there is but a single just *politeia*, that's because all the others are more or less bad imitations of reality. From then on, the royal man alone, endowed with this *epistēmē*, will know how to define it and fix it in place. But what *epistēmē*?

Let's return to the first postulate. This *orthē politeia* is unique because all the others can only be systems of laws—which laws suffer both from being, ontologically, only *mimēmata*, imitations for want of the true things, and from always wearing themselves out in trying to "cover" reality. One cannot fix on paper, and especially not once and for all, characteristics like the community of goods and of women (the *Republic*) or the initial equal division of lands (the *Laws*). All these things are ceaselessly and everywhere different. One never steps into the same river twice; a city never remains like itself; an individual is never twice the same. Therefore, one can never lay down the same rule. But the whole problem concerns precisely the distance that is put between this whole flux, this multiple, and the universal rule. And Plato's sophism here is in the absolutization of the terms. Aristotle later saw this in the *Politics*, as well as in book 5 of the *Nichomachean Ethics*: the opposition between the abstract universal and concrete reality—the Heraclitean flux, let us say—is presented as absolute, totally incompatible. Seeing that an abstract universal rule can never be perfectly congruent with a reality, because things always change, Plato wants to conclude from this that it cannot even be so during fifteen years, or fifteen weeks, or even fifteen days. It cannot be so in a radical way, and there's no recourse.

Now, that's not correct. First of all, of course, there's the possibility of changing the law. In the second place, there's the whole theory of equity Aristotle later introduced in book 5 of the *Nichomachean Ethics*.[4]

Aristotle's theory of equity is as follows: There's always a gap between the written laws and what the jurists call the concrete consistency of the case. Formally, the law punishes someone who has killed someone else. But in reality, it's never just "someone" who kills "someone else." It's, for example, Mr. Smith who, exasperated with Mrs. Smith, slits her throat. Or it's Mr. Jones who, discovering arsenic in his soup, strangles Mrs. Jones. But it's always something other than what the law describes. Only, this essential gap between the rule and the concrete case isn't absolute, and it's the judge who is going to fill it in. That's the meaning of equity. It restores the universal in the singular; it reestablishes the general spirit of the law in the concrete case. Aristotle's celebrated observation is that it's the judge who settles the matter; he decides in the way in which the legislator would have settled matters had he known, had he been present. The judge puts himself in the place of the legislator.

This means that in a society, in a rights-based State, one ruled by laws—I point out to you that a rights-based State, a State ruled by laws, was, in fact, defined for the first time in the *Statesman*—the legislator is not the sole one to be legislator. And that's another huge weakness of Plato's argument. The judge, too, is the legislator: he necessarily has to stand in for the law, which is indeed like an "ignorant and brutal man" who always repeats the same thing, whereas reality is always different. And legislation has foreseen this itself by establishing courts, *dikastēria*, and giving them not only the right but the duty to interpret the laws. And behind the interpretation of the law, in fact, is hidden a laying down of rules. Ultimately, in a sense it can be said that not only the judge but every individual lays down laws. This is so from the moment there's a law that says: Each has the right to act in the sphere that is acknowledged as being hers individually. Let's take a trivial example: a cafe terrace, empty tables, chairs. I sit down on one of these chairs. I thus exercise my right, which passes by way of a whole series of rules, to sit down on this chair. From the moment I'm seated on this chair, I have created a legal situation. I can't be told, "Get out of that chair." I sat there because the seat was free, because there were no other places. The concretization of the legal system goes so far as to include the concrete acts through which, by operating within the network of rights and duties conferred upon me by legislation, I concretize them. If someone rushed into this room right now and said, "We've decided to hold a seminar in Sanskrit here at half past twelve," he'd be committing an infraction against the legal system that organizes, covers, and protects what we are doing: the whole pyramid that starts with the French Constitution and reaches down to the regulations of the École des Hautes Études en Sciences Sociales.[5]

But what does that mean? It means that no human system can stay alive—I shall return to this point at length, and it is, moreover, as you perhaps know, one of the major themes to be found in my criticism of totalitarianism and even of the soft forms of bureaucracy—unless it postulates, even under slavery, some minimum capacity for autonomy among its subjects. And this is, as a matter of fact, the ultimate contradiction of heteronomous systems, at least from the moment when these systems are not completely internalized by their subjects. So long as a slave, in the southern United States, picks cotton devotedly because that's the way things are, because for him it's nearly a divine mission, heteronomy prospers. But let him say, "I am picking cotton for that bastard of an owner," starting from that moment it's over; there's already an antinomy in the system. In fact, such total internalization has existed. It's another task to see where and when and up to what point. The fact is that it happens to break down in certain societies starting from a certain moment.

So, Plato, absolutizing the distinction, the gap between the abstract universal and the concrete particular, doesn't see the necessary participation of each in the concretization of the law. But neither does he see, certainly, something else. And here, you can have some fun, if you want, in observing how the pseudo-Moderns are absolutely in thrall to Plato and one of the reasons why they spend their time trying to refute Plato, rising up against logo-phallo-whatever-centrism. Roland Barthes says: All language is fascist.[6] Why? Because I cannot speak while saying, "Broum-bram-groum." I have to pronounce French phonemes, and I have to say them in the order [*consécution*] of phonemes imposed by French phonetics. These series [*consécutions*] of phonemes also have to form words that are in the French lexicon. And these words have to be arranged according to French syntax. Here one stops, because even Barthes would not dare to say that semantics is fascism. Now, where does this asininity that "All language is fascist" come from—it being, moreover, a typically provocative and stupid paradox formulated on the basis of a phrase lifted from Roman Jakobson? As a matter of fact, where it comes from is the inability to see that the social being of man (*anthrōpos*) implies at once a rule and a distance from the rule. A life in which we had rules made to fit us the way a good tailor makes our clothes fit would indeed be total slavery. It would

be the ideal penal colony. But it's precisely in the twofold existence of a
rule and of a certain gap in relation to this rule that what we can have as
autonomy qua social beings is established. It's a gap, first of all, because
the rule not being able to cover all the cases obliges us to find our way in
concrete situations, not only legally immaterial ones but even legally pertinent, important ones, in which nothing is prescribed. And it's a gap, in
the second place, precisely because, the rule never being able to be
adapted to reality, we are called upon from time to time to call it into
question. But in order to call a rule into question, there has to be a rule.
And if we are to be able to call the rule into question, we mustn't be the
rule, or the rule mustn't be us. It mustn't stick to us the way the tunic of
Nessus clings to Hercules. And Hercules is killed by it because it's a poisoned tunic. That's really the image; it would be a poisoned tunic. We
would be able to rip off such a shirt only by ripping off our skin. It's in
and through this gap that we can live socially and individually. This is
what is totally absent from Plato's text and what, for centuries and centuries and still today, has handicapped philosophy in general and political
philosophy in particular. And this is tied up with some very profound
questions, like the whole question of creation and the creativity of the
singular human being and of society taken as a whole.

I come to the second implicit postulate: This unique *orthē politeia* is
defined by *epistēmē*. But one can only ask: What *epistēmē*? Given the
character of public affairs, it is pretty much clear that this *epistēmē* is, at
least potentially, an *epistēmē* of the totality. Moreover, this is said more or
less explicitly in the dialogue, since ultimately it's a matter of having a
knowledge that decides what particular art is to enter into action, at what
moment, and under what conditions; it's a knowledge, as Plato says, that
is *epitaktikē* {260c}, that orders the other forms of knowledge.

It is here, moreover, that the Stranger hangs the apparently obvious but
in fact perfectly fallacious corollary, that if that's how things are, it's impossible for this *epistēmē* to be shared by the totality or by the greatest
number. Remember the comparison, which is logically quite intolerable,
with the art of playing the lyre. Then with medicine and navigation. This
is an intolerable comparison, not so much on account of the patient's vol-
untariness or involuntariness, as Diès's translation somewhat foolishly
says, but on account of the inexistence of a *technē* that is recognized by
Plato in the *Protagoras* and that is occulted here when he speaks of this

gap between the universal and the particular—occulted, that is, in the principal thesis.

So, *epistēmē* of the whole. But to what does this idea of the *epistēmē* of everything refer? Here we're completely in chaos, fully in the abyss. For, this idea of the *epistēmē* of the whole contradicts what is nevertheless one of Plato's central theses, and what is the Greek remainder in Plato— which is granted in the *Timaeus* and which returns in the *Statesman* apropos of that story about the abstract universal law and the concrete. That is to say, the idea that there's an ineliminable matter, called *chōra* in the *Timaeus*, the *aei ginomenon*, the eternally becoming, the always becoming, or the *apeiron* in the *Philebus*, or not-being in the *Sophist*. That is to say, a huge portion of indeterminateness in what is, the recognition of this fact. Therefore, a contradiction between this *epistēmē* of the whole and this *chōra*, this unknowable part of matter.

I am not harking back upon the metaphysical, properly ontological aspect of this, which we have already spoken about. That is to say, the fact that, ultimately, the two elements were there from the origin in the Greek imaginary: the idea of a total knowledge; the idea of a matter that is in part resistant to such a knowledge. And this has yielded two major options in the philosophical tradition, beginning already with the pre-Socratics. One of these options, the Parmenidean option, was to say: Matter, the indeterminate, is not. Alone is what is; and what is is what is entirely determined. This was later taken up by Plato, with the result that the other path, the tradition of Heraclitus, Democritus, and the Sophists, has more or less been set aside throughout the history of philosophy. But Plato, like Aristotle, nevertheless retained something of this Greek trace. In their ontology, there is an irreducible portion of matter, that is to say, an ultimately unknowable portion. That portion can be formed; it is formed, moreover, by the demiurge, but it's formed only to the extent that it can be. It isn't the demiurge who created matter; he simply formed it (*Timaeus*). And it therefore remains something indeterminate or irrational. Later on came Christian theology's desperate struggles with all that and its attempts to eliminate it.

~

But the paradox here, and it's even a double paradox, is that:

1. This *epistēmē* of the whole, which is recognized in general in Plato and

here in particular hintingly [*à mi-mot*] as being in fact impossible, unrealizable, nevertheless becomes the measure for defining the correct regime, the *orthē politeia*.

2. And the other paradox is that the *epistēmē* of this *anēr basilikos*, the knowledge of this royal man, which makes him superior to the law and leads him to offer his *technē* as law, is, as a matter of fact, a knowledge of the singular and of the concrete. That is to say, something quite the contrary of what was thought of as *epistēmē*.

Of course, Plato doesn't say, as Aristotle said later on, that there is no science of the universal. But the idea is already in him. It's the Socratic definition of knowledge, which is found, for example, in the *Theaetetus*: One must always try to condense the plurality of things into a single *eidos*. In the *Theaetetus*, the discussion is: What is *epistēmē*? Intelligent though he is, Theaetetus foolishly responds by enumerating the knowledge of this, that, and the other thing. And Socrates corrects him by saying: OK, but I wasn't asking you how many kinds of knowledge there are but what the meaning of knowledge is and what nevertheless makes all these kinds of knowledge you are enumerating knowledge. What is being sought is the *eidos*, the Idea of knowledge.

So, there's a second paradox. Whereas, according to Plato himself, there is knowledge only of *eidos*, here the statesman is presented to us as someone who is *epistēmōn* precisely by virtue of the fact that he can closely follow each singular situation.

These are Plato's difficulties, which weren't resolved in the *Republic* (written prior to the *Statesman*) and won't be resolved in the *Laws* (written after it). They will simply be covered over by the recognition of the fact that there cannot in reality be, or that it is very improbable that there might ever be, an ideal regime; that, therefore, there can be only an approximation, a *mimēsis*. Plato says this clearly in the *Laws*; and in light of the *Statesman*, it would be true even for the *Republic*.

～

What I mean is that, from the political point of view, Plato's thought yields the absolutely inaccessible regime of the *Statesman*, where an individual, this *epistēmōn*, is at the bedside of each person to tell him what to do. That isn't even a coherent fiction—which the *Republic* is—but it's in relation to this noncoherent fiction that reality is judged. This is the besetting sin of every idealist philosophy—one constructs a fiction that doesn't cohere and then says: The real world is false, bad, inadequate in relation to this noncoherent fiction. Next, there are two other fictions, coherent ones, indeed, but very improbable. The first (the *Republic*) is impossible by Plato's own admission. As for the *Laws*, the regime described therein is even less close to the perfect State than the one in the *Republic*. But these difficulties, these aporias of Plato's thought as they are centrally expounded in the *Statesman*—which people don't generally look at; they look at the *Republic* or the *Laws*—are just simply covered over by the "solution" given beforehand, in the *Republic*, and afterward, in the *Laws*. We shall talk about this story again. I still have a number of things to say to you about the *Statesman*, but I'm stopping here to leave room for discussion.

Questions

1. *It seems to me that what Jean-Pierre Vernant and others have studied under the name of* mētis *in Greek thought is the meaning of conjuncture or of* kairos. *Doesn't that play a role in Plato? Here, when you say that it's knowledge of the singular and of the concrete, one assumes that it's the same thing as* mētis.[7]

—Yes, but *mētis* is, as a matter of fact, opposed to *epistēmē*.
—*Has he completely eliminated* mētis?
—The capital, primary, *princeps* example of *mētis* is Ulysses—*polumētis*, as Homer says. Ulysses is someone who is capable of finding his bearings again [*se retrouver*] in each concrete situation, most of the time by inventing solutions, stratagems, crafty tricks, and so on. Remember Polyphemus's cave, Ulysses' companions hidden under the bellies of the sheep, and so on. "What's your name?" "My name is Nobody." Then, it's the Cyclops who yells that it's Nobody who blinded him! {cf. *Odyssey* 9.355–365} *Mētis* is the capacity to invent, to find one's bearings again in each particular situation. And that gift, in the Greek mind-set, is not shared equally by all men. Otherwise, Ulysses would not be the example of the person who can invent something in all situations, and there wouldn't be any examples of particularly stupid people, in this regard at least.

Now, in Plato, the question isn't really posed like that. Plato never talks about *mētis* but contrasts, juxtaposes, *phronēsis* and *epistēmē*. And in the

Statesman, this yields something entirely incongruous that doesn't hold up: the royal man is he who has *epistēmē* but who is to govern *meta phronēseōs*. Why? It comes in here like a hair in your soup. If he has *epistēmē*, he doesn't need *phronēsis*. In Aristotle and among the Greeks in general, there's *phronēsis* precisely where there is no *epistēmē*. It cannot be said of a mathematician who proves a theorem that he is making use of *phronēsis*; it's *epistēmē*. One can speak of the *phronēsis* of a mathematician in the objectives he sets for himself. And when David Hilbert tried to prove at all costs noncontradiction in mathematics, he transgressed *phronēsis*. He said something that wasn't very prudent. It was very fertile, very fecund, but it came tumbling back down upon Hilbert's head because the opposite was proved: that one couldn't show this noncontradiction.

But as for *mētis*, it's a domain in which *epistēmē* can say nothing. If *epistēmē* can say something, it's a certain knowledge; there's nothing to make do about [*à se débrouiller*]. That's what I tried to underscore, but without introducing the term *mētis*—you're not wrong to have done so; but once again, Plato doesn't talk about *mētis*. That's the paradoxical situation of the *Statesman*, where the sole true regime and the man who incarnates it are defined by *epistēmē*, whereas the critique of the laws is grounded upon the fact that there can be no universally valid laws. This is something that poses a huge question, and Plato is obviously aware of it; otherwise, he wouldn't have written the *Republic* or the *Laws*. And if one makes of the royal man of the *Statesman* someone who has *mētis*, then one makes Themistocles into one of them—he who commissioned the mob to row at Salamis. It's truly an abomination, but that's *mētis*. No science could tell Themistocles: Here's the stratagem to get the Persians to fight in the strait of Salamis rather than on the high seas. I don't know if I have answered your question, but it's one of the text's large aporias.

2. Apropos of medicine. Can't one just conclude that men are not sick, and so, as a consequence, the comparison falls apart—and then medicine isn't a science?

—Of course, medicine isn't a science.
—*Is this something implicit in Plato?*
—Quite so. It's in the implicit part of the argument. In the text of the *Statesman*, medicine or navigation are as a matter of fact on the side of *technē* in the sense defined in the *Protagoras*. That is to say, a type of know-how specific to an object that is able to take particular circum-

stances into account. The whole passage that runs from 298 to 300 is pre-cisely that. It is absurd to say in advance to a captain of a ship how he'll have to navigate. According to the winds, the tides, the currents, the moon, the state of the ship, and so on, he'll make do and will decide how to run the ship. That's why Plato lodges this ironic charge against the Athenian democracy, that it has decided once and for all how the ship of the city is to be governed; next, it draws by lot people who are going to govern it according to these written instructions—the height of ridicu-lousness!—and then anyone, once these magistrates' terms in office are over, can drag them before the court and accuse them, saying: You have violated the laws because you didn't continue to fire, whereas the laws or-der it, and so on and so forth. This charge is unacceptable. And Plato knows it very well.

In the text, navigation and medicine are completely on the side of knowledge that deals with the concrete. And this, in my opinion, only underscores the aporia, the antinomy between *epistēmē* in the general sense—that of the *Theaetetus*, but which is used in the *Statesman* without any warning—and those *technai* that are *technai* of particular things. There are two distinctions that include an element of professional knowl-edge. And that's the discussion from the *Protagoras*: the *stratēgoi* were or-dered to sail to Sicily, but no one at Athens required that they get there in ten days or by setting the sails in this or that way. That's the question: only true navigators can do it. Now, there's a double shift. There's an *epistēmē* that knows everything. And the *technai* that are used as examples in the *Statesman*—medicine, navigation—are types of know-how that do, after all, include some portion of knowledge. If one doesn't positively know the anatomy of the human body, one can't do medicine. But know-ing anatomy and pharmacology is far from being sufficient for treating a patient. If one doesn't know the cardinal points, one cannot navigate, but that isn't enough either. Here, then, you have two parts: one part that is almost or completely codifiable and another that involves adaptation to the circumstances.

And then you have politics properly speaking, where one doesn't truly know what is codifiable. This implies a familiarity with things: if the Athenians decide to send an expedition to Sicily, they have to know that Sicily is an island, that there are so many inhabitants, that the Syracusans are like that, and so on. But all that is a contingent type of knowledge. Today, it's Sicily; tomorrow it'll be Egypt. So, one can "inform oneself about," but one doesn't know in advance. No one can know all those things just like that. Even the CIA had to learn that there was a leader of the Iranian Shiites who was called Khomeini. And then this acquired knowledge involves above all a judgment that adapts itself to particular situations to a much greater degree than in the case of *technē*, which includes an instrument of knowledge.

Now, these three articulations aren't made in the text. They are crushed or covered over by the idea of a total *epistēmē* that could be seated beside each person and tell him with certainty what he has to do or not do.

3. *Has Plato chosen, between the* Republic *and the* Laws, *democracy, then the enlightened despot?*

What he offers in the *Statesman* would be an enlightened superdespot. An enlightened despot or a technocrat has never claimed to tell each person what he has to do. Now, that's Plato's literal expression: *parakathēmenos*, at the bedside of each. When we leave this {seminar} room at 1 P.M., it's the royal man who's going to tell us whether or not we should go to lunch. So it's beyond enlightened despotism. As for the *Laws*, it's not democracy; it's a regime of another type.

4. *Apropos of Barthes and the fascism of all language.*

Barthes and all of structuralism, this is an enormous abuse surrounding a phrase from Jakobson that was correct for one part of language. Jakobson had said that, from the point of view of structure, language is like totalitarian regimes: everything that is not obligatory is forbidden; and everything that is not forbidden is obligatory. What did he mean? He was wrong, moreover, save perhaps from the point of view of phonetics. And still there, I don't know. It is said that in French certain sequences [*consécutions*] of phonemes are forbidden. But even that is quite relative. "Doukipudonktan," Raymond Queneau writes at the beginning of *Zazie dans le métro*. And this order [*consécution*] of phonemes belonging to different words is forbidden a priori and yet perfectly pronounceable by a Frenchman. If one spoke like that for ten minutes, one would line up fifty series [*consécutions*] of phonemes that are absolutely forbidden in French phonetics. For, French phonetics is valid only for the construction of each lexeme. Here we have the obligatory part of the forbidden. But that ceases to be true for the sequencings [*consécutions*] in spoken French.

And even assuming that that would be true for phonetics and for grammar, this rule of "everything that is not obligatory is forbidden and everything that is not forbidden is obligatory" is no longer true of semantics. For, semantics is precisely a domain in which other relations are constantly being created by the living speaker of a given tongue. It's in this sense that Barthes's phrase is an asininity and a bad interpretation of what initial structuralism in language was, Jakobson himself very clearly tracing out some lines between the part I'd call *ensidic* and what he himself called the *poetic* part of language.

Seminar of April 30, 1986

V. The Three Digressions (Continued)

I hope today to be able to finish with this *Statesman*, which has cost us so much labor. After having commented on the two and a half definitions, the eight incidental points, and the first two digressions—the myth of the age of Cronus and the form of regimes—we were right in the middle of the third digression, which is, in a sense, like a third definition of the statesman.

The third digression defines the statesman on the basis of the idea of science (continued).

And we were saying that this third digression has at least two hidden presuppositions. The first is that there exists one republic, one city, one *polis*, one just *politeia*, and only one. That may seem evident, but it's just as well contestable. For, a sea of questions then opens up: A straight and upright *polis*, an *orthē* one, but *orthē* in relation to what? And under what conditions? Herodotus had already spoken of each regime's adaptation [*appropriation*] to each people; as for Montesquieu, he speaks of adaptation to "natural" conditions; and Marx, of the state of the forces of production, although he assumes that there will be a single *orthē politeia* at the end of history. This is, therefore, an enormous problem. Plato doesn't discuss it and instead decrees: One *orthē politeia*, and only one. This obviously presupposes that there exists what in mathematics would be called a good hierarchical ordering of the different types of *politeia*, of city, with the *orthē politeia* at the summit.

A second implicit postulate: This *orthē politeia*, this correct, straight, upright city—upstanding, with the others recumbent—is defined by *epistēmē*. And here the criteria for this *epistēmē* that Plato is constantly using are sometimes a sort of absolute knowledge, sometimes a knowledge that also implies some techniques for its application. In short, it could be said—but with some question marks—that this knowledge of the statesman, of the royal man, that defines this city has to be made of a scientific, "epistemic" knowledge, of something that concerns the essence of things, and at the same time has to include, in light of the examples Plato brings in to support his thesis (medicine, the "governance" of a boat), a *technē* in the practical sense of the term, a knowledge of the particular circumstances, a knowledge that contains in itself the virtual possibility of adapting to every set of circumstances that might present itself.

So here we have a first paradox concerning this *epistēmē*, concerning this knowledge: that, while being—sometimes hintingly and elsewhere explicitly—recognized all along as inaccessible, it becomes an absolute measure of reality. Why inaccessible? Well, we already know why in the *Republic*: There are the essences, the *ousiai*, and there is something that is beyond essences and that is the Good, genuine being, which itself is not accessible to knowledge. Plato says himself that this Good that is beyond essences, this *agathon*, "can hardly be seen" {517b–c}. (And this "seen" is certainly metaphorical, but not that much so: in all this, the metaphor of vision plays a cardinal role. Vision, speculation, contemplation, *theōria*, all that comes from the verb *to see*.) In any case, what truly is isn't visible with the eyes of the body. As for the eyes of the soul, they can hardly catch a glimpse of it. And anyway, this *agathon* is not discursively demonstrable.

Plato says the same thing in many other texts. In the *Phaedrus*, for example. And in the *Seventh Letter*, which is perhaps authentic, perhaps inauthentic, but which in any case was written by someone who knew his Plato very well. The central philosophical passage could have been written by Plato. It's the historical details of this text that are improbable, as M. I. Finley rightly says.[1] And what this *Seventh Letter* describes is, as in the *Republic*, a labor of preparation, on the order of discussion, study, discursiveness, definition, proof; but the sight of the *agathon* itself comes *ex-aiphnēs*, suddenly, like a flame that rises up after one has rubbed oneself with the thing for a long time. This much talked-about image from the *Seventh Letter* fully reminds us of certain passages from the great mystics about periods of drought and the need for an ongoing effort [*travail per-manent*], during which nothing is guaranteed, but at the end of which, perhaps, the deity or the light or transcendence appears to the mystic. All that is already there in the *Seventh Letter*.

And that means what, ultimately? That genuine *epistēmē* is practically inaccessible for those who are human. Or accessible in very contingent fashion. Whence the paradox that arrives when this inaccessible knowledge becomes the measure of something real. We are obliged to measure our earthly cities, what we do, our Constitutions, and so on, by the yard-stick of this knowledge.

But there's more, for how are the rest of us, we who are neither this philosopher nor this royal man, this statesman, going to recognize him when he turns up? The best-case scenario—it's not explicitly said, but it's the only conclusion to be drawn—is that we're dealing with an act of faith: That's the royal man; what he says is better than the law. The only thing is to follow him.

It must be said parenthetically that Aristotle, who is always for the reign of law, takes up a rather analogous idea in a rather strange passage from the *Politics* when, in the middle of his discussion of the different forms of city, he suddenly speaks of the possible appearance in the city of an exceptional man. And Aristotle says that, starting from the moment when that man appears, all the rest comes to a halt. The citizens recognize him as such, as an exceptional man, and what he says becomes, in a certain fashion, law. One can go on and on about that. What does Aristotle, who always remains very pragmatic, have in view? Is this exceptional man exceptional perhaps in his ability to convince people, to carry them away? In any case, this idea is also there in Aristotle. And do we need, in addition, to mention Alexander the Great, whose accession to power was contemporary with the *Politics*?

OK, but the problem remains: it's not enough to have this royal man in the city; the city must still—and Plato doesn't talk about this, except in one place to say that it's practically impossible—recognize this royal man. Or else it would be necessary to count among the royal man's faculties—which would perhaps be a more favorable interpretation—the ability to convince the city that he's the royal man, that his authority must therefore be accepted. This is in no way discussed here, and it is highly doubt-ful, because, according to everything Plato says elsewhere, the qualities that according to him are necessary in order to convince people are not at all the ones that make the true philosopher, he who possesses true knowledge.

Thus, this first paradox is doubled:

1. How could someone possess this absolute, inaccessible *epistēmē* that nevertheless is the measure of the real?

2. And if someone can possess it, how will he be recognized by the others as possessing it?

And there's a second paradox concerning this *epistēmē*, to which I drew your attention last time. It's this sort of combination of the universal and the concrete. The knowledge of the royal man, the knowledge that renders him superior to the law and that ensures that he can "furnish his art instead of and in place of the laws" {297a}, well, it's precisely a knowledge that includes the singular and the concrete—and even the outer limit of the concrete, since the statesman has to be at the bedside of each citizen, *parakathēmenos*, that's the Greek expression. And that's completely the contrary of what one generally understands, and of what Plato himself understands, by *epistēmē*—that is to say, a knowledge that really intends the universal. And it is defined as such in the *Theaetetus*, in the *Republic*, and so on.

Thus, we have here a kind of vacillation with respect to the prior conception. That is the conception in particular from the *Republic*, where it's the philosophers who govern the city, after having been selected as such, after having spent the bulk of their lives preparing themselves from the standpoints of dialectic and mathematics for the theory, the vision, the intuition of the Ideas.

And we find here, once again, the same paradox: nothing says that, as such, these Ideas, these essences, render the philosopher of the *Republic* capable of managing, as is said today, of governing in singular, concrete situations. And that, indeed, is something Plato catches a glimpse of as his work unfolds—perhaps also as a function of the direct or indirect experience of his affairs in Sicily, as a function of his relations with Dion. This is perhaps also what later led him (thinking of his captivity at Dionysius's?) to wax ironic in the *Philebus* about someone who knows the Idea of justice but who doesn't know his way home. This is indeed an old theme in Greek philosophical anecdotes: remember Thales, who looks up

at the sky and falls into a hole. In the *Philebus,* Plato continues this be-
nign, benevolent sort of disparagement, by citizens, of the philosopher
who misses what's right in front of him because his gaze is elsewhere. And
there is perhaps a trace of that in this kind of vacillation in the *Statesman.*

But you see the strange logical situation created at this point: the third
digression criticizes the law for its essential deficiency, for the gap it cannot fill in between universality and the concrete. And in the *Statesman,*
the law is taken as the abstract universal. Once again, it is defined as "the
ignorant and arrogant man" who is always repeating the same thing.
Therefore, it cannot adapt itself to concrete situations. Whence our rather
intense sense of unease, almost like an emptiness: the Idea of justice qua
eidos cannot be transformed into law, into a simple abstract universal rule.
But at the same time, this royal man is presented to us as he who is the
Idea of justice, he who makes that Idea present in reality in order for each
citizen, at each moment and under all his life circumstances, to be told
what is to be done and what is not to be done. But on what basis can he
do so, if not on the basis of both a knowledge of the Ideas and a knowledge of singularities?

And all that ultimately leaves us wavering, which no doubt prepares us
for the regime later described in the *Laws,* where you have magistrates
who are more or less elected by the rest of the citizenry but at the same
time you have the much talked-about "nocturnal council" whose composition and recruitment are rather precisely defined, but whose role is not.
It's a sort of secret oligarchy that watches over and keeps under surveillance what is done in the city, that also practically watches over the magistrates and keeps them under surveillance, and that brings together in a
group some people who are chosen in terms of their *cursus honorum.* Indeed, this is the first time such an idea appears in a Greek text, whereas it
was quite basic in Rome, because the Roman Senate was made up of people who had followed a *cursus honorum,* performed a series of magistracies. This is a necessary condition even if it is not a sufficient one. And
the first time we have this in a Greek text is in the middle of the fourth
century, in the *Laws,* apropos of this nocturnal council. In the Platonic
context, that council is, as far as possible, composed of people who combine some universal knowledge [*un savoir universel*] with a sort of business acumen [*une sorte de connaissance des affaires*], as the journalists
would say today. The {French} Socialists failed {it is said} because they

didn't have "business acumen" when they came in back in 1981; and then they learned business after two or three years in government, and so on and so forth.

So the vacillations of the *Statesman* can be understood if they are placed back within this evolution in Plato's thought, which begins with the *Gorgias*, when Socrates says to Callicles, who is presented as a politician: It isn't you who are the true statesman, it's me {521d}. The true statesman is the philosopher, he who knows how to tell the definition of the just and the unjust. From there one goes on to the *Republic*, with the philosopher who governs. Then the *Statesman* gives us this definition of the royal man—an inaccessible definition, however, and one that combines heterogeneous and even contradictory elements. And finally we touch down in the city of the *Laws*, where the government is almost democratic—or aristocratic, in Aristotle's sense, since the magistrates are elected and not drawn by lot—but in which, at the same time, there's this nocturnal council.

Now, this text also contains some completely opposite implications. One sees here how extraordinarily rich a text can be and how vastly far-reaching thought can outstrip [*dépasser*] the explicit intentions of the author and even lead to conclusions completely opposed to his own. Such inexhaustibility would perhaps rightly be one of the criteria for great works of art, which one can reread or listen to for the one hundred and seventeenth time while still discovering therein a little something more. Of course, in all this, it's Castoriadis who's talking, who's reading Plato, and who begins by picking out a few cherries or pulling on a variety of strings that are in it in order to see what comes along with them. And I have the right to do so provided that it not be arbitrary and also because clearly, as we have tried to show, the text is full of anomalies.

Let's take this argument then that Plato sets against himself in order to say that, ultimately, the government of a royal man isn't possible (287a–b): How could someone be at the bedside—*parakathēmenos*—of all the citizens so as to order each person exactly and rigorously to do what he is to do? That isn't possible. No governor, no government can be everywhere at the same time and attend to each case. And here, I'm asking you to enter into the skin of the philosopher, of philosophers, of philosophy, and to take ideas absolutely. To say that there is only one man in the city who knows statesmanship means literally that he has to be hovering over everyone's head twenty-four hours a day in order to tell each person what he is to do. And that is, moreover, the inference Plato draws. For, Plato isn't like writers today in 1986: when he says *a b*, he concludes *c*. And here he sees that *c* doesn't hold up. And he therefore deduces from this that one must retract *a b*: no one man—be he royal—can govern the city. So, there's a second navigation, a second best: written "letters," those *grammata*, those immobile, dead rules, laid down once and for all on paper, which always repeat the same thing "like an ignorant peasant." But anyway they're a substitute, the least bad one possible, for the inability of the royal man, were he to exist, to carry out his role effectively.

Therefore, on the one hand, we have this inability, this impossibility: The royal man *parakathēmenos* is untenable. The only solution is the *grammata*. But on the other hand, there's a second impossibility: These *grammata* are necessarily and by their essence distant from reality, incapable as such of managing reality's details and of adapting to the way reality evolves. And that is something that Plato was the first to remind us of, to teach us, to unveil to us. There is therefore always a necessity, if we have laws, to fill in this gap between the abstraction of the law and the concreteness of the real. And this point is of capital importance, for, as I have reminded you, Aristotle's whole theory of equity in the fifth book of the *Nichomachean Ethics* was later going to come along and be grafted on top of it; next, it yielded Roman *aequitas*, then the whole theory of legal interpretation for century upon century. This entire theory, and the whole philosophy of law, is based upon these two paragraphs from the *Statesman* and their innumerable implications.

By way of consequence, if we don't simply want the judge with his equity to intervene after the fact and as a correction, what are we to conclude? Obviously, that each citizen is interpreter of the law for her own life. Each citizen has before her this set of abstract rules, but she lives in a diverse, changing reality, a Heraclitean reality, and she's the only one who might be able to bridge the two. Also by way of consequence, the task, at that very moment, of the much talked-about legislator, whoever he might be, is the education of citizens, *paideia*, in such a way and with such an orientation that these citizens might themselves constantly make up for the law, that is to say, fill in the gap between the abstraction of the legal universal and reality. Each citizen has herself, in a sense, to be judge *ex ante* (as is said in Latin), in advance, of what's going to happen.

Let's recall, then, how Aristotle defines what the judge does when he finds himself before a concrete case that doesn't as such fit the very abstract mold of the law: At that moment, the judge has to settle things as the legislator would have done had he been obliged to be familiar with [*connaître*] some particular case. The judge brings the legislator back into actuality; he gives specificity to the law; he makes a sublaw of it in the particular case. And this sublaw for the particular case is made in the spirit of the general law; that is to say, it takes into account the particular circumstances but also the spirit of the law, the intentions of the legislator—as one says in philosophy of law. The judge performs this combination, makes this synthesis. Let's transpose to the situation described by Plato: the city can truly function with written laws, the much talked-about *grammata*, only if each citizen is capable of performing this labor Aristotle imputes to the judge when resolving disputes in litigation, that is to say, only if she is capable of acting in each case as the legislator would have acted had he been familiar with the particular case in question. This is also to say that the city can function only if each citizen is constantly capable of raising herself up to the level that defines the good legislator.

In still other words, there are two mutually exclusive alternatives:

1. Either the mass of citizens is this sort of hopeless morass, *anthrōpon agelai*, flocks for ever; and that's what Plato envisages most of the time. In that case, there's nothing to be done, because, with or without *grammata*, the gap between the law and reality will always be filled in badly anyway; and, what's more, these *grammata* will be laid down badly at the outset. In addition, and still within the hypothesis that human beings are this hopeless herd, these hopeless cattle that Plato takes pleasure in describing to us, one must then be a democrat, and this is so according to Plato himself, since democracy is, amid corruption, the least bad of regimes. It's a regime that "can never do anything great," as he wrote black on white in the *Statesman* {303a}. (He wrote that at the foot of the Acropolis and in the shadow of the Parthenon! But, well, that's how things are; a philosopher has a right to a certain amount of arbitrariness.) And it can do nothing very bad either. Therefore, so long as you live under a corrupt regime, it might as well be a democracy.

2. Or else, then, it is granted that the mass of citizens is not for ever merely a morass—which, moreover, Plato himself recognizes by contradicting himself in 300b, when he says that where there are written laws in cities, they mustn't be violated, firstly, because one needs written laws—it's better than illegality or total anomie—and, secondly, because these

written laws have been laid down on the basis of experience. Plato says this himself; and he who says *experience* says *subject capable of acquiring an experience.* This table I'm leaning on now acquires no experience. If the laws are what they are, let them be respected, because they crystallize, embody, incorporate a certain experience—this experience of living men in the city who have learned, over centuries and decades, that such laws are less bad than others. And at the same time, he says, they have been laid down because a few intelligent, wise, and subtle persons have known how to persuade the crowd to adopt these *grammata.* And here again, a crowd can be persuaded to adopt good laws only if the crowd is "persuadable," can be persuaded to accept these good laws. If the crowd were such that it always flung itself upon the most corrupt laws presented to it, what Plato says in 300b would be an absurdity.

Once we accept that there might be some little glimmer of hope for this host of human cattle, the consequence of the Platonic text is obvious: it's the permanent democratic self-institution of society. Why? Because people must be educated so as to enable them constantly to fill in themselves this gap between the *grammata,* the dead letters of the law, and reality; to seat themselves at their own bedsides—since no one else can do it for them: Plato has acknowledged that. Therefore, each person must, as much as possible, be able to act almost like a royal man in the affairs that regard her. And the argument Plato himself develops starting at 295d must be understood in the same sense: remember the doctor who has gone on a trip, leaving you a prescription [*ordonnance*], and then comes back and wants to change the treatment. But stupid you, you respond: "No, no, I've got your orders [*l'ordonnance*]." Of course, the doctor here is the royal man. And if the laws are—as Plato himself says—laid down by the crowd itself with the advice of the wisest men, the crowd, like the doctor, can go back over its decisions; the *dēmos* can collect itself and reconsider the question. And given the essential gap between the *grammata*—the dead "letters"—and ever-changing reality—the always different circumstances, and therefore the need to modify the laws in order to take into account these changes in reality and the variation in circumstances—it follows that legislation cannot be something that is made once and for all; it's a permanent activity. All legislation has to be capable on a permanent basis of collecting itself and going back over things— that's what I call permanent self-institution. And the subjects of this permanent self-institution, the active, acting subjects, have to—if we are to stick to the potentialities of the text—be the whole set of citizens; this has to be the *dēmos* itself.

You see then that, if these ideas are taken seriously—on the one hand, the essential gap between the written law and a diverse and changing reality; on the other hand, the impossibility of any government being seated constantly at everyone's bedside[2]—the potentialities of the text paradoxically but, I believe, quite rigorously lead, in light of the impossibilities Plato himself posits, to the idea that ultimately the *politeia* that corresponds to the nature of things, to the nature of laws, is a democratic *politeia*, which self-institutes itself in permanent fashion.

~

Before passing to the part that concerns the division of regimes, I'd like to insist upon the fact that it's really with Plato and with this passage from the *Statesman* that we have the beginning not only of all discussion about the interpretation of the laws, hermeneutics, but also—and here, it's along with a passage from the *Phaedrus*—of all discussion concerning objectivation as alienation. There is something that is the living subject, living *logos*, living speech, discussion, dialogue; and this is the genuine "life of the mind [*vie de l'esprit*]," to employ an anachronistic expression. And then there's the dead deposit of that, which are letters, the *grammata*, artifacts, which the spirit [*l'esprit*] has constituted, in which it has crystallized itself, but from which it has withdrawn. And this later became one of the great themes of subsequent philosophy, in Hegel and Marx: These objectivations are thenceforth there as a sort of dead product of a living subject; the dead product stands in the way of this living subject like an obstacle to its subsequent realization or to its subsequent life. It's Hegel's "becoming exterior to oneself": the works of the spirit from which the spirit as living spirit has withdrawn. And the point of departure for this distinction, for the opposition between the spirit that breathes, that is alive, and dead works, is in this passage from the *Statesman*.

Reprise of the second digression on the form of regimes.

I don't want to linger very long over this. There's the beginning of an exposition in 292a, interrupted by the long digression on the law, the royal man, and so forth, and then Plato goes back over the subject between 300d and 303b. He begins by dividing political regimes according to the old criteria, already known in Herodotus, of one, several, all. Or, monarchy, oligarchy, democracy. Here, indeed, is a *topos* extending across the history of political theory and the history of philosophy. The equivalents in logic are singular, particular, and universal judgments. And Hegel said later on that Asians knew the freedom of a single man, Greeks knew the freedom of a few, the Germano-Christians knew the freedom of all. Then, after the definition of the statesman in terms of science, and, starting from there, the reintroduction of the laws, one ends up with a bipartition of these three regimes. Plato's text is often jarring, and I don't want to linger too long over it. Let's say that we have at this moment a single correct city, the one ruled by the royal man. And for the three regimes, there are the forms that are rights-based States, States ruled by laws, and there are the forms that are in a state of illegitimacy. That is, if in monarchy we have someone who governs according to laws, that will give us a genuine kingship; if not, we have a tyranny. When in the regime where a small number reign, we have a government according to laws, we'll have an aristocracy; if not, an oligarchy. Finally, when the crowd governs, there are no preestablished names, but here again one can distinguish between the case where the crowd governs without laws and the one where it governs with laws. But Plato refuses to name these two regimes as such.

In my opinion, there's not much to say about this discussion—except, here again, to admire Plato's rhetoric and sophistry. For, the way in which he describes the Athenian democratic regime in the paragraphs preceding the third digression is a wholly unacceptable, grotesque caricature. He presents it as if it were a regime that arbitrarily decides upon what is good or bad in medicine, that designates by the drawing of lots the people who are to carry out instructions [*réaliser les prescriptions*] and then asks them to account for it, and so on. This argument is utterly inadmissible and dishonest, because as a matter of fact at Athens the city does not decide the problems, the questions, the subjects on which there is a technical knowledge of some sort. The city decides upon laws in general or decides upon governmental acts, but there are no laws concerning government as activity. The whole parallel Plato is drawing with the "governance" of a ship or with the activity of a doctor is aimed at presenting the Athenian *dēmos* as having decided in its stupidity upon what the "governor" of a ship is to do and as forcing him to stick to the instructions of the *dēmos* in this regard. Now, that wasn't the case at Athens: there were no instructions given concerning government as activity. The activity of the *dēmos* concerns points that are absolutely not technical in nature. And Plato himself knows that very well, since he already discussed this, among other things, in the *Protagoras*, as I told you last time. But we don't have to be concerned any further with these distinctions among types of regime.

VI. Conclusion: On the Composition of the *Statesman*

I'd like to conclude now with a few considerations concerning the overall structure of the *Statesman*—what, from the outset of our reading, I have called the "strangeness" of this structure.

What, indeed, is one to think of this very bizarre composition, in which Plato sets out to define the statesman and gives several successive definitions, only to abandon them along the way, in which there are numerous incidental points that concern very important issues and digressions that touch upon entirely basic points, like the third digression on the law, for example? How is one to understand these strange goings-on in the composition of the *Statesman*? The question is all the more compelling because we know that Plato was eminently capable of writing dialogues that are perfectly composed, from the standpoint of dramatic form as well as from the standpoint of the very tight ordering of the argument. Think of the *Symposium*, a literary as well as philosophical masterpiece, but also of the *Protagoras*, the *Phaedrus*, the *Crito*, the *Gorgias*, the *Euthydemus*, and the first book of the *Republic*. And there are dialogues like the *Theaetetus* or the *Parmenides* that are absolutely perfect, whose plan is crystalline in its hardness and transparency, and in which the exposition of doctrine is admirably mastered, with regiments of argumentation that march to the assault in totally ordered fashion, following a perfect battle plan.

On the other hand, what we have to keep in sight is that Plato—as much, indeed, as Aristotle and Thucydides—doesn't worry, when he's writing prose, about considerations of form and composition the way the Moderns do, especially after Rousseau and especially after Kant. Plato, Aristotle, and Thucydides follow their own thought and allow themselves to go into incidental points and to make digressions. The way we let ourselves go when we find ourselves in a fecund moment: we're writing, other thoughts come, and we want at any price to record them, it mattering little whether or not they lie along the central axis of what we are expounding.

And this is tied up with the more general problem of form in written work. What was the case in Greece from this standpoint? Of course, one had a perfect and strict form from the outset in poetry, in epic poetry as well as in lyric poetry. And obviously in tragedy, too: no more "forceful" form could be imagined—in the sense that one talks about the *force* of a work of art—than the form of a tragedy. But things are different with prose. And this is clear in Herodotus, who, as I told you last year {in the seminar}, can't resist the pleasure of telling a good story, even in the middle of a "serious" bit of narration. As for Thucydides, he weaves his story from general reflections, either in the form of pure digressions of his own invention [*de son cru*] or in the form of speeches attributed to characters who participate in the action.

But even taking account of that—taking account of the fact that the Ancients weren't writing essays for teacher recruitment exams [*dissertations d'agrégation*], with the risk that a grader might note "off the subject" in the margin—the composition of the *Statesman* remains very bizarre. This is so above all because the two definitions at issue—that of the statesman as pastor, then as weaver—aren't concerned about what is essential to the dialogue. And here, there's the precedent of the *Sophist*, where one starts off by defining a whole series of activities that deal only in a secondary way with the Sophist; but in this *Sophist*, it can be said that Plato's interest in his subject, the Sophist, is relatively secondary, whereas it would be wrong to say the same thing in the case of the *Statesman*. Who could maintain that the *politikos*—as royal man, as political man— or the political—as field—doesn't interest Plato as such?[3] We know very well that he wrote on this topic upon several occasions!

Now, there's one way of approaching the *Statesman* that perhaps renders the strangeness of its composition less opaque. And it's that the considerations expressed in the two major digressions aren't secondary but constitute, rather, the substance of the dialogue.

Thus, the first digression, which introduces the myth of Cronus, as I told you a few weeks ago, has a quite strategic importance, not only in the *Statesman* itself but in Plato's political and philosophical oeuvre. For, it's with this myth that Plato builds up what could be called his political-philosophical strategic reserves, with the idea of a divine pastor and also of a terrestrial world that, abandoned by the god, is doomed to decay and corruption. Set in the middle of the *Statesman*, this myth of the age of Cronus, and therefore of a present era that is no longer the age of Cronus but the age of Zeus, gives, for he who believes in this myth or who wants to let himself be impressed by it, all the strategic depth—as one talks about a territory's defensive depth—necessary for the rest of what Plato is advancing to seem as if it has been defended with sufficient force.

And likewise it may be thought that introducing the third digression was also one of the dialogue's objectives. For, it was necessary for Plato to introduce this critique of the law that comes here to intensify, to give resonance and bring reinforcement to, his whole critique of written speech as opposed to living speech. And it was also necessary for him to ratify in advance, if I may say so, the rights of a royal man who might suddenly appear and who would therefore be, due to this very fact, like the doctor who comes home from a trip and who can tear up the orders he has left and write another set or say in person and out loud [*de vive voix*] what the patient is or is not to do.

It is also in view of this digression that one is to understand the introduction of the image—later to be abandoned—of the pastor and of the paradigm of the weaver. That paradigm, as I have already said to you, introduces other aporias and paradoxes relative to the question of what ultimately this much talked-about weaver weaves together and from what, what his raw material is.

So, finally, it's from this point of view that one must see, I believe, the strange features in the composition of the *Statesman*. We have here a construction that is baroque, though willed as such, done in a concerted way, conscious. For, even if the way the dialogue unfolds isn't subjected at every moment to strict logical control (by which I mean, formal control), the publication of the dialogue—the fact that Plato accepted this manuscript as his own, without which we wouldn't have it; it wouldn't have been handed down to us—is well and truly a conscious, deliberate, responsible act, as one would say today. Therefore, everything happens as if, in leaving this dialogue in the state it is in, Plato had wanted as a matter of fact to furnish a written example of living thought—as if he had wanted to give us *grammata* that show how the mind, thought, *logos* functions when it is left to itself and when it doesn't worry about problems of formal presentation or outward comprehension. It's as if he were saying to us: Here's how this works when it works; here's how one thinks.

The Statesman is a dialogue that can be criticized—I have done so amply during this discussion—but it must also be seen as being, to my knowledge, one of the closest specimens we possess of the genuine course of an important thought, of a great thought, of an authentic thought when it operates without caring about criticisms, examiners, formalists, the grammarians of Alexandria or the French academicians, and so on. It operates like that; it unfolds, it goes off on tangents, and then it recovers its balance [*se récupère*] as it can. We may recall the remark of André Gide's about the difference between talent and genius: "When one has some talent, one does what one wants; when one has some genius, one does what one can." And it's true that Plato, in this dialogue, does what he can. And he can let himself go off expounding a course of thought just like that without having to correct it. He makes us see in this way some of the most profound aspects of the labor of thought—aspects that we also find again, for example, but in an entirely different fashion, in the *Timaeus*, when, right in the middle, the dialogue is again interrupted there by the sudden discovery that it has started off on the wrong foot and that everything must be started over from the beginning. The same thing happens again in the *Theaetetus*, with consecutive resumptions, and in the *Laws*, although this last text raises other questions. Aristotle, too, was in the habit of making these sorts of digressions, which head off in a certain direction that seems important to him at the moment he's writing something, but he did so in a much more moderate way, and never with the intensity we encounter in the *Statesman*.

I don't want to make superficial and facile parallels, but I'd like you to understand what I mean: here we have something that offers a bit of an analogy with dreams. There is a sort of latent content in the *Statesman*, which isn't singular [*unique*]; it's multiple. And it's no more singular, whatever Freud might sometimes say about it, than it is in a dream. What uniqueness [*unicité*] there is in a dream is much more the result of the working out of secondary features [*élaborations secondaires*], because the latent content itself tends to go off in all directions—as Freud knew perfectly well. And that is more or less always the case each time the creative imagination is truly laboring, even when it's the theoretical imagination as grasped by us before formal constraints come to impose themselves upon it in a certain fashion from the outside—when, therefore, this imagination labors, creates, solely with the aid of formal constraints it has already incorporated into itself, for example, the fact that it can speak, that it is not reduced to mumblings but, rather, articulates something.

And I believe that we have here something that is analogous to what can be called the latent content that is at the start of all music, which perhaps initially includes only a rhythm and an intensity coupled with another latent content that is melodic, all of that being subject from the outset to a first-order secondary elaboration [*une première élaboration secondaire*], that of expression; then, next, to a second-order secondary elaboration, that of genuine fixation, that is to say, of formulation or composition.[4] It is this second-order elaboration that might have been able to come to "correct" the *Statesman*: one can imagine Plato or someone else going back over the dialogue in order to give it that formal outward coherence it doesn't have at present. But that wasn't done. As such, nevertheless, I'll say that reading the *Statesman*—and it is for this reason, too, that I have been lingering over it—is a bit like listening to Chopin improvise one of his *Nocturnes*, one of his *Ballades*, before having written it down. Contrary to some wrongly widespread ideas, the works of Chopin are written out to a great extent; they aren't pure improvisations. He went back over them, constructed a very rigorous, very large architecture. But we also know that he was a great improviser. And it's that difference that I am trying to mark; and it's that difference the *Statesman* gives us.

I am going to stop on this point, on this theme of the authentic presentation of works of thought, and invite you, too, to discuss all these theoretical contents that we have seen deployed through it and that will justify, in your view as well as mine, the fact that we have devoted all these seminars to this dialogue. It has, at the same time, allowed us to see an example of what is called—more or less abusively—"reading" a philosophical work. But I mean really reading it, by respecting it yet without respecting it, by going into the recesses and details without having decided in advance that everything it contains is coherent, homogeneous, makes sense, and is true.

Questions
1. *On the royal man, the providential man, and his modern avatars . . .*

You cite {the Socialist politician} Michel Rocard and the mystery of his popularity. But I myself have alluded to cases that are, if I may say so, much more worthy of hanging: Hitler, Mussolini, or whoever you want. What's going on? Suddenly, someone appears who embodies the answer to all problems. Perhaps he doesn't embody it for the majority of the population, but for a enough of a segment for him to be imposed by violent means upon the others. This is the way, moreover, that Aristotle, always very pragmatic, analyzed the appearance of tyrants. The cities were in a moment of crisis, of decomposition of the dominant oligarchy—of *stasis*, of a halt to the normal functioning of the city. And the person who knew how to seduce the people imposed himself. Pisistratus at Athens, for example. But there are plenty of examples elsewhere.

One can also think of Bonaparte for the France of 1798–1800. He knew how to do it: from Egypt, he organized his propaganda machine in order to make the French believe that he was this exceptional man, this great general capable of bringing France out of the situation in which it found itself.

So, this is a recurrent figure in history, and Weber has himself insisted upon his charismatic, religious aspect. Take Mohammed. One can then value or not value this or that personage, consider him a monster or a savior, but the phenomenon exists. Likewise, there really exists a tendency, a predisposition of populations, to hope for a providential man who will relieve us of our responsibilities as citizens.

Moreover, you're talking to me about the role of the media, which, in the modern world, are, you say, insidiously imposing their choices. For my part, I would much more willingly tie the *epistēmē* of the Platonic royal man to certain modern pretensions to knowledge about society and history. I am thinking obviously of Marxist-Leninist parties: it isn't just by chance that Stalin got himself awarded the title of "coryphaeus of science" by his toadies. But one can just as well mention our alleged experts, whether or not they've been to a top public-management school like the École Nationale d'Administration [*énarques ou pas*]. Why do those people govern us? Because they "know." What do they know? Most of the time, nothing at all.

As for the media, and to remain within the Platonic vocabulary, I would file them under the heading: presentation of the simulacrum. The image instead of the truth. This is now something well established. I myself argued all that as early as 1959, in a text on modern capitalism:[5] a president of the Republic is sold to the population as one sells a tube of toothpaste. And it's truer than ever now in 1986. {Take the advertising man} Jacques Séguéla, with {his slogan for the 1981 presidential election campaign of} François Mitterrand, "the tranquil force." *Le Monde* offering serious commentary on the {TV political news-show appearances} of

Jacques Chirac and Laurent Fabius.[6] This is really the manipulation of images and nothing else. It's what comrade Guy Debord gallicized and plagiarized when talking about the "society of the spectacle."[7] And to come back to Rocard,[8] I believe that his popularity dates back to election night 1978. For the first time, French television viewers saw a politician who didn't say, "We lost but we won anyway," or else, "We lost because the others cheated," or "because it was raining," or something else like that. No, Rocard said: We lost, and it's our fault, and we have only ourselves to blame if we screwed up. That was unheard of! It was so strong, this against-the-current use of the media, that it won him the hatred of the Socialist Party and the Communist Party, and that was enough to keep him ahead in the polls for eight years.

And Reagan! His political maxim isn't, "Is it good or not?" but, rather, "Is it news or not?" It happens that I was in New York at the moment of the attack on Libya. And the thing had been prepared like a live television program. The attack took place in such a way that it was going to monopolize the evening news. All the networks talked about nothing but that. A half hour later, Larry Speaks, the White House spokesman, came on. And at nine o'clock, the culmination: Reagan addressed the American nation. "From now on, the world will know that you can't walk over us." And the polls, to top it all off: Did you like it? Five to one, the Americans approved of the attack. Or liked the program; it's about the same thing.

That said, I shall never let contemporary society off the hook by saying that it's getting raped by the media. It's getting raped because it really wants to get raped. The same thing goes for French readers who let themselves be abused and stupified by the "new philosophers."[9] They have the authors they deserve. From this standpoint, the role of the media isn't decisive: if there's manipulation, that's because there's "manipulability."

2. On the equivalence, the identity, between, on the one hand, the gap separating the laws from daily reality and, on the other, the difficult participation of things in the Ideas—as the Parmenides *treats this issue, for example.*

Quite right. And Plato's great merit is to have raised this problem as early as the *Parmenides*. Without giving an answer, I might add. And later this was Aristotle's principal war-horse against Plato. What is the relationship between the singular *anthrōpos* and the Idea of *anthrōpos*? Plato says: It participates in the Idea. And Aristotle replies: But what does that mean, *participate*? It's a metaphor. Whence the "third man" argument.

And this problem of the singular being [*l'étant singulier*] and the universal is still with us. The nominalist solution doesn't hold up for long. One can, of course, decide by convention to call "dogs" all mammals that have such and such characteristics. But it happens, as Aristotle already said, that a dog and a bitch make puppies, not pelicans. Now that doesn't depend upon the conventions of language. Therefore, there is something like a "canitude." What the biologists say about it is that it's in the genes, and in any case it goes beyond [*dépasse*] the conventions of language.

And the problem of singular/universal relationships hasn't made any headway toward a solution. I believe that in the abstract not much more can be said. I'd like to add only that this relationship between the instances of a concept and the concept differs according to the regions of being [*les régions de l'être*] under consideration. This is to say that the relationship of a dog with the notion of dog is not the same as the relationship of the entity "twentieth-century French society" or "fifteenth-century Florentine society" with the notion of society. Each time, the domain of being in which we find ourselves must be explored, as well as the relation that, within this domain of being, unites the universal to the singular.

Moreover, in the *Statesman*, this Platonic preoccupation with participation is coupled with another question I have already insisted upon a great deal: the distance between the dead letter and the living spirit. That is also one of the themes of the *Phaedrus*: the superiority of living dialogue over the written, which fixes thought in place and forbids dialogue.

Translator's Afterword

"Great minds think alike"—or so the saying goes. Often this adage is said in jest or to compliment both speaker and interlocutor who have fallen into agreement. Behind humor or mutual flattery, however, lies the idea that if a mind is great, it would (could, should) think *the same thing* as another great mind. As Pierre Vidal-Naquet points out in his Foreword, another Plato commentator, Leo Strauss, "followed the text quite closely—to the point of modeling himself upon it"; in that case, he explains, "the result is a constant justification of the most minor details of the argument." And this, despite the fact that Strauss, one of the principal proponents of the "great books" school of learning—"Liberal education consists in listening to the conversation among the greatest minds"— confessed that these "great minds" often disagree with one another, thus placing us poor Moderns in a situation of "overwhelming difficulty."[1] An impossible nostalgia for a consensual "meeting of the [great] minds" that, despite their "conversation," never occurred would therefore seem to rule Strauss's mind and to direct him toward mimetic "modeling," as well as "constant justification."

One would be hard pressed to find a more adamant—and fecund— refutation of the view that "great minds think alike" than the dissident writings and speeches of Cornelius Castoriadis. Castoriadis regarded Plato as by far the "greatest philosopher who ever existed" (*CR*, p. 372). But as he already said in 1981, "to honor a thinker is not to praise, or even to interpret, but to discuss his work, thereby keeping it alive and demonstrating that it defies time and retains relevance."[2] Speaking earlier, in 1974, of Marx's as "a great work," Castoriadis called not only for discussion but deep interrogations: "It is ambiguous. It is also contradictory: there are different strata. An immense labor is required to begin to make something out of it—that is to say, to find therein especially some questions" (*CR*, p. 25). Later, when taking a more general view in his 1989 "critical/political reflection upon our history," he related that view back to relevant reading of great philosophy:

> To reflect upon historical eras and processes critically . . . is to strive to find therein some germs of importance to us, as well as also limits and failures which, to begin with, put a halt to our thinking since they had served within reality itself as actual stopping blocks. (This is also the way one reads—or, rather, the way one ought to read—a great philosophical text, if one wants to make something of it for oneself.) It is certainly not to look in them for models, or for foils. Nor is it to look in them for lessons. (*WIF*, p. 73)

A great work of philosophy can, moreover, be greatly mistaken, Kant's assertion that he "could furnish the 'conditions of possibility for experience' by looking *uniquely* at the 'subject'" being "one of the most astonishing absurdities ever registered in the history of great thought" (*WIF*, p. 345).

Yet we are not offhandedly to dismiss a great thinker for his great mistakes any more than we should simply learn "lessons" therefrom. Castoriadis intensely reflected upon the reception of great works—which, he informs us, "is never and can never be a matter of mere passive acceptance; it is always also re-creation" (*CR*, p. 346). Indeed, these works invite us to think through their immense absurdities, flagrant errors, and bald contradictions so that we may think further ourselves, just as these thinkers have done—although without always knowing or acknowledging it. It is worthwhile quoting him at length on this matter to see how he conceives this process of reception (*IIS*, p. 174):

> It is not these conceptions, as such, that truly matter, nor their critique, and even less the critique of their authors. With important authors, conceptions are never pure; the application of such conceptions in contact with the material these authors are attempting to think reveals something other than what they explicitly think, and the results are infinitely richer than their programmatic theses. A great author, by definition, thinks beyond his means. He is great to the extent that he thinks something other than what has already been thought, and his means are the result of what has already been thought, which continually encroaches on what he does think, if only because he cannot wipe away all that he has received and place himself before a tabula rasa,

even when he is under the illusion that he can. The contradictions that are always present in a great author bear witness to this fact; I am speaking of true, raw, irreducible contradictions, which it is just as stupid to think cancel by themselves the author's contribution as it is useless to try to dissolve or to recuperate at successive and ever deeper levels of interpretation.

Those familiar with Castoriadis's thought know his thesis that, just as politics challenges instituted ways of being and doing in society, "the truth of philosophy is the rupture of closure, the shaking of received self-evident truths, including and especially philosophical ones" (*CR*, p. 371). Its characteristically radical creativity is that "it is this movement, but it is a movement that creates the soil upon which it walks." In being determinative rather than determined in advance—even in the case of "the whole of Greco-Western philosophy," whose soil "is the soil of *determinacy*"— such creation must always also determine itself as something particular: "This soil is not and cannot be just anything—it defines, delimits, forms, and constrains." Thus,

> the defining characteristic of a great philosophy is what allows it to go beyond its own soil—what incites it, even, to go beyond. As it tends to—and has to—take responsibility for the totality of the thinkable, it tends to close upon itself. If it is great, one will find in it at least some signs that the movement of thought cannot stop there and even some part of the means to continue this movement. Both these signs and these means take the form of aporias, antinomies, frank contradictions, heterogeneous chunks. (ibid.)

The present seminars offer us an exemplary instance of this pragmatic, pertinent, and discriminating approach to thinking and reading through great works. Castoriadis himself concludes his seminar of April 30, 1986: "I mean really reading it, by respecting it yet without respecting it, by going into the recesses and details without having decided in advance that everything it contains is coherent, homogeneous, makes sense, and is true." His respected and disrespected adversary here is Plato, the great philosophical opponent of Athenian democracy—which, Plato himself claimed, "can never do anything great" (*Statesman* 303a). Castoriadis, we know, saw the capacity for human greatness not only in isolated individuals but especially in collective democratic endeavors that may foster rather than stifle creativity.[3]

∼

Castoriadis examines the "quirky," "bizarre" structure of Plato's *States-man*, situating it historically in a key position between the *Republic* and the *Laws*. But what is to be said of this series of transcribed seminars? While not aberrant in structure, they are indeed curious. Like the *States-man's* many digressions and incidental points, they do have their excur-suses (e.g., on Chomsky and Chopin). And like the *Statesman*, they hover between the written and the spoken—but not, as Castoriadis says of that dialogue, in the same deliberate, *signed* way.

To form an idea of where, within Castoriadis's overall oeuvre, to situate these transcribed talks, let us start with his own humorous response that he didn't know that he had written a new book. Not only that, but Cas-toriadis never wrote a book all the way through. The eight-volume Édi-tions 10/18 series (excerpted translations in *PSW1-3* and *CR*) reprinted ar-ticles from his revolutionary journal, *Socialisme ou Barbarie* (*S. ou B.*), along with new introductory pieces. The six-volume *Carrefours du labyrinthe* series (excerpted translations so far in *CL*, *PPA*, *CR*, and *WIF*) reprinted separate articles and interviews, as well as including previously unpublished material. Even what we call his magnum opus, *The Imagi-nary Institution of Society*, isn't a conventional book but four chapters added on to a five-part *S. ou B.* series. With the exception of one other transcription—his 1980 *De l'écologie à l'autonomie* public talk along with Daniel Cohn-Bendit, which now appears in *CR*—these seminars in fact constitute the first book-length Castoriadis volume published at one time on a single theme. (The first part of his pseudonymous contribution to *Mai 68: La brèche*, coauthored with Claude Lefort and Edgar Morin and now in *PSW3* with a twenty-year retrospective in *WIF*, was first distrib-uted to protestors as a mimeographed pamphlet during "the events" themselves; *Devant la guerre*, his 1981 analysis of Russia as a "stratocracy," began as a 1980 magazine article.)

Castoriadis thus was an ever-engaged and evolving writer and speaker, "striving to find some germs of importance to us," rather than an author of weighty or slight tomes on, say, madness and civilization, capitalism and schizophrenia, or, perhaps, postcards. His speeches became moder-ate-length published essays, his essays became public talks and interviews, worked and reworked throughout his life. A good example is the se-quence starting out as a 1965 lecture for British comrades printed as a London Solidarity pamphlet, "The Crisis of Modern Society" (*PSW3*), reappearing as an updated 1979 French-Canadian journal article, "Social

Transformation and Cultural Creation" (*PSW3*), and adapted for a 1987 American audience as "The Crisis of Culture and the State" (*PPA*).[4]

Castoriadis also wrote in 1979 "Socialism and Autonomous Society" (*SAS* in *PSW3*), an introductory essay to the 10/18 volume on the content of socialism in which he formally abandoned the much-abused term *socialism* in favor of *the autonomous society*. Similarities to *On Plato's "Statesman"* establish that *SAS* is indeed a precursor text for the Plato seminars.

First, Castoriadis's only substantial prior discussion of the *Statesman* appeared in *SAS*.[5] There, Castoriadis examined Plato's idea of the law acting as an "arrogant and ignorant man" and stressed that a power "unbound by law . . . cannot purely and simply be dismissed out of hand," for this "discussion of law in the *Statesman* cannot be underestimated either in its profundity or as to its relevance today" (*SAS*, p. 329). As in the March 26 seminar, he attacked communist dictatorship, linking Marx back to Plato while affirming the necessity of rules and institutions (ibid., pp. 328–30). There is, however, not only the rule but a distance from the rule, an "ineffaceable *gap* which opens [society] to its proper question, the question of justice" (ibid., p. 329), an "essential gap between the rule and the concrete case [which] isn't absolute" (April 23). At the end of the last seminar, he drags out, against its manifest intention, the "consequence of the Platonic text": "it's the permanent democratic self-institution of society," just as, in *SAS*, he draws therefrom his conclusion about "a society . . . constantly in the movement of explicit self-institution" (*SAS*, p. 329). We can, in this way, even supply one last unattributed reference: it was Edward Bellamy (ibid., p. 317; Castoriadis adding, "I think") who gave the Platonic "critique of the law . . . a socialist form: The law, for example, just as strictly forbids rich people from sleeping under bridges as it does poor people" (March 26).[6]

We nevertheless must trace these roots even deeper. The key texts in the volume *SAS* introduced were the first two parts of "On the Content of Socialism" (*CSI* and *CSII*, now in *PSW1* and 2). Following preliminary remarks, Castoriadis deliberately began his classic 1957 text on council-based workers' management with a "positive definition of socialism": "The very content of our ideas leads us to maintain that, ultimately, one cannot understand anything about the profound meaning of capitalism and the crisis it is undergoing unless one begins with the most total idea of socialism" (*CSII*, p. 92). Similarly, after opening remarks on the *Statesman*, he explains: "I offer here and now these anticipations . . . because, if we don't have in sight this central kernel of the dialogue—the positions developed there and the problematic to which they give birth—we cannot understand the genuine stakes that are there during the discussion of the two [statesman] definitions" (February 26). These seminar "anticipations" concern "self-government at all echelons" as well as "a radical and entirely justified condemnation of every utopia" (*CSII* being based upon projections from actual experiences of the workers' movement and also resolutely opposed to "a backward-looking type of utopian thinking" [p. 101]).[7]

~

Now, there is a tendency to contrast an early, "political" or "revolutionary" Castoriadis to a later one, described variously as "intellectual," "academic," a "philosopher," and so on—as if these two sets of terms must always be mutually and totally exclusive.[8] To see that such a dichotomous temporal division of Castoriadis's oeuvre doesn't hold, let's examine how a number of apparent anomalies in *On Plato's "Statesman"* can be illuminated by reading these seminars in light of what I call its precursor texts.

First, a minor point concerning an error in Diès's translation that stole into the transcribed text. Here is the restored passage for *Statesman* 292e, one of Young Socrates' most significant responses to the Stranger from Elea, the former uttering more than his usual few words of agreement yet still reinforcing the latter's idea of the statesman as single "royal man":

> STRANGER: But in a city of a thousand citizens, would it be possible that a hundred or even fifty citizens might possess this [political] science?
> YOUNG SOCRATES: By this count, statesmanship would be the easiest of all the arts. Out of a thousand citizens, it would already be quite difficult to find fifty or a hundred who knew how to play checkers well. So, for this art that is the most difficult of all, if there were one citizen to possess it, that would already be miraculous!

Intriguingly, Castoriadis, who knew the difference between the correct "a thousand" (*chilioi*) and Diès's incorrect "ten thousand" (*murias*) perfectly well and noted the mistake in his copy, may also have had this specific passage in mind back in 1957 when he spoke about the deep-seated irrationality, contradictions, wastefulness, and perpetual conflict of "the capitalist organization of society [which] denies people's capacity for self-organization": "If a thousand individuals have among them a given capacity for self-organization, capitalism consists in more or less arbitrarily choosing fifty of these individuals, vesting them with managerial authority and deciding that the others should just be cogs" (p. 93). Not only "a thousand" but "fifty" appears in both passages![9]

Is this numerical comparison between *Statesman* 292e and *CSII* farfetched? Castoriadis had already alluded two years earlier to the *Statesman*'s likening of the law to "an ignorant and crude man," concluding that "a socialist solution can only be socialist if it is a concrete solution that involves the permanent participation of the organized unit of workers in determining this solution" (*CSI*, p. 300). He was thus already working through the *Statesman*, its ambiguous critique of law, and its determined denial of the self-organizational capacities of (finite, specific) people when he composed his landmark mid-1950s texts on the content of socialism.[10] The idea that Castoriadis was once an engaged political activist who later became an academic philosopher enthralled by Greece therefore cannot withstand sustained scrutiny of continuities and developments in his thought.

Were one nevertheless disposed to contrast an early, "councilist" Castoriadis to a later "academic philosopher" merely commenting on Plato, many of these seminars' intricacies would defy comprehension. When, for example, Castoriadis states (April 30) that Plato presents the Athenian democracy "as if it were a regime that arbitrarily decides upon what is good or bad in medicine," one might surmise that he is also abandoning the absolutist "all power to the councils" position one imagines he formerly championed. In fact, an advocacy of the "dictatorship of the proletariat," already attenuated in *CSII*, was mercilessly criticized in *SAS* (p. 326): "the present-day partisans of the 'dictatorship of the proletariat' should have the courage to explain that they are, in principle, for the abolition of the political rights of farmers, craftsman, massage therapists working at home, and so on; also, that the publication of medical, literary, and other such journals should depend on ad hoc authorizations granted by 'the workers.'" *CSII* argued that a radical system of councils requires not only extensive decentralization but also central decision-making—a thoughtful, sober position, upsetting to many anarchists and liberals. His central socialist goal, however, was to foster a set of institutions that would allow for a *self-integrated articulation* of participatory democratic rule at all levels under modern conditions (*CSII*, p. 99), not aggregation around the center or disaggregation at the "margins." (It is, rather, in a totalitarian society that, for example, scientific issues—e.g.,

Lysenkoism—are transformed systematically into objects of governmental decree.) Castoriadis's insistence in these seminars upon the relative autonomy of workers in various technical fields is thus consonant with earlier remarks and in fact extends and refines them.

In this last seminar, Castoriadis judges Plato's argument "utterly inadmissible and dishonest, because as a matter of fact at Athens the city does not decide the problems, the questions, the subjects on which there is a technical knowledge of some sort." Again, some may be tempted to think that a now mellowed Castoriadis is attempting to remove certain issues from the purview of direct-democratic organs, whereas before he would have favored such solutions. But the relevant issue here refers directly back to *CSII*'s distinction between *technique* and *technology*: technology is the societal choice—among "a 'spectrum' of techniques available at a given point in time"—of "a given group (or 'band') of processes," for example, capitalist technology's selection of techniques that seek to *exclude* workers from the management of their own work so as to "fit in with capitalism's basic need to deal with labor power as a measurable, supervisable, and interchangeable commodity" (p. 104). Not just the use but the choice and orientation of a technology is a *political* question of the first magnitude, whereas technical questions are not to be settled in "democratic-centralist" fashion (though demarcations between "the political" and "the technical" themselves remain ever-open political questions). The whole discussion of Greek *technē* in these seminars and elsewhere must be read in light of *CSII*'s key distinction.

Castoriadis explains that "the city decides upon laws in general or decides upon governmental acts," adding, "but there are no laws concerning government as activity . . . there were no instructions given concerning government as activity. The activity of the *dēmos* concerns points that are absolutely not technical in nature" (April 30). This particular explanation might appear merely empirical, a nostalgic appeal to the practices of his beloved Athens, as if he had become enamored of ancient Greece at the expense of the practices of workers' management. But in fact he had already brought out the same point when generalizing from the 1956 Hungarian Revolution's creation of councils, *even within governmental departments*, as a way for workers' to manage their own affairs democratically (*CSII*, p. 151).

During the previous seminar, Castoriadis mocked one French military-industrial-complex leader's caricature of self-management (*autogestion*),

paraphrasing him thus: "They want the hospital's cleaning ladies to operate on us! And it's these general assemblies of surgeons, nurses, the
cashier, the social worker, and the women who wash the floors that will
decide by vote whether the patient has an appendicitis rather than bronchitis!" But does this mean that Castoriadis was abandoning the idea of
sovereign decision-making councils and general assemblies? Certainly
not. The same year, he praised the May '68 student-worker rebellion in
France for its "sit-ins and teach-ins of all sorts, in which professors and
students, schoolteachers and pupils, and doctors, nurses and hospital
staff, workers, engineers, foremen, business and administrative staff spent
whole days and nights discussing their work, their mutual relations, the
possibility of transforming the organization and the aims of their firms"
(*WIF*, p. 48). Again, *CSII*'s distinction between technical and political
matters and its idea of an articulated set of institutions capable of self-
governance (and thus self-limitation) at all levels are of prime importance
for understanding the direction of his thought and the tenor of his voice.

In the aftermath of May '68 (whose premises he and his revolutionary
group were so instrumental in preparing) and with the generalization and
popularization of *S. ou B.*'s theses and ideas on workers' management, *autogestion* became a slogan on the French Left.[11] To the extent that this slogan entailed mitigations of those theses and ideas, he expressed reticence:

> The domination of a particular group over society could not be abolished
> without abolishing the domination of particular groups over the production
> and work process. . . . [T]he only conceivable mode of organization for pro-
> duction and work is *collective management* by all those who participate, as I
> have not ceased to argue since 1947. Later on, this was called "self-manage-
> ment"—usually in order to make of it a reformist cosmetic for the existing
> state of affairs or a "testing ground" while carefully remaining quiet about
> [its] colossal implications, upstream and downstream. (*SAS*, p. 320)

Thus when he spoke (April 23) about what the late Marcel Dassault would
have said fifteen years earlier about *autogestion*, he not only wasn't abandoning principles and practices behind *autogestion* but defending them,
rather, against their post-'68 reformist watering-down, as well as against
the conservative caricatures formulated in reaction to such bastardizations.

One irony is worth mentioning here. In *CSII*, Castoriadis still spoke
ambiguously about *representative democracy*. Citing advances in the "technique of communication" well before the advent of the Internet, he

ridiculed the claim "that the very size of modern societies precludes the exercise of any genuine democracy. Distances and numbers allegedly render direct democracy impossible. The only feasible democracy, it is claimed, is representative democracy, which 'inevitably' contains a kernel of political alienation, namely, the separation of representatives from those they represent" (*CS II*, p. 144). This argument is quite familiar to readers of the "later" Castoriadis. Yet he also allowed in 1957 that "there are several ways of envisaging and achieving representative democracy. A legislature is one form. Councils are another, and it is difficult to see how political alienation could arise in a council system operating according to its own rules. If modern techniques of communication were put in the service of democracy, the areas where representative democracy would remain necessary would narrow considerably" (ibid.). Clearly, the relevant issue here is not labels but the existence or nonexistence of "political alienation." Later in life, however, Castoriadis condemned "representative democracy" *even more clearly, radically, and adamantly*, stressing its "opposition" (*WIF*, p. 75) to direct democracy—an opposition he terms "immediate and obvious" (ibid., p. 89)—while championing the latter (and allowing for delegation by lot, rotation, or revocable election, not "representation," in cases where on-the-spot participation isn't feasible).

Upon close examination of precursor texts, we see how these Plato seminars continue to explore the "colossal implications" of popular management of the economy and of society as a whole—what Castoriadis (*CR*, p. 30) came to call "no longer simply collective management ('self-management') but the *permanent and explicit self-institution of society*; that is to say, a state in which the collectivity knows that its institutions are its own creation and has become capable of regarding them as such, of taking them up again and transforming them." Each Wednesday from 11 A.M. to 1 P.M. during the French academic year, Castoriadis's seminar brought together an impressive number of people—50 to 100—at the École des Hautes Études en Sciences Sociales.[12] Participants included not only students, whose studies he conscientiously directed, but also a wide variety of persons of all ages: academics and anarchists, ex-Trotskyists and former members of S. ou B., as well as many others interested in his work and the topics he was discussing. Thus, as subsequent planned volumes will also show, the seminars allowed him to try out his evolving ideas on a large, diverse, critical, and attentive audience.[13]

Audiotapings as well as transcribings of seminars by Castoriadis and other participants commenced early on. Transcriptions began to circulate informally. Starting in 1991, Agora International, a group dedicated to fostering the project of autonomy as elucidated by Castoriadis, made photocopied transcriptions available to all at cost.[14] Castoriadis's only proviso was that circulation of unpublished work remain limited to interested parties and not itself become a form of publication: he had already seen his ideas plagiarized and debased too many times,[15] he said, and he didn't want unfinished work turned into someone else's fashionable book.[16]

In previous presentations, I've experimented with the form of the translator's foreword. In light of Castoriadis's praise for Thucydides', Plato's, and Aristotle's tendency to follow their own thought wherever it leads them, it certainly would be tempting to emulate here that particular aspect of the text through extended improvisation, riffing on the seminars' motifs. Let me instead simply express my satisfaction at seeing in print Castoriadis's own thoughts on improvisation, "jam sessions," Chopin as a "great improviser," and so on, in relation to the *Statesman*, its errant structure, and its "turbulences," which land us "smack dab in the chaos." From my very first translator's foreword (*PSW1*), I have been underscoring this jazz theme of improvisatory creation as a basic feature of Castoriadis's elucidation of the project of autonomy.[17]

It is with regard to Barthes and structuralism that Castoriadis decried an "inability to see that the social being of man implies at once a rule and a distance from the rule" (April 23). Similarly, in response to a questioner, he responded the following week that "Plato doesn't see the problem of the institution—and neither does Derrida, indeed, in *Speech and Phenomena*. He doesn't see the relationship of the play between subjectivity and its works." It is neither that all language is "fascist" (Barthes utilizing precisely language to make this dubious claim) nor that we are ensnared in logo-, phono-, or whatever-centrism. Our inherited philosophy—with its tendency, even among those who make the most conspicuous denunciations thereof, to maintain subject-object dualisms—has yet to assimilate Castoriadis's original contribution concerning the imaginary institution of society, as well as its political, social, philosophical, psychoanalytical, and other implications. The project of autonomy isn't an exclusive autonomization of the written or an alleged absoluteness of the oral but the capacity to adopt *another relation* to our works, and to ourselves. One's ca-

pacity for improvisation—like that of societies fostering such creativity—
is no more exclusively subjective than it is fully objective; it is historical,
always tentative, and ever to be renewed.

There is in the end perhaps something apt as well as evocative in the
unfinished nature of Castoriadis's oeuvre. Castoriadis envisioned two
great multivolume works, *L'Élément imaginaire* (The Imaginary Element)
and *La Création humaine* (Human Creation). As a series of 1986 notes explained (*WIF*, pp. 213, 416 n. 4, 428 n. 6), *L'Élément imaginaire* was to be
a written work on the imagination. The same year (ibid., p. 413 n. 1) he
spoke about *La Création humaine*, which was to be based upon his seminars. As it turns out, even this separation between the written and reworked oral presentations couldn't be maintained. He eventually folded
both tomes into one huge Human Creation project. It was never published. The present seminars form the first published part of that unfinished work.

Ultimately, it's up to us to continue this unfinished project of autonomy and to find "some germs of importance to us," speaking, writing,
reading, and acting today with our fellow human beings on and around
this planet. The possibility of human greatness is not to be reserved for a
few but is open to all engaged in dialogue with great works who dare to
think differently, more deeply, further than what has been thought so far,
as Castoriadis did in relation to Plato—and as we may in turn do in relation to him by relevantly discussing his work. Not to "discover," beneath
some "new" interpretation, the merits of representative democracy, to be
sure, nor by blithely opposing "earlier" and "later" Castoriadises. More
than ever, we are "incited to go beyond" what his unfinished work and his
times were able to think; to think through, in this new millennium he
never reached, the issues he raised and the ideas he formulated; to broach
a "re-creative" reception of his work; to foster the greatness of the democratic project of individual and collective autonomy he helped advance.
Merely assenting to his propositions would make him *monumental*, not
great. It is in unearthing and sifting through Castoriadis's "aporias, antinomies, frank contradictions, heterogeneous chunks" as well as in smash-
ing "actual stopping blocks within reality itself" that we can lay down
new foundations upon soil we shall create, raise new edifices thereupon,
and, perhaps, discover in him one of the great thinkers of the past two
and a half millennia.[18]

Reference Matter

Notes

N.B.: The abbreviations of titles of books by Cornelius Castoriadis used in the notes are listed preceding the Foreword by Pierre Vidal-Naquet.

Foreword: Castoriadis and the Statesman, by Pierre Vidal Naquet

1. On the "Cercle Saint-Just," which became the "Centre de Recherches et d'Études Sociales et Politiques" (CRESP), see pp. 19–20 of Vidal-Naquet's "Souvenirs à bâtons rompus sur Castoriadis et *Socialisme ou Barbarie*," *Revue Européenne des Sciences Sociales* 86 (December 1989), reprinted in *Autonomie et autotransformation de la société: La Philosophie militante de Cornelius Castoriadis*, ed. Giovanni Busino (Geneva: Droz, 1989), with the same pagination.—Trans.

2. Jean-Pierre Vernant, *Les Origines de la pensée grecque* (Paris: Presses universitaires de France, 1962), trans. as *The Origins of Greek Thought* (Ithaca, N.Y.: Cornell University Press, 1982).

3. François Châtelet, *La Naissance de l'histoire: La Formation de la pensée historienne en Grèce* (Paris: Minuit, 1962), new ed., 2 vols. (Paris: Seuil, 1996).

4. Pierre Lévêque and Pierre Vidal-Naquet, *Clisthène l'Athénien: Essai sur la représentation de l'espace et du temps dans la pensée politique grecque de la fin du VIe siècle à la mort de Platon* (Paris: Les Belles Lettres, 1964), trans. David Ames Curtis as *Cleisthenes the Athenian: An Essay on the Representation of Space and Time in Greek Political Thought from the End of the Sixth Century to the Death of Plato* (Atlantic Highlands, N.J.: Humanities Press, 1996).

5. Karl Popper's *The Open Society and Its Enemies* (2 vols., London: Routledge, 1945) was translated into French only in 1979.

6. Charles Maurras (1868–1952), a relentless polemicist who exercised a great influence over many intellectuals in France, was an author whose writings in-

spired the anti-Dreyfusard and royalist nationalism of the ultrareactionary group Action Française, of which he was a principal leader.—P.V.-N. / Trans.

7. In 2.41 of the Funeral Oration in Thucydides' *History of the Peloponnesian War*, Pericles calls Athens the "educator of Greece."—Trans.

8. Thucydides 2.63, 3.37.

9. Vidal-Naquet is referring to Castoriadis's discussion of this passage from Thucydides in *IIS*, p. 208.—Trans.

10. See Victor Goldschmidt, *Le Paradigme dans la dialectique platonicienne* (1947; reprint, Paris: Vrin, 1985).

11. See John Scheid and Jesper Svenbro, *The Craft of Zeus: Myths of Weaving and Fabric* (1994), trans. Carol Volk (Cambridge, Mass.: Harvard University Press, 1996), and, for the Homeric poems, Ioanna Papadopoulou-Belmehdi, *Le Chant de Pénélope* (Paris: Belin, 1994). [See also Jean-Pierre Vernant's "Weaving Friendship" (1995), trans. David Ames Curtis, *Salmagundi* 130–31 (Spring–Summer 2001): 75–87.—Trans.]

Introduction: "Living Thought at Work," by Pascal Vernay

1. The first volume of *Carrefours du labyrinthe* appeared as *CL*. Selections from volumes 4 and 5, mentioned here, appeared in *WIF* and *CR*. Additional texts from these two French volumes, as well as the entirety of the sixth, posthumous volume in this series, *Figures du pensable: Les carrefours du labyrinthe VI* (Paris: Seuil, 1999), are forthcoming in Stanford University Press volumes translated and edited by me. Prior *Carrefours* texts—selections from the second and third volumes—were previously translated as *PPA*.—Trans.

2. With the valuable aid of Stéphane Barbery, Olivier Fressard, and Nikos Iliopoulos in 1992, and then of Myrto Gondicas in 1998.

3. See now "The Greek and the Modern Political Imaginary" (1991), *WIF*, pp. 84–107.—Trans.

On the Translation

1. For an overview of the problems I've encountered and the solutions I've offered when translating the work of Cornelius Castoriadis, I refer the reader to "On the Translation" in WIF. See also the glossaries found in *PSW1*, app. B, and *PSW3*, app. G.

2. These include: Herodotus (February 19 seminar); the "much talked-about story of the lice in the *Parmenides*," Demosthenes exhorting Athenians, and Adam Smith speaking "of our poets" (February 26); Aristotle on *nous* and Nietzsche's phrase "The desert is growing" (March 5); Aristotle criticizing Plato for

"using poetic metaphors" (March 12; cf. March 5); "Mannheim" on Plato's "reactionary utopia," which I take to be an allusion to Karl Mannheim's *Ideology and Utopia* (April 23); Plato "waxing ironic in the *Philebus*," as well as André Gide talking about the difference between talent and genius and Aristotle saying that a dog and a bitch make puppies, not pelicans (April 30).

3. Paul Berman, "Waiting for the Barbarians," *New Republic*, December 21, 1998, p. 38.

4. Castoriadis explains his invention of *comitant* in "Discovery" (*WIF*, p. 216), referring the reader to *IIS*, p. 328 and p. 395, n. 22, and *CL*, pp. 322–24. For his explanation in the present volume, see the two parenthetical paragraphs immediately following its first appearance (February 19).

5. In "Time and Creation"'s English original (*WIF*, p. 391), Castoriadis refers in passing to "Plato's *Politicus* (a title wrongly rendered in the standard English usage as 'Statesman')."

6. See my discussion of Castoriadis and Lefort's usages of *le/la politique* in the Translator's Foreword to Claude Lefort's *Writing: The Political Test*, trans. David Ames Curtis (Durham, N.C.: Duke University Press, 2000), pp. x–xi.

Seminar of February 19, 1986

1. The Athenians took away his command of the military expedition against Sicily.—Pascal Vernay (P. V.)

2. M. I. Finley, *Ancient Sicily* (1968; rev. ed., London: Chatto & Windus, 1979), p. 92. From memory, Castoriadis says: "minorité entêtée des *scholars*." Only "dogged minority" (*minorité obstinée*, in the French translation) and not "scholars" appears in Finley. But Finley had contrasted "most modern historians" who "accept this saga" about Plato's three Sicilian voyages to "a dogged minority" that "continues to insist on the discrepancies and improbabilities, concluding that the saga is largely, perhaps wholly, fictitious (apart from the early, private visit by Plato in 387)" (ibid., pp. 92–93). Castoriadis shares Finley's skepticism and offers in his seminar talk a summary of the reasons Finley, too, cites for such skepticism. This added insistence here that he is not an academic "scholar" should be retained.—Trans.

3. This is an allusion to Finley, *Ancient Sicily*, pp. 92–93.—P. V.-N.

4. In France, philosophy is taught already at the high-school level.—Trans.

5. In *Cleisthenes the Athenian* (p. 189, n. 89), Vidal-Naquet and his coauthor Pierre Lévêque explain their adoption of *mia deuterōs*: "We retain here—as the context, moreover, demands—the text of manuscripts A and O. E. des Places . . . adopts Apelt's conjecture, τιμία. We owe this suggestion to M. H.

Margueritte (from his course at the École des Hautes Études, 1952–53)." See p. 93 of *Cleisthenes the Athenian*, where this reading is adopted.—Trans.

6. On ancient and modern conceptions of movement, see also Castoriadis's "*Phusis* and Autonomy" in *WIF*, pp. 334–35.—Trans.

Seminar of February 26, 1986

1. Following Castoriadis's classic distinction of directors (*dirigeants*) vs. executants (*exécutants*) in bureaucratic-capitalist society, someone in an "executive" position is defined, not as a person fulfilling a top managerial role, as one says today, but as a person carrying out orders formulated by others—and usually by having to contravene those directorial orders, since such orders are formulated from the outside and thus don't benefit from the executant's experience, which always goes beyond what that experience is defined as being. See *PSW1-3.*—Trans.

2. I have added, as per Castoriadis's usual practice, quotation marks around "Soviet." (Milan Kundera has quoted him as saying, "U.S.S.R.: four words, four lies.") Similarly, in the second sentence of the present paragraph in the text I have added, to this translation of the transcription, quotation marks around the adjective "socialist." In light of this discussion of national accounting procedures, it is also to be remembered that, before his retirement from the Organization for Economic Cooperation and Development in 1970, Castoriadis had been promoted director of the Branch of Statistics, National Accounts, and Growth Studies.—Trans.

3. French- and English-language translators and commentators give different, indeed opposite, titles to this lost work. Kathleen Freeman's *Ancilla to the Pre-Socratic Philosophers: A Complete Translation of the Fragments in Diels, Fragmente der Vorsokratiker* (Cambridge, Mass.: Harvard University Press, 1948; paperback ed., 1983), p. 127, states that "Gorgias . . . wrote one of the earliest Handbooks on Rhetoric; an essay *On Being* or *On Nature*; and a number of model orations. . . ." The content of what she calls here *On Being*, and which Castoriadis entitles *On Not-Being*, does indeed concern not-being. In Jean-Paul Dumont's *Les Présocratiques* (Paris: Gallimard/Pléiade, 1988), p. 1022, Gorgias's text is listed as *On Not-Being, or On Nature* (my translation of Dumont's French).—Trans.

4. The three principal theses of what Freeman entitles *On Being* or *On Nature* are translated very similarly by her in *Ancilla to the Pre-Socratic Philosophers*, p. 128, as follows: "I. Nothing exists. II. If anything exists, it is incomprehensible. III. If it is comprehensible, it is incommunicable."—Trans.

5. This seems to be Castoriadis's partial paraphrased translation of two consecutive fragments from Parmenides of Elea. I provide below Kathleen Free-

man's translation of fragments 2 and 3 from her *Ancilla to the Pre-Socratic Philosophers*, p. 42:

> 2. Come, I will tell you—and you must accept my word when you have heard it—the ways of inquiry which alone are to be thought: the one that IT IS, and it is not possible for IT NOT TO BE, is the way of credibility, for it follows Truth; the other, that IT IS NOT, and that IT is bound NOT TO BE: this I tell you is a path that cannot be explored; for you could neither recognise that which IS NOT, nor express it.
>
> 3. For it is the same thing to think and to be.

Freeman adds a footnote to fragment 3, stating: "Or, reading ἔστιν: 'that which it is possible to think is identical with that which can Be' (Zeller and Burnet, probably rightly)." As rendered into English by me, Castoriadis's paraphrased French translation of Parmenides' Greek adopts language closer to this "probably right" reading of Zeller and Burnet than to the first alternative reading Freeman presents in the text.—Trans.

Seminar of March 5, 1986

1. The Diès translation, which Castoriadis was using, provides references here (p. 49) to *Phaedrus* 265e and *Philebus* 16d.—Trans.

2. These appear to be Castoriadis's paraphrases from Xenophanes of Colophon's fragments 16 and 15, as they are listed in Freeman's *Ancilla to the Pre-Socratic Philosophers*, p. 22.—Trans.

3. In "The Discovery of the Imagination" (*WIF*, p. 220), Castoriadis refers to these *Zoological Treatises* as "*Short Treatises on Natural History (Parva Naturalia)*," adding that "'Short Treatises on Psychical History' would in fact be the correct title."—Trans.

Seminar of March 12, 1986

1. The precise location of this quotation from Aristotle is *De Anima* 3.3.428a11–12. In "The Discovery of the Imagination," Castoriadis offers a slightly different paraphrased translation of Aristotle, which was translated by me from Castoriadis's French as follows: "Sensations are always true, whereas most of the products of the imagination are false" (*WIF*, p. 224; see also p. 226 for a partial direct quotation). There he gives a broader citation of *De Anima* as 428a5–16; more narrowly, it's cited as 428a11–12 on p. 226.—Trans.

2. *Ensidic* and *ensidizable* are neologisms introduced by Castoriadis to designate the "ensemblistic-identitary" dimension.—P.V. As I noted in "On the Translation" in *WIF* (p. xxiv): "The term 'ensemblistic-identitarian' . . . has been developed by Castoriadis in *The Imaginary Institution of Society* and in *Crossroads*

in the Labyrinth to designate the world of logical, ordered relations. To give an idea of what he is driving at, we may note that another translation of *ensembliste* (from *ensemble*, 'set') would be 'set-theoretical'—that is, relating to set theory (*la théorie des ensembles*), but the 'set-theoretical/identitary' of the *Crossroads* translation seems to me to be too heavy a phrase." See, more recently, the many references to "ensemblistic-identitary" found in the indexes to *WIF* and *CR*. —Trans.

3. Castoriadis quotes this thirty-third "Proverb of Hell" from Blake's *The Marriage of Heaven and Hell* on p. 373 of *WIF*, at the end of "The Ontological Import of the History of Science," and in n. 44 (p. 437) to that essay, dated December 9, 1985—i.e., just three months prior to the present seminar. In that note, he thanked Cliff Berry for having found this citation and, subsidiarily and too kindly, myself for simply having communicated to him Berry's discovery of the exact reference.—Trans.

4. What Aristotle specifically says is, *Metabolē de pasa phusei ekstatikon* ("Now, every change is by nature undoing" [*Physics* 4.13.222b16]). But change is intimately tied up with time, and Aristotle speaks in 221b2 of destructive time, in effect, by employing the terms *phthoras* {destruction, decay} and *existēsi* {to remove, to displace}.

5. See Thomas Cole's excellent book, *Democritus and the Sources of Greek Anthropology* (1967), Monograph series/American Philological Association, no. 25 (Atlanta, Ga.: Scholars Press, 1990).

6. Jean-Paul Dumont, *Les Présocratiques* (Paris: Gallimard/Pléiade, 1988); partial reissue, *Les Écoles présocratiques* (Paris: Gallimard/Folio, 1991), pp. 496–97.—P.V.

7. See Cornelius Castoriadis, "Anthropogonie chez Eschyle et autocréation de l'homme chez Sophocle," in *Figures du pensable*.—P.V. This essay on "Anthropogony in Aeschylus and the Self-Creation of Man in Sophocles" is forthcoming in one of the Stanford University Press volumes of English translations of *Figures*.—Trans.

8. *Protagoras* 320d–322d.—P.V.

Seminar of March 26, 1986

1. One can add to this the beginning of the *Timaeus* and the *Crito* (the myth of Atlantis).—P. V.-N. [Pierre Vidal-Naquet has himself commented, upon many occasions, that Plato's myth of the cave, with its projections of shadows on the cave's wall, is itself an anticipation of the projection technique of cinema.—Trans.]

2. Probably an allusion to the English nursery rhyme "Humpty-Dumpty."— P. V.-N.

3. On Plato's phrase "moving image of eternity," see *IIS*, p. 188, and *WIF*, p. 235.—Trans.

4. I take the "besides" (*d'ailleurs*, in French), to which Castoriadis refers here, to be his translation of the Greek *de*.—Trans.

5. See "Value, Equality, Justice, Politics: From Marx to Aristotle and from Aristotle to Ourselves" (1975), in *CL*, pp. 260–339.—P.V.

6. Jacques Derrida, *Speech and Phenomena: And Other Essays on Husserl's Theory of Signs*, trans. David B. Allison (Evanston, Ill.: Northwestern University Press, 1973).—Trans.

7. In *Process and Reality: An Essay in Cosmology* (1929; rev. ed. [New York: Free Press, 1978], p. 39), Alfred North Whitehead explains that "the safest characterization of the European philosophical tradition is that it consists of a series of footnotes to Plato."—Trans.

Seminar of April 23, 1986

1. See the antepenultimate and penultimate chapters of Tocqueville's *Democracy in America*.—Trans.

2. M. I. Finley, "The Ancestral Constitution," in *The Uses and Abuses of History* (London: Chatto & Windus, 1975), pp. 34–59.—P. V.-N.

3. As noted above, see *Protagoras* 320d–322d. The equal distribution of *technē politikē* appears at 322c–d.—Trans.

4. Again, see "Value, Equality, Justice, Politics . . . ," in *CL*.—P.V.

5. Castoriadis was giving his seminar there at the École des Hautes Études en Sciences Sociales precisely at that time.—Trans.

6. In Barthes's *leçon inaugurale* at the Collège de France.—P. V.-N. Originally published as *Leçon* (Paris: Seuil, 1978), this January 7, 1977 *leçon inaugurale* was translated by Richard Howard as "Inaugural Lecture, Collège de France" for *A Barthes Reader*, ed. Susan Sontag (New York: Hill & Wang, 1982), pp. 457–78. On p. 461, Barthes asserts that "language—the performance of a language system—is neither reactionary nor progressive; it is quite simply fascist; for fascism does not prevent speech, it compels speech."—Trans.

7. The book in question is Marcel Detienne and Jean-Pierre Vernant's *Cunning Intelligence in Greek Culture and Society* (1974), trans. Janet Lloyd (Chicago: University of Chicago Press, 1991).—Trans.

Seminar of April 30, 1986

1. This is again an allusion to Finley, *Ancient Sicily*, pp. 92–93.—P. V.-N.

2. This is, in addition, the kernel of every critique of totalitarianism. For, the totalitarian utopia is that. I have spoken to you about it. With the closed-circuit

television surveillance of George Orwell's *Nineteen Eighty-Four* and other fantasms of this type that have been expressed, whether in literature or in reality. The total internalization by each citizen of the ideals of the totalitarian State ultimately means that each becomes—and there are interpretations from Jean-Jacques Rousseau through Hannah Arendt that head in this direction—his own surveillant and his own informer in relation to . . . the general will, in relation to the State, in relation to the Party, in relation to whatever you want; here you have an *x* you can fill in to your own liking. In these observations from the *Statesman* are found, then, the kernel of the criticism of every totalitarian regime and even of all bureaucratic power, including management of labor in factories, regulations, foremen, and so forth.

3. Here I've translated the one appearance of "le politique" as both *politikos* (the original Greek term for *statesman*) and as "the political" in general, so as to fit with the dual meaning of this French term, as I believe it is intended here. —Trans.

4. On musical composition, see, e.g., "The Social-Historical: Mode of Being, Problems of Knowledge," *PPA*, pp. 44–45, and "From the Monad to Autonomy," *WIF*, pp. 182–83.—Trans.

5. "Modern Capitalism and Revolution," *PSW*2, pp. 226–325.—Trans.

6. The Socialist-Communist alliance had just been defeated in the March 16, 1986, legislative elections. French President François Mitterrand, a Socialist, was forced into a "cohabitation" (divided government) arrangement with the neo-Gaullist leader and Paris mayor Jacques Chirac, who became his new prime minister. Thus, Chirac as well as the outgoing prime minister, Laurent Fabius, a Socialist, had just been doing the rounds of the television news shows, including *L'Heure de vérité* (The Hour of Truth), which Castoriadis mentions here in the French original.—Trans.

7. The Situationist International leader Guy Debord, author in 1967 of *The Society of the Spectacle*, trans. from the French (Detroit: Black and Red, 1983), was briefly a member of Castoriadis's revolutionary organization, Socialisme ou Barbarie. For a former S. ou B. member's close-up view of Debord's year-long passage through S. ou B., see Daniel Blanchard (known as Canjuers in the group), "Debord in the Resounding Cataract of Time," trans. Helen Arnold, in *Revolutionary Romanticism: A* Drunken Boat *Anthology*, ed. Max Blechman (San Francisco: City Lights, 1999), pp. 223–37; for a historian's analytical view, see Stephen Hastings-King, "*L'Internationale Situationniste, Socialisme ou Barbarie*, and the Crisis of the Marxist Imaginary," *SubStance: A Review of Theory and Literary Criticism* 90 (1999): 26–54; for the view of a Situationist 'zine also sympathetic to Castoriadis and S. ou B., see Bill Brown, "Strangers in the Night. . . ." *Not Bored!* 31 (June 1999): 74–83 <http://www.notbored.org/strangers.html>. —Trans.

8. Michel Rocard, who had quit Fabius's cabinet in a staged protest the year before (1985), was later appointed prime minister by Mitterrand during the latter's second presidential term in office. Such resignations are a common practice for *presidentiables*, potential presidential candidates, as has occurred again recently with the departure of the *énarque* Jean-Pierre Chevènement, who has resigned from Socialist governments in 1983, 1990, and 2000.—Trans.

9. For Castoriadis's views on the "New Philosophers," see "The Diversionists" (1977), in *PSW3*, pp. 272–77, and "L'Industrie du vide" (his response to "New Philosopher" Bernard-Henri Lévy), *Nouvel Observateur* 765 (July 9–15, 1979): 35–37. The latter text was reprinted in *Quaderni di storia* 11 (January 1980): 322–29, along with the June 18 and 25, 1979, *Nouvel Observateur* letters of Pierre Vidal-Naquet (ibid.: 315–17, 319–21) and the June 18, 1979, *Nouvel Observateur* letter of Lévy (ibid.: 317–19). A second reprint of Castoriadis's text alone appeared in his *Domaines de l'homme: Les carrefours du labyrinthe II* (Paris: Seuil, 1986), pp. 28–34.—Trans.

Translator's Afterword

1. Quoted in Lefort, *Writing*, p. 188.

2. "The Destinies of Totalitarianism" (1981), *Salmagundi* 60 (Spring–Summer 1983): 107–22, correcting a grammatical error and, in light of the French translation, what appears to be a typo (p. 107).

3. Compare his remarks on Plato and the Parthenon on April 30, 1986, to *CR*, p. 348, on postrevolutionary Greek, French, and American democratic creativity: "tragedy and the Parthenon," "Stendhal, Balzac, Rimbaud, Manet, and Proust," and "Poe, Melville, Whitman, and Faulkner."

4. See my essay "Castoriadis on Culture" <http://www.costis.org/x/castoriadis/culture.htm>.

5. See, however, n. 5 of "On the Translation," this volume, and *CSI*, mentioned below.

6. Similarities appear even in tiny details, e.g., his paraphrasing of Hegel about the freedom of one, a few, and all (*SAS*, p. 322, and April 30).

7. The most convincing evidence, though, is the final seminar's added note about the *Statesman* containing "the kernel of the criticism of every totalitarian regime and even of all bureaucratic power, including management of labor in factories, regulations, foremen, and so forth."

8. The most egregious, sustained example is Philippe Gottraux's Bourdieu-inspired sociology thesis, *"Socialisme ou Barbarie": Un engagement politique et intellectuel dans la France de l'après-guerre* (Lausanne: Éditions Payot Lausanne, 1997).

9. Although Plato was developing a deeply antidemocratic argument, he re-

mained profoundly Greek. Ten thousand in Greek is *murias*, and *murios* means "countless." We know from the last chapter of *Cleisthenes the Athenian*—Vidal-Naquet and Lévêque's classic work, much admired by Castoriadis, on the birth of democracy—that Plato developed his negation of the Athenian democracy by borrowing therefrom, and especially from its numerical features—three, five, ten, and their multiples being privileged Cleisthenic numerals. (My English-language translation, *Cleisthenes the Athenian*, includes as an appendix *On the Invention of Democracy*, the proceedings of a 1992 conference in Paris with Lévêque, Vidal-Naquet, and Castoriadis that was organized by myself and Clara Gibson Maxwell along with Pascal Vernay and Stéphane Barbery and chaired by former S. ou B. member Christian Descamps; this minicolloquium was held to celebrate and critically examine the 2,500th anniversary of Cleisthenes' reforms. It was Castoriadis himself in 1991 who first recommended that I take a look at *Clisthène l'Athénien* in preparation for this anniversary.) Even Plato didn't describe the crowd of citizens here as "myriad." Rather, it is in relation to the disturbing unendingness of not-being that the term "ten thousand," meaning "innumerable," appears: "Ten thousand times ten thousand, being is not and not-being is," as Castoriadis quotes *Sophist* 259b.

10. In *CSII*, p. 142, contemporary denials of the possibility of "real democracy" were also linked to Plato's *Protagoras*, a dialogue mentioned several times in the 1986 seminars too.

11. Appropriating *S. ou B.*'s distinctive red and white cover, *Autogestion et Socialisme*, for example, became an influential journal in the 1970s.

12. Castoriadis took pride in the fact that his teaching post resulted not from a state "appointment" but from election by fellow EHESS members.

13. Another volume of transcribed Castoriadis seminars is now forthcoming from Éditions du Seuil under the general series heading *La Création humaine*. The April 29, 1987, seminar from this volume had already appeared as "La Vérité dans l'effectivité social-historique" in a special issue of *Les Temps Modernes* (609 [June–July–August 2000]: 41–70) devoted to Castoriadis.

14. See app. E/19910, *PSW3*, p. 346. Agora International—27, rue Froidevaux 75104 Paris FRANCE; <curtis@msh-paris.fr>—has now ceased photocopy distribution of these transcriptions.

15. See, e.g., April 30, n. 9 on the "New Philosophers."

16. The name he cited, seemingly out of the blue, was Gilles Deleuze's. Only later did I form the hypothesis that Castoriadis may have felt that Deleuze/Guattari's book on capitalism and schizophrenia may have taken over, without attribution or the same depth of revolutionary purpose, his own ideas on the contradictory nature of capitalism, which simultaneously *excludes* workers' participation and *solicits* it.

17. Six months before his death, Castoriadis spoke on the theme of musical

improvisation at a La Villette (Paris) colloquium organized by the jazz musician and classical composer Ornette Coleman. Another Coleman friend who participated was the artist Jean-Jacques Lebel, organizer with S. ou B. members and others of Paris "happenings" in the mid-1960s.

18. I thank Max Blechman, Zoé Castoriadis, Clara Gibson Maxwell, Pierre Vidal-Naquet, and Dominique Walter for their helpful comments and suggestions concerning this Afterword's earlier drafts and my editor Helen Tartar for her ongoing interest and much welcome support.

Index

thought/thinking activity, 121–22, 166; voice, 123

Logic, logical, 3, 7, 13, 15, 34, 36, 38, 50, 65, 100, 106, 116, 157, 163, 166; binary, 34; formal, 34; of the human, 57; of living beings, 57; ordinary, 36

Logo-phallo-whatever-centrism, 143

Logos, 14, 76, 80, 162, 166

Lots, drawing of, 138–39, 149, 158, 163

Lying down and resting, 49–51

Lymphocytes, 72

Macedonian king, 35. *See also* Philip of Macedon

Mafia, 43

Magistrates, magistracies, 138, 149; drawn by lot, 138–39, 149; elective/elected, 10, 47, 139, 157–58; in *Laws*, 10, 114, 157

Magmas, magmatic, 9; semantic, 66; of signification, 66

Magna Graecia, 11

Mahler, Gustav, 86

Maieutic, 23

Making/doing, 116

Male/female, 58–59

Manifold, chaotic, 74

Manipulation and "manipulability," 170

Mannheim, Karl, 137

Manufacturers, 43; of false images, 21; of simulacra, 3

Manufacturing, manufacture, 41–43, 84–85

Manufacturing god, 88, 96–100, 110. *See also* Demiurge

Marks, 72

Marriages, 89, 93

Marx, Karl, 6, 113, 153, 162; his theory of value, 43

Marxism, Marxist, 43

Marxist-Leninist parties, 169

Materialists, 82

Mathematics, mathematicians, mathematical, 13, 24, 75, 100, 148, 153, 156

Matter, materiality, material, 19, 42–45, 75–76, 79–80, 89, 95, 97–98, 100, 103, 111, 113, 116, 123, 145; ineliminable, 145; its unknowable portion, 145; nature of, 19; not pure, 75; of the object, 34; pure, 80–81; raw, 98, 166; unformed, 80–81; weaving/to be woven, 24, 27, 44–45; without, 76, 80

Measurable, 86

Measured, 87

Measurement, measuring, measures, 25, 55, 85–88, 146, 156; absolute/non-relative, 25, 41, 85–88, 126, 154; relative, 25, 41, 85–88, 126

Mechanics, mechanical, mechanizable, 36, 72, 74, 107–108

Media, 169–70

Medicine, medical knowledge, medical, 72, 87, 131, 134, 137–39, 144, 148–49, 154, 163; not a science, 148

Megabyzus, 128

Megara, 11

Megarites, Megarians, 11, 21

Memory, 121, 131; letters as poison for, 121; without/loss of, 93–94, 111.

Metaphors, 70–71, 130, 133, 154, 171; mere, 75; poetic, 80

Metaphysics, metaphysical, 23, 66, 84, 145

Methexis (participation), 80. *See also* Participation

Metonymy, 71

"Metretics," "metretic," 86–87

Metrētikē (art of measure, "metretics"), 85

Metrion (measured), 87

Metriōs (judicious), 119

Mētis (capacity to invent), 147–48; *polu-*, 147

Mia deuterōs (second in unity), 17, 189n5

Russell's paradox, 57
Russia, Russians, 43

Sache selbst, die (thing itself, the), 84
Salvation, savior, saving, 111–12, 118,
132, 169
Same, the, 62, 67; as supreme kind, 20
Savagery, savages, savage, wild, 64,
94–96, 105, 112–14
Savoir faire, 5. *See also* Know-how
Scarcity, 96
Schemata, schemes, 71, 78, 84; creative
new, 83; universal imaginary, 92
"Science alone defines the statesman,"
26, 29, 44, 91, 104, 115, 128–29
Science fiction, 106
Sciences, science, scientific, 26, 29–30,
33–35, 37, 44, 53, 56, 58, 88, 91, 104,
115–16, 118–20, 128–32, 136, 138, 148,
153–54, 163, 169; directive/executive,
34; directive/self-directive, 33; gen-
uine, 131; modern, 81; natural, 131; of
human things, 30; of things in gen-
eral, 30; royal, 45; theoretical, 33; the-
oretical/nontheoretical, 58; theoreti-
cal/practical, 34; of the universal,
146. *See also* "*Epistēmonōn tis, tōn*";
Political science
Scientists, 35, 118, 131; true, 131
Second best, 114, 128, 134, 159
Seeking, 23, 65; for what one doesn't
know, 64–65
Séguéla, Jacques, 169
Self-altering, 31
Self-constitution, constituting itself,
95, 102, 112–14
Self-correction, 121
Self-corruption, 137
Self-creation, creating itself, 73, 78, 95,
102, 114
Self-directive, directing oneself, 33, 92.
See also Directive
Self-government, governing them-
selves, 114, 127; at all echelons, 31

Self-institution, 5; democratic, 161; ef-
fort to stop it, 5; permanent, 161–62
Self-management, 139
Self-organization, organizing oneself,
73, 102, 110–11
Semantics, 66, 143, 151
Sensation, 80
Senses, 49; data of, 80
Sensoriality, sensorial, 67–68, 74, 82; as
organizing, 74
Separation, 36, 66–67, 69–71, 81–83,
98, 100, 108
Sequencing, 107, 150
Services, 43
Sets, 34, 57
Set theory, 69
Several, 19, 58, 60, 70, 82, 128–30, 163
Sexual reproduction, 91–92, 94
Shame, 7
Shepherd, 9, 37, 101, 110; divine, 101,
114; of humans, 37; true, 101. *See also*
Definitions of statesman; Herdsman;
Nomeus; Pastor
Ships, vessels, boats, shipbuilding, 42,
113, 135–36, 138, 149, 154, 163
Shortage, 89–90
Sicily, 3, 11–12, 149, 156; no kings there,
35, 119
Significations, 66, 80; imaginary, 95
Silence, 7, 21
Similarities, similar, alike, like, 61–62,
69–71, 97, 134
Simulacra, 3, 169
Singularities, singular, 8, 29, 73, 76, 82,
142, 146–47, 156–57, 163, 167, 171
Skepticism, 54
Slaves, slavery, 2, 45, 143; in the *Meno*,
23, 64; total, 143
Sleep, sleeping, 49, 63, 74–75, 80
Smerdis, 128
Smith, Adam, 43
Social: assignment, 6; being, 143–44;
fabrication of the individual, 47; po-
sition, 6; sphere, 73

Crossing Aesthetics

Emmanuel Levinas, *Proper Names*

Alexander García Düttmann, *At Odds with AIDS: Thinking and Talking About a Virus*

Maurice Blanchot, *Friendship*

Jean-Luc Nancy, *The Muses*

Massimo Cacciari, *Posthumous People: Vienna at the Turning Point*

David E. Wellbery, *The Specular Moment: Goethe's Early Lyric and the Beginnings of Romanticism*

Edmond Jabès, *The Little Book of Unsuspected Subversion*

Hans-Jost Frey, *Studies in Poetic Discourse: Mallarmé, Baudelaire, Rimbaud, Hölderlin*

Pierre Bourdieu, *The Rules of Art: Genesis and Structure of the Literary Field*

Nicolas Abraham, *Rhythms: On the Work, Translation, and Psychoanalysis*

Jacques Derrida, *On the Name*

David Wills, *Prosthesis*

Maurice Blanchot, *The Work of Fire*

Jacques Derrida, *Points . . . : Interviews, 1974–1994*

J. Hillis Miller, *Topographies*

Philippe Lacoue-Labarthe, *Musica Ficta (Figures of Wagner)*

Jacques Derrida, *Aporias*

Emmanuel Levinas, *Outside the Subject*

Jean-François Lyotard, *Lessons on the Analytic of the Sublime*

Peter Fenves, *"Chatter": Language and History in Kierkegaard*

Jean-Luc Nancy, *The Experience of Freedom*

Jean-Joseph Goux, *Oedipus, Philosopher*

Haun Saussy, *The Problem of a Chinese Aesthetic*

Jean-Luc Nancy, *The Birth to Presence*